Rebel Angels
IN
Exile

"If it is true that the Urantia Revelation accurately depicts our pre-history, then this new volume—like the previous two in the series—is an astonishing revelation in its own right. The high drama and vivid characters he depicts riveted my attention from beginning to the end."

BYRON BELITSOS, AWARD-WINNING PUBLISHER
AND COAUTHOR OF *THE ADVENTURE OF BEING HUMAN*

"Timothy has done us all an important favor by sharing his well-developed, extensive, and carefully considered personal cosmology in his many books. Based in part on the Urantia framework, he has taken its concepts and made them relevant and accessible for us all. His personal stories illustrate esoteric concepts in remarkable ways. The power of the elegant artistry in his words is reflected in the memes he has created that have become part of our current culture. Timothy Wyllie is an important and underappreciated elder who has much to offer anyone who takes the time to read his works."

SCOTT TAYLOR, AUTHOR OF
SOULS OF THE SEA: DOLPHINS, WHALES, AND HUMAN DESTINY

Rebel Angels

IN

Exile

PLEIADIANS, WATCHERS, AND THE SPIRITUAL QUICKENING OF HUMANITY

TIMOTHY WYLLIE

Bear & Company
Rochester, Vermont • Toronto, Canada

Bear & Company
One Park Street
Rochester, Vermont 05767
www.BearandCompanyBooks.com

Bear & Company is a division of Inner Traditions International

Library of Congress Cataloging-in-Publication Data
Wyllie, Timothy, 1940–
  Rebel angels in exile : Pleiadians, watchers, and the spiritual quickening of
humanity / Timothy Wyllie.
      pages cm
  Includes index.
  Summary: "A rebel angel's revelations on the angelic quarantine after the Lucifer
Rebellion 203,000 years ago" — Provided by publisher.
  ISBN 978-1-59143-188-6 (pbk.) — ISBN 978-1-59143-770-3 (e-book)
  1. Angels—Miscellanea. 2. Devil—Miscellanea. 3. Demonology—Miscellanea.
4. Extraterrestrial beings—Miscellanea. 5. Earth (Planet)—Forecasting. I. Title.
  BF1999.W958 2014
  133.9—dc23
                                                                    2014011729

Printed and bound in the United States by McNaughton & Gunn, Inc.

10 9 8 7 6 5 4 3 2 1

Text design and layout by Virginia Scott Bowman
This book was typeset in Garamond Premier Pro with Baskerville used as the
display typeface

To send correspondence to the author of this book, mail a first-class letter to the
author c/o Inner Traditions • Bear & Company, One Park Street, Rochester, VT
05767, and we will forward the communication, or contact the author through his
website at **www.timothywyllie.com**.

Contents

Whereas angels were once the epitome
of beauty and goodness,
now, in our time, they are irrelevant.
Materialism and science have banished them to nonexistence,
a sphere as indeterminate as purgatory.
It used to be that humanity believed in angels implicitly,
intuitively, not with our minds but with our very souls.
Now we need proof. We need material,
scientific data that will verify without a doubt their reality.
Yet what a crisis would occur if the proof existed!
What would happen, do you suppose,
if the material existence of angels could be verified?

DANIELLE TRUSSONI, *ANGELOLOGY*

The Gnostics might well have said:
We who are in the know, who think for ourselves
and see through the sham,
have been enlightened by a hidden God far above,
who is free of all this impossible system
under which the world suffers.
This hidden God frees us—He does not enslave us.

JAMES M. ROBINSON, *THE SECRETS OF JUDAS*

Acknowledgments

Although it might seem odd to some, my most heartfelt appreciation must first go to the Watcher Georgia, who came into my life just when I thought I'd completed the obligation I'd taken on to write the three books of *The DETA Factor*. It was to be one book every ten years to explore and record the impact nonhuman intelligences were having at this crucial point in Earth's history. Then I could get out of this writing business and back to my drawing board. But along came Georgia with her need and desire to tell all. How could I possibly refuse?!

This series of Georgia's *Confessions,* of which this book, *Rebel Angels in Exile,* is the third volume, have been an all-consuming passion for me these past few years, so I've appreciated the work that Anne Dillon, who edited my previous books, has put into this volume. Celestial and interplanetary politics are complex and not easy to grasp, so Anne's input has been an invaluable help in showing what needs further clarification.

Once again I've been fortunate to work with my project editor, Chanc VanWinkle Orzell, who not only appears adept at keeping an improbable number of balls in the air simultaneously, bringing the focus of a ballet dancer and a sensitive, first-class intelligence to bear on the final and most important stage of the editing process. She pulls it all together, and quite magically (from a writer's point of view) she is guaranteed to improve it. Many thanks, Chanc, for your patience and caring, and I look forward to working with you again if we have the opportunity.

As I've done with Georgia's previous books, I sent this volume in manuscript form to Susan P. Marie for her to dowse each sentence and concept in Georgia's reporting for its truth content. I find this helpful and encouraging when there are only a small handful of queries in a book. Writing as I do with Georgia has some of the qualities of skydiving (the faith it's going to work this time); surfing (the confidence to think I can stay on the wave); and tight-rope walking (it's all a question of balance), so I'm indebted to Susan for her encouragement in uncharted territories. It was in the latter part of this volume that her dowsing showed positive on one of Georgia's most intriguing speculations—one I hardly dared think might be so—a revelation that deeply affects every one of us.

Robert Davis of the Daynal Institute is one of the few people who has read all Georgia's volumes to date and has been consistently encouraging for the work to get into print. Robert's profound and unique understanding of that most difficult of cosmologies, *The Urantia Book,* and his approval of Georgia's insights and the questions she seeks to tease out of history have helped give me courage to continue.

As my avocation is graphic art I always like to drop in a handful of my graphic pieces that I find can connect with the reader, sometimes in a more direct way. I also include two of the more elaborate graphics (plates 3 and 5) that Juno (June Atkin Sanders)—my beloved "Artner"—and I do collaboratively. These are large Prismacolor on watercolor paper that we send back and forth through snail mail, each adding our contributions until it's finished. Juno and I have been working together for almost thirty years, and I believe we've drawn out the best in one another—and that could not make me happier or more grateful.

As these books of Georgia's are gaining a readership, I've started to receive the most supportive and encouraging letters from an unexpectedly wide group of people who find some resonance in her narrative and that her words are helping open up their own secret doors. As you've been waiting long for this volume, you'll be likely reading these words, and, as you know who you are, I won't mention names. But I do thank you, all of you for your open-hearted responses. Having said that, how could I not express my appreciation to Kathleen B. M.; to Jason H.; to Roberta G; Gordon P.; Martin G.; to Urszula B.; and to Magi, and Viola, and Yana; to my friends in Europe and new friends in Santa Fe; and to all my readers not mentioned, my gratitude for your encouragement and support—and keep reading. They get better by the volume.

I continue to feel blessed to have my books picked up by Inner Traditions • Bear & Company, the very publisher I would have chosen had they not got to me first. For that I can thank Jon Graham, the publisher's acquisitions editor, in particular, for recognizing the value of this work and constantly surprising me by accepting the next volume; and to John Hays, the director of sales and marketing, and his team, for having the confidence to sell them. Making a book takes many talents, some of which an author is unaware and others—like Peri Swan's continuingly inventive cover design and Virginia Scott Bowman's elegant text design and layout—are more visible; but regardless, I'm deeply thankful for the love and attention you put into my books. And to those who make the final decision as to whether to publish or not—to the publisher Ehud Sperling, to Jeanie Levitan, the editor in chief, and to Janet Jesso, the managing editor—goes my deepest gratitude for choosing to publish these volumes of Georgia's *Confessions* when you must receive so many excellent books. I'm also most grateful to Manzanita Carpenter for the diligent work she does to publicize my books. Having once worked in that field myself, I can admire her persistence. I know what it entails.

I also express my special appreciation to Barbara Hand Clow, who I sense is working behind the scenes to see these books of Georgia's get into print. She has long been a supporter of my work, republishing my first book, *Dolphins ETs & Angels,* in 1992 and publishing my second, *Dolphins Telepathy & Underwater Birthing,* in 1993, so I was delighted and thankful she also took a liking to Georgia's writings.

It may seem a little ingenuous to thank Georgia when she herself is so thankful to have an outlet for her words and that she can be of help to others, but I'm thankful to her anyway. Neither of us could have written it without the other. And I've been writing with angels long enough to know the help I receive from them over the long and lonely haul of writing books. Whether I perceive you or not, I know you're there, and I thank all of you, my invisible allies, for your love and the constancy of your enthusiasm.

As readers will know from my books over the past thirty years, as well as from the work of others who can see beneath the fear and confusion of everyday life, I have no doubt we've chosen to incarnate on Earth at this absolutely fulcrum point in human development. To all appearances, life is getting worse. Yet if I read Georgia correctly there are now well over one hundred million rebel angels incarnated as human beings, and as each wakes up to her or his true heritage and their reason for being here, the helping hand the planet so desperately needs will reveal itself, as naturally as a flower opening, to effect a transformation so gentle and profound we'll laugh at our preposterous fantasies of Armageddon.

And for knowing that I am truly grateful to my angels.

Note to the Reader
Regarding a Glossary of Terms
and the Angelic Cosmology

In this work the author has coined or provided specialized definitions of certain words, some of which are derived from *The Urantia Book*, a key source text. A list of these terms and their meanings has been provided in the glossary at the back of this book for your ready reference. The reader will find a brief overview of the Angelic Cosmology, also drawn from *The Urantia Book*, in the appendix.

My Collaboration
with a Watcher Angel

Georgia, as those who have read the first two volumes of her *Confessions* will know, represents herself as a discarnate Watcher, an angel who aligned herself with Lucifer at the time of the rebellion among the angels some 203,000 years ago. She claims she first came to this planet as an observing angel 500,000 years ago, accompanying the first of the off-planet interventions. She has written extensively about those early times in the two previous volumes of this series.

Professional skeptics, if they were ever to pick up this book, are likely to dismiss Georgia's *Confessions* at the very sight of the word *angel,* so I feel no need to justify or try to prove Georgia's ontological existence to those who would so thoughtlessly deny what they may not yet understand. I've no doubt there are as many other explanations for the phenomenon I experience as Georgia as there are languages for dismissing me as delusional. I'm not naive. Yet as so much of her material is clearly original and covers many of the realms of existence of which humans are generally unaware, her narrative will have to stand or fall on the authenticity of her words and the relevance of her perceptions. And that, in turn, will depend on the state of consciousness of the reader. While it is clearly sensible to be cautious, skeptical even, I believe we are all equipped spiritually—if we are not too clouded by lies and delusions—with the ability to discern the truth in what we observe and feel. Absorbing a book such as this can also be an opportunity to fine-tune your intuition—that currently somewhat discredited capacity for knowing the truth—if the narrative is taken in with an open heart.

As Georgia and I collaborate on this, the third volume of her *Confessions,* it will be of interest to new readers for me to briefly recap how Georgia and I came to take on this project together.

My own work for the past thirty-five years has been almost entirely focused on nonhuman intelligences: dolphins, angels, nature spirits, and extraterrestrials, and their interest in and involvement with this planet. This interest had been galvanized by a profound near-death experience (NDE) I had in 1973. The unquestionable authenticity of what I experienced during my NDE finally convinced me of the reality of other levels of existence.

When I started writing my books in the 1980s I became more familiar with the active presence of angels in my life when I made contact with my two companion (guardian) angels. By the time, some fifteen years later, Georgia made her presence known to me, I felt well prepared to relate to a discarnate entity, yet the fact that Georgia claimed to be one of the rebel angels meant we had to tackle the trust issue. Rebel angels are traditionally believed to be malicious and tricky creatures, and I needed to be sure about what I was getting myself into, while Georgia had to be certain I could tolerate her presence without freaking out or giving away my power. It required an extremely delicate balance. It wasn't surprising that it took another seven years of testing one another before we were able to evolve an effective way of writing together. This turned out to be a true collaboration. It's not me just taking dictation. We discuss the issues as they rise to consciousness and settle together the best way to express the narrative Georgia is weaving. This process is quite different from the books I'd previously written in which the angels merely gave me a frisson of delight when I got the words correct; and it isn't the automatic writing with which I received *The Helianx Proposition* in a single unbroken six-hour stretch of writing.* Working with Georgia on these books is far more like collaborating with a deeply knowledgeable colleague whom I experience as autonomous and external to myself and yet who feels as close to me as a heartbeat.

The Helianx Proposition: The Return of the Rainbow Serpent, Sewannee, Tenn.: The Daynal Institute, 2012.

Just how we managed to accomplish this is a whole story unto itself and will have to wait until Georgia's narrative reaches the point in my life that I'm ready to receive it. The younger me, the man whom Georgia describes in this volume, has no conscious awareness of angels at all and would have skeptically dismissed any thought of their existence.

The near-death experience will change all that, but that remains a couple of years in the future.

Georgia tells me she has accompanied me over the course of this lifetime and a number of other ones also, although I didn't come to know this until we started working together. What I'm learning over the course of this collaboration is allowing me to see how long and thoroughly I've been prepared so as to be able to form an intimate creative relationship with a discarnate entity. I have needed to sacrifice family life: no wife and children to distract the necessary equanimity of my mind and heart. I live alone with my cat, and for the past twenty-one years I've been required to make my home in the wilds of the New Mexican high desert. I have no complaints; I'm aware I chose this path prior to incarnation. Its rewards have been more spiritual than material.

In retrospect, I can see how this period of my life has been about learning how to work with angels. *Ask Your Angels,* which I wrote with my two coauthors, Alma Daniel and Andrew Ramer, from 1988 to 1992, would never have come together without the guidance and help of Abigrael. She was an angel assigned to us for the work, who skillfully coordinated the material the three of us were developing separately. Over the course of writing my second book, *Adventures Among Spiritual Intelligences,* I became aware of two other angels, Zophiel and Zadkiel. They were the angels I mentioned earlier who gave me that frisson of delight. They gave me confidence, of course, but it was still wholly my book.

Yet neither of these books was a true collaboration.

These books with Georgia are of a different order of magnitude altogether, and the process we have developed of working together is a curious one. After settling down at my keyboard, I clear my mind and invoke Georgia's presence. I can feel a slight transition of consciousness, but I'm so familiar with it by now that I barely notice it. Then I put on my earphones and listen to the BBC talk radio. This, Georgia informs me, is designed to absorb and distract me from my chattering thoughts. It keeps my monkey-mind occupied so we can get down to business.

Then I wait and listen to a play or a comedy show until her words drift into my consciousness, perhaps half a dozen at the same time, which I then type out. Mostly I don't know where the sentence or concept is going, and at other times she'll give me some leads, which I then follow up on by doing the relevant research.

At the end of the day I, Timothy, can seldom recall what's been written during the session. And when I read through the entire book at the end, which I don't do until it's complete, it's as if I am reading a book that, although vaguely familiar, feels as if it's composed of words I've not read before.

My Life as a Watcher

The life of a Watcher would feel most strange to a human being for many reasons, because we Watchers locate the core of our existence in an essentially timeless domain. Humans find it convenient to believe time moves in an orderly forward direction. But this is only a convenience and one to which the human sensorium is tuned. As Einstein said, "The only reason for time is so that everything doesn't happen at once."

When Einstein coupled time and space into an inseparable space-time continuum—no space without time; no time without space—he was, of necessity, speaking about the space and time to which his sense apparatus, and that of most other humans, is tuned. This serves your purposes insofar as it concerns your normal material existence. Trains arrive on time, the trajectory of spacecraft can be calculated accurately, you are born before you die. Thus time's arrow appears to move in one direction— from present to future. The space-time continuum works—within the described limits.

But what if those limits are merely the result of the limitations of the human sensorium? As an ant's senses are tuned to an environment that can ensure its survival, so will the insect's experience of time and space be subject to the limitations of its sensorium. In this way it's possible to visualize how the perception of space and time depends on the sense apparatus of the perceiver.

As a Watcher, my sense apparatus is different from that of a human. My senses are tuned to the space-time continuum in which I find myself, and that continuum is best described as one in which everything is happening at once. It's a dimension I believe a Yaqui Indian shaman would call the nagual, and it's also starting to make its appearance in contemporary physics within the holographic model of the Universe.

Understand please, that as a Watcher, I am not a causative principle. I cannot make anything happen. Consequently, my sense of continuity only exists inasmuch as I observe *your* dimension. This is why I need to work through Mein Host's consciousness—his expanded sensorium—because it allows me a sense of sequence, of causes preceding effects. In a very down-to-earth way, this work would have been impossible without my ward's neural circuitry, his memory banks, as well as his typing fingers.

Yet, as I embark on this volume of my *Confessions,* I find I'm approaching it in rather a different manner. Whereas previously I wanted to narrate primarily what I've observed, without drawing conclusions or challenging accepted wisdom, I now feel that my viewpoint is subtly shifting. I assume this is, in part, the result of the progressive trust Mein Host and I have been able to establish with one another over the course of writing these books. Now I want to cut deeper, to be more adventurous in my questioning, and to allow the narrative to reflect the best of what our unusual venture has to offer.

I feel—as I'm launching off into my story again—that I'm just starting to get a handle on the narratives I'm weaving, or perhaps are being woven through me. (As, perhaps, Mein Host would say that I'm weaving *my* narratives through *him!*) It's as though another intelligence, a meta-process perhaps, is busy deciphering and decoding this work, plucking its words and images from some vast astral library of everything that ever occurred. My own memories aren't stored sequentially but seem to flow in to one another and, from them, associations over which I have little control are made. Like atomic particles once in contact with one another and now light-years apart, memories separated by millennia seem to resonate in ways that I and Mein Host would never have thought of on our own.

Being able to relate events in a linear fashion like this, whatever the mechanism, allows me to see patterns of behavior—both in social groups and in individuals on Earth and on Zandana—that were previously invisible to me. Perhaps this is akin to the familiar maxim "not seeing the forest for the trees," which may be thought of as one of the functional limitations of the angelic intelligence. Under normal circumstances, on a normal world, an angel like me has no need to see the forest; it's enough to know the forest is there. We generally are not given any more information than we need for our tasks.

With the advantage of being able to observe progress on the planet Zandana, I've been able to draw some comparisons to life on Earth. I've had the chance to examine in retrospect something of the early history of these two worlds, and in so doing, I've become convinced that Earth has been, for a long time, in the throes of unknowingly preparing for some special destiny. I was aware of nothing of this "special destiny" in the early days of my time here and could only stand back and watch human life on the planet stumbling forward in the dark. Sometimes I would observe groups of people coalescing into a promising civilization, which surged for a moment into the light before collapsing in on itself or was overrun by a more dominant crowd.

Humans have always been a hardy species; fearful yes, but also feisty and capable of great courage, as well as being ingenuous and wildly creative. Fine cultures have flowered briefly in different parts of the world, but because they tended to build their cities on ocean coastlines, a modest rise in sea level put an end to a number of budding civilizations.

Let's not forget that the period I'm covering in this and coming volumes—between eighty thousand and twelve thousand years ago—was marked geologically by the withdrawal of the ice age. Over the millennia, as the glaciers withdrew and melted, enormous amounts of freshwater spilled into the oceans, and the planetary temperatures finally stabilized. This occurred approximately ten thousand years ago. A vast amount of landmass was lost worldwide by the rising oceans, which erased almost all trace of those ancient civilizations.

Within the past few years and with the fortuitous invention of the Aqua-Lung, divers have discovered that some enigmatic undersea rock formations are, in reality, the ruins of cities that flourished tens of thousands of years before the so-called Bronze Age. This defies the conventional archaeological time line. Largely due to the geophysical activity that occurred throughout that long period, there was nothing of the continuity that a contemporary archaeologist or anthropologist might assume from their studies of the comparatively recent history of the past six or seven thousand years.

Despite prevailing assumptions, progress was never the steady march from the bronze spearpoint to the Atlas rocket of the modern historical record. Civilizations had risen and fallen all over the world well before some ingenious Chalcolithic smithy was presumed to have alloyed copper and tin approximately five thousand years ago. Some of those civilizations reached high levels of social organization, as I've previously described in the case of the exceptionally long-lasting Lemurian culture. Other ones—like those to whom Prince Caligastia and his midway minions had introduced the technological know-how to split the atom—were not so long-lasting, both having destroyed each other after a few hundred years.

Thus, by the time I'm picking up my narrative some thirty-eight thousand years ago, Earth's natural disasters had already been taking their toll. However, if there was any truth to the warning that the Lemurians received from the Pleiadean Star People, there would be worse devastation to come.

As I have no choice but to report the truth of what I've observed, I also have to be open and honest about the medium through which I'm expressing my truth. The medium in this case is, of course, Mein Host's delicate state of consciousness, which allows our collaboration to flourish, or diminish. I say this because I can sense a certain reluctance in my ward to dive in to my examination of the next stage of his spiritual journey. He is aware of the personal value of my observations, yet I've noticed he's previously chosen to brush over what was evidently a dark and challenging period in his life.

If I'm revealing a certain reticence on the part of my collaborator to continue this narrative, it is only to bring it out into the open, or to "communicate on the block," as my ward calls it; and it seems to have done the trick. Of course he will have his moments of fear or doubt, it would be too much to expect otherwise. I know how challenging it must be for him to maintain the integrity of our contact. Those readers already familiar with the first two volumes will know that I intersperse my narrative of Earth's history with my observations of my ward's life. This can be extremely confronting for him, because I'm able to reveal his many foibles as well as what was happening around him that impacted his life, and of which he was quite unaware.

Having said that, and I know my ward appreciates my recognition of the difficulties he faces in working so closely with a discarnate entity, we are both ready now to continue my narrative. We'll start with another look at his progress as he settles into community life in London.

1

The Raison d'Être
of the Process Church

Malicious Onslaughts, the Nephilim, and Vanu's Doubts

The mansion in Balfour Place hummed with activity throughout the middle 1960s as the Process community—not yet a formal church—felt driven to make its way as an uncharacteristic voice in swinging London. As a Watcher, I was fortunate to witness all of this. My ward—whom I also affectionately refer to as Mein Host—spent the years from 1963 until the late winter of 1977 as part of this spiritual community, which also included a number of chapters in different parts of the world.

In London, the Process community's highly disciplined spiritual life—free of drugs, sex, and alcohol—and their all-consuming dedication to a higher cause made an unlikely contrast to their increasingly liberated, and licentious, peers in the outside world. The British stoicism that had served so well throughout the turbulent twentieth century and its terrible wars was starting to break down by the 1960s, and Mein Host's generation was becoming increasingly skeptical of authority. The establishment was starting to realize all this.

In a way that members of the Process didn't fully acknowledge—or even notice—they were becoming curiosities: living anachronisms; devotees of the Goddess in a godless city; living like monks in a world they believed had become corrupted beyond redemption.

The Process was gaining in popularity and, in the process, was becoming a very effective moneymaking machine. This is not an unreasonably cynical way to express the community's success in a materialist culture. In spite of the challenges inherent in being part of such an organization, young people were now actively engaging with the group. They were joining up after attending a course of classes in telepathic development, for example, or a series of sessions with one of the senior members who had been trained to use the E-meter. (The E-meter is a simple device that detects the electrical conductance of the skin in order to measure the emotional energy vested in the responses to specific questions.)

These new people were not directly invited to join the community as Internal Processeans (IPs) but were required to "work their way in." This "working their way in" predominantly entailed selling the community's highly offbeat publication, the PROCESS magazine, which the group created and over which Mein Host was appointed art director. Those at the top of the organization had recognized his innate artistic and design talents and had, quite rightly, designated him to oversee this important aspect of their media mouthpiece to the world.

Mary Ann MacLean and Robert Moor, the founders and leaders of the Process community (who were also known as the Omega), were pleased that money was flowing in, and evidently believed it was time to take advantage of it. Bringing a couple of their favorites with them, they had recently set off for a long research trip to the Middle East. They told no one in Balfour Place their exact itinerary except for two of the young women who were closest to Mary Ann, whom they'd left in charge in London, and whose silence they'd ensured with the promise of a trip to visit them.

It gradually leaked out that the Omega was visiting Turkey, Greece, and Israel. Mary Ann and Robert had been traveling around the Middle East doing their so-called research for three months before it became obvious to those back in England that they weren't coming back anytime soon.

The reason given seemed so counterproductive and strange that many Processeans found it hard to believe. They were going to be looking for a new center for the community somewhere in Europe! Just when Balfour Place was thriving and the group was becoming more widely known, they would be packing up and starting all over again somewhere entirely new—in a place no one knew them and where there'd be no shared language.

That's how it sounded to Mein Host, anyway, and it made absolutely no logical sense. His friend Peter, recently appointed as editor of the magazine, was just starting to work on the next issue. Mein Host's art department was gearing up with new equipment for the darkroom. Magazines were selling well, and the organization's numbers were swelling. The group's primary hub, the coffee house, previously Satan's Cavern and now more sensibly renamed the Cavern, was doing excellent business.

It must have seemed a crazy time to think about uprooting the entire operation just as it was becoming successful.

But, of course, the Process was never really about business. It was never about worldly success either, although it was certainly about *striving* for success. In reality, the Process was always about failure—about learning and growing from failure and to be able to then push further and deeper into the unknown aspects of the self. Mein Host has since said that understanding and overcoming the roots of failure *was* the process. "The Process was the process of awakening from our limitations" is how I've heard him express it.

This has been hard for me, Georgia, his Watcher angel, to understand, because I wanted to see my ward flourish and succeed. It pained me to see him suffer. Because I didn't have access to his mind at that point in the way I do now, I was unaware of how much emotional baggage he needed to work through from his previous, troubled incarnation before his real work could begin. I hadn't fully comprehended this until Mary Ann's instructions came through to start the search for a fine new center in Europe.

Whatever rationale the other members of the community had for joining the group, it was now becoming clear to me that the Process could very well have been designed specifically to challenge Mein Host to face and release his demons. And to do this quickly and effectively, he'd needed a teacher—a guru to put it in Eastern terms—who was prepared to be utterly merciless with him. Although I was reluctant to admit it, with what I knew about Mary Ann MacLean, I was slowly realizing that his devotion to the Goddess—in the form of Mary Ann—might well be just what he needed at this point in his life.

Odd though it may sound, because I have been somewhat critical of Mary Ann and her pretensions, this was one of those occasions when I did well to recall how positive my ward's companion angels had been about his being a part of the Process community. I was starting to appreciate that, despite Mary Ann's personal agenda and the decisions she made to enforce that agenda, the ramifications of those decisions as they devolved down to her followers often took the form of rigorous tests and challenges, which were naturally part and parcel of any authentic Mystery School.

If there was a sign, for example, that members were becoming too secure in their positions in the community, or if they were becoming too successful at whatever they were doing (although excelling at bringing in money seemed to be an exception), or later on, when some peoples' relationships were becoming too close, Mary Ann would be sure to intervene in a way that would reverse, change, or collapse that person's hopes and dreams. These were stern lessons, often harshly administered, but if I may not have liked them, they certainly proved an effective way of dislodging peoples' illusions.

Just as there was nothing timid about the underlying raison d'être of the Process, there was nothing reticent about the confrontational nature of its message—that humanity is bringing about its own destruction. However, this message, coupled with the resounding financial success of PROCESS magazine and the sight of an increasing number of uniformed Processeans cruising the streets with armfuls of these same periodicals, was starting to ruffle some conservative feathers.

There had already been a couple of critical articles written about the community, which had appeared in the English press when the group had been operating out of Nassau in the summer and early fall of 1966. Mary Ann and Robert were aware of these articles and their negative nature, but they'd told no one about them. It was therefore a complete surprise to Mein Host and the others when one of the less respectable Sunday newspapers appeared on England's newsstands featuring the caption "The Mindbenders of Mayfair!" along with a story and photos showing the community in the very worst light imaginable. It was a further surprise that the headlines were two inches high, thereby underscoring the hostility that the prickly English establishment apparently felt toward the unconventional organization.

However, this media salvo made absolutely no difference to the way the Process conducted itself. In fact, it had rather the opposite effect. The malicious headlines became a badge of credibility that made the group far more intriguing and attractive to those who were already aware of the establishment's intolerance toward it.

The medium through which the Process responded to this attack was, naturally, PROCESS magazine. Its second issue, dedicated to Freedom of Expression, featured a long list of questions under the provocative banner "Now. The Process Paranoids' Course," which set a satirically defiant tone in response to the barbs of the British press. A few questions posed by the Paranoids' Course will serve to show an editorial policy of refusing to take the malicious rumors and accusations seriously. Mein Host, who designed and laid out the pages, was aligned with Mary Ann in being an enthusiastic supporter of the policy of dismissing the absurd allegations with humor.

Forty questions contained in the magazine mocked each accusation with a heightened, feigned sense of alarm. The first one, in bold-type asks: "Do you have nightmares about giant bats sitting on top of Process House?" (The spread featured a black-and-white photograph of their Balfour Place mansion, vigorously foreshortened and topped by a photo of Chris—a fellow Processean and my ward's longtime friend from architecture college—dressed in a black cloak, with arms up in mock emulation of a large black bat.) Other questions inquire immodestly: "Have you decided whether members of the Process are incredibly stupid or diabolically brilliant?" and "Are you convinced that members of the Process get inside your head and control your actions?"

There were some more pointed questions too: "Have you wasted a lot of money taking legal action against members of the Process?" and "Are you considerably more interested in your own reputation than in your children's welfare and fulfillment?" There were sardonic questions: "Are you afraid the Process will take over the world?" and "Would you love to be able to accuse the Process of taking drugs and having orgies?" This was a good one: "Do you feel you have had your mind 'bent' by the Process?"

The Process proudly took its stand; it was not about to be bullied. The false accusations (they never "bent" anyone's mind that I observed) and the ridiculous lies told about them merely bonded its members more closely and simply confirmed their low opinion of the establishment.

Besides, PROCESS magazine was being sold by the thousands. The Cavern was thriving (Mein Host particularly enjoying working there as a waiter on busy nights); the courses and classes were drawing people in; and money was pouring into its coffers—with, of course, a healthy cut being passed on up to the Omega for Mary Ann and Robert's personal use.

* * *

The angelic revolution was raging, and conditions on Earth had long been deteriorating under Prince Caligastia's corrupt and self-serving dominion. By this time I, Georgia, had already observed signs that Caligastia had been way out of his depth in his role as Planetary Prince and was now even more at sea with his claims to be "God of this world." His greed for absolute power was becoming the dominating feature of his life, with those under his command starting to emulate their Prince's obsession with power and control.

As you might recall, one of the main impulses behind the angelic revolt was Lucifer's call for greater autonomy at the local level of Multiverse Administration (MA). You might think of this as a plea for greater decentralization, for more individual freedoms. When Lucifer split from MA, the Planetary Princes of thirty-seven worlds in this System of planets chose to follow him. One of these worlds was Earth, with Prince Caligastia and his deputy, Daligastia, serving as Earth's two Planetary Princes.

When the angelic revolution initially broke out on Jerusem, the administrative capital planet of this System, the uprising only spread to these thirty-seven third-density worlds and not to the entire System of between six hundred and seven hundred inhabited worlds, as Lucifer would have hoped, expected even. I believe it was then that he must have realized he was bracing for a fight. After all, Lucifer had been appointed by MA as System Sovereign, and he had served honorably in that capacity long before the revolution started. So I believe he had every right to hope that a far larger number of Planetary Princes would have aligned with him.

The post of Planetary Prince is a relatively junior position in the celestial administrative hierarchy and Lucifer, as their commander and overseer, had clearly anticipated swaying them with the power of his rhetoric and his personal charisma. It's my belief that it was this failure to garner more support for his cause that doomed Lucifer's ambitions before his new policies of "greater freedom for all" could take root. Now, more than two hundred millennia later, the fruits of this demand for independence can be seen most clearly acted out, for better and for worse, on Earth.

The Prince's mission—MA's first official "intervention" on the planet—arrived with the Princes Caligastia and Daligastia and their staff of one hundred about half a million years ago. When the angelic uprising broke out on Jerusem 297,000 years later and then spread to Earth, the staff became bitterly divided. Sixty of them elected to support Caligastia and Lucifer's rebel faction, while the remaining forty chose to stay loyal to MA. Shortly after the uprising on Earth those of the Prince's staff remaining loyal to MA were removed back to Jerusem, leaving only Vanu and his assistant Amadon on the planet to "keep the light of truth burning through the terrible times ahead."

This put Vanu in direct opposition to everything Caligastia hoped to achieve as the self-styled God of the World. It wasn't long, therefore, before Vanu and Amadon, and a small group of humans who had kept the faith with Vanu, left Dalamanta, the proud city they had built on the Persian Gulf, and struck out across the eastern desert. Their numbers would grow over the centuries as they created numerous settlements stretching from the Black Sea, across northern India, and all the way to China. They learned from their almost godlike teachers, Vanu and Amadon, and in the main, they stayed free of Caligastia's baleful dominion. These were the people, more interested in trade than in warfare, who were the first to travel the Silk Road. As they were also the people who followed Vanu and Amadon across the southern Pacific to the Islands of Mu, to found one of the finest and longest-lasting civilizations this world has known.

Yet deep trouble awaits the Lemurian civilization, and the first rumbles of the impending disasters start casting their shadows as we begin this part of our journey's tale.

In the meantime, Prince Caligastia, with the majority of his staff remaining aligned with him, moved north and west to set up two main command centers, one in the hills of Salem, in Palestine, and the other in the area that would later become buried deep beneath the city of Alexandria, in Egypt.

More significantly for what was to happen on the planet was the decision of more than 41,000 of the total of 50,000 midwayers to join with Prince Caligastia in the revolution. Midwayers, as the name suggests, exist in a dimension slightly higher than the third density you're familiar with, somewhat less than midway between angels and humans. They were created by the Prince's staff after the mission arrived on the planet, and because they aren't discernible to human senses, midwayers form a valuable surveillance asset serving the mission's purposes. It has been the persistence of these revolutionary midwayers gradually slipping out of Caligastia's control that has been, and will continue to be, the cause of so much mayhem among the mortals of this world.

I too came to this world as a member of Prince Caligastia's support team all those half-a-million years ago. As an observing angel I was responsible to the Prince, although by the time the revolution broke out I was already feeling estranged from him. However, I chose to follow Lucifer and thus found myself, rather to my dismay, still under Caligastia's authority. That was a nasty realization, I can tell you. I'd lost much of my respect for Caligastia well before the revolution, and I hoped the principles that Lucifer was espousing would redirect the Prince into more thoughtful and caring ways.

How wrong I was!

Fortunately, as a Watcher of the Seraphic Order, I was not as closely affiliated with the Prince as those, like the rebel midwayers, who were more directly under his thumb. Perhaps it was this that allowed me to stay here, with a mere handful of Watchers, when all the other angels on the planet who sided with Caligastia were quietly removed to what I hear referred to as "prison planets." It has been a strange and rather puzzling privilege, I suppose, to be one of the very few of the mission's original host of angels left to serve on Earth. As it is also an unsettling thought that Earth may be just one of those prison planets, I am still "technically" responsible to Prince Caligastia, but in reality he has very little direct control over me, and I've been starting to take pains to avoid being in his presence. When I've felt my life here becoming too uncomfortable, I've been able to journey to Zandana, a neighboring world that started out at approximately the same stage of development as Earth. On Zandana too, both Planetary Princes aligned themselves and their planet with Lucifer. Their names were Prince Zanda and his deputy Prince Janda-Chi, with whom I have a far warmer relationship than I do with either of the princes on my world.

Meanwhile, on Earth, matters had been spinning from bad to worse, if that was even possible. Caligastia's demands, made through his rebel midwayers, to be worshipped as the supreme God, and his obsession with destroying Vanu, were consuming him to the point of madness. The primary purpose of MA's original intervention was to gently help improve the standard of life and in doing so raise the consciousness of the indigenous natives. In this way the plan was to ready the planetary population for the second mission. This is perfectly normal and occurs on all inhabited third-density worlds when they are deemed ready by MA.

Yet all those plans had been forgotten in Caligastia's lust for power.

So it was that when MA's second intervention arrived around 40,000 years ago, instead of finding a planet beautifully prepared for them by the Prince and his staff from the previous mission, they arrived to discover a world in chaos and the reality of having to immediately face the Prince's subtle opposition. They found that their garden paradise on the peninsula, prepared for the mission by Vanu, was now fending off the aggressive interest of the local Nodite tribes on the mainland.

The intention of MA's second mission was, in part, to add a specific refinement to the human genome to upgrade the intelligence and make the genome more disease resistant. The two leaders of the mission and the main protagonists were a pair drawn from the celestial Order of Material Sons and Daughters and will become known in biblical history as Adam and Eve. They were accompanied by a small host of angels and were also served by their own cadre of midwayers, a far lesser number than the original group, and known as "Secondary Midwayers."

They are a formidable team, and it will be absolutely essential for Caligastia to subvert this mission as it represents the most serious of threats to the Prince's lawless hegemony.

Whether Prince Caligastia will be able to corrupt or destroy the second of MA's interventionary missions, and what the long-lasting consequences are of this epochal confrontation, are where we begin as we join the two magnificent "visitors" as they carry out their formidable plan. . . .

My story starts here with two mysterious and powerful visitors having arrived to participate in the second of MA's interventions, this time settling on a verdant peninsula now long sunk under the waters at the eastern end of the Mediterranean. The visitors reported to Lanaforge, the System Sovereign who had succeeded the disgraced Lucifer and was now in administrative control over the approximately 670 inhabited planets in this System. While I'm sure that Lanaforge, as well as those who prepared the visitors, would have briefed the visitors most carefully on the condition they would encounter on Prince Caligastia's world, I still doubt if any being could have rightfully prepared them for the chaos and opposition they met when they got here.

I was aware, as I'm sure Caligastia was too, that one of the primary functions of this magnificent couple—and even in my eyes they were magnificent—was generative. They were bringing a genetic boost of what was called "violet blood," which was designed to contribute an important, added refinement to the human genome. I've called this pair magnificent, and that was no understatement. They were humanoids, of course, but both the male and the female stood over nine feet tall. They were beautifully formed, with broad shoulders and strong, muscular, long-legged bodies. Their skin was fairer than any I'd yet seen, almost translucent, and as they moved around I could discern that their auras were tinged with a tone of light violet. Their fine-boned faces were dominated by a pair of the brightest of cornflower-blue eyes—the first such strikingly blue eyes I'd seen on the planet—and their long blond hair blew wildly in the offshore sea breeze.

The pair was evidently closely bonded, and from what I could observe they appeared to dislike spending time apart. Frankly, they couldn't keep their hands off one another. They were obviously reveling in the beautiful new bodies the Avalon surgeons had grown for them, which, I remember thinking at the time, was most fortunate for them when I recalled from the tutorials I'd attended on Jerusem that the visitors were here to make children—hundreds of thousands of children. The tutors had explained it would be these children, and their direct progeny, who, once their number reached one million, would then begin to interbreed with the indigenous mortals on Earth. This would deliver violet blood into the genetic stream of all the planetary races. Our tutors had impressed on us that this approach to instilling a genetic uplift, while slow and somewhat tedious, was regarded as the most natural way of accomplishing the uplift. Cloning, we were taught, and a variety of other reproductive techniques had been explored on earlier experimental worlds. However, nothing had been as successful over the long term as what they'd called this "more natural technique," as it allowed a decent period of time for the human races to become accustomed to the presence of the visitors and their steadily expanding family numbers.

Vanu, together with his team of loyalists had prepared a beautiful home for the visitors on the peninsula, and I was privileged to observe one of the first interactions between Vanu and the visitors. I was curious to determine whether the couple really knew what they faced here, dropped down as they had been, right in the middle of Caligastia's domain.

"We've been well taught, Vanu," reassured the female, and although her voice was soft and consoling, her words didn't make me feel particularly confident.

Then it was the male visitor's turn to speak. His voice was deep and melodic—and yet strong. "We were informed that Prince Caligastia was utterly exhausted. They were certain of that. We'd have no problems from him, they assured us."

Vanu and Amadon exchanged a look, which I don't think the visitors saw. Vanu turned to them directly, and when he spoke there was impatience in his tone. "It's not Prince Caligastia you need be concerned with right now. It's the northern tribes: the Nodites. The wall isn't going to hold them back if they attack. We'd be overwhelmed. You will have to do more to protect yourselves. You've no idea what those tribes are capable of . . ."

The male visitor's voice cut across Vanu's. When he spoke, he defended the decision that had been made by Lucifer's replacement, Lanaforge. "Do you really believe we would be sent here unprepared? That we would be ill-equipped? Do you have so little faith in Lanaforge's judgment? Have you been so infected by Caligastia's lies that you've lost confidence in your System Sovereign?"

It was a harsh criticism of Vanu, even if essentially true. I knew Vanu had been forced by circumstances to make some compromises he must have regretted. And I don't believe that Vanu had ever had the chance to meet with Lanaforge directly, so after his experience with Lucifer, he probably felt he had good reason to be suspicious of Lanaforge, Lucifer's replacement.

Being a Watcher, I was never permitted to peer too deeply into Vanu's character, so I assumed the visitors were telepathically aware of Vanu and Amadon's true state of mind regarding Caligastia; he had been their cruel and cunning enemy for the past 164,000 years. I had no doubt that Vanu and his followers were bone tired and heartily fed up with carrying MA's banner for so long without much help from Lanaforge's administration. But the visitors' sharp tone really *was* unfair. I watched Vanu and Amadon shrinking into themselves as they sat on their side of the obsidian table.

All of us working on Earth knew that the northern Nodite tribes were extremely belligerent and particularly jealous of their land. It would just be a question of time before they descended on the peninsula in force. Admittedly, there were a few Nodites whom Vanu had managed to co-opt to help him prepare for the visitors. Originally the Nodite elite had approved of these defections, because these individuals could, in their view, act as spies in Vanu's camp. However, due to the exceptional intelligence of Nodite stock, the defectors had risen to positions of responsibility in Vanu's entourage and became loyal to him in the process. Some of them had even relocated their families to the Islands of Mu, thanks to Vanu's influence.

This had infuriated the Nodites, as it seemed to threaten their treasured image of themselves. They were the descendants of Nodu and the sixty rebel staff who had left Dalamatia just before the city was inundated by the waters of the Persian Gulf. As such, they were a racially proud and arrogant people convinced of their own superiority. Because all the staff and their companions—their clone-donors—were biologically structured to have almost limitless life spans, their progeny too were singularly long-lived.

The Nodites were Caligastia's "special people," his darling ones. In addition to their long lives, they were endowed with higher intelligence and stronger physical constitutions than any other tribe on the planet. Caligastia's command that Nodu and all the other staff aligned with the Prince should have as many children as possible before they passed away was predicated on his understanding that something of the staff's great longevity would be passed down to their progeny. He evidently believed he could continue to manipulate and influence this select tribe and bend them to his plans.

The purity of their Nephilitic bloodlines became an obsession for Nodu and the Nodites, resulting in the severest penalties for any member who procreated outside the tribe. Although Nodu and the other rebel staff were long dead by the time the visitors arrived, these honored ancestors lived on as the central iconic figures of the tribes who were the direct descendants of the staff's auspicious bloodlines. Down through the ages and long after their demise, those original members of Caligastia's staff continued to receive a worshipful reverence, as was their capacity to inspire fear and violence. These beings, the Nephilim, are those the Bible maintains were the "Sons of God" who descended to mate with the "daughters of men." And it was their children, and their children's children, who became known as the "mighty men of old."

It seems appropriate here to clear up what may be a source of confusion to some scholars. The Hebrew word "Nephilim," the Sumerian "Anunnaki," and the Enochian concept of the "Grigori" all originally referred to the one hundred of the Prince's staff and their clone-donors. These were the true supermortals, the biblical "Sons of Heaven," some of whom had been living continuously for more than 300,000 years before they died in the millennia following the revolution. It was only after Caligastia's instruction for the sixty members of his staff who sided with the revolution to sire as many children with mortals as possible that their exceptionally long-lived offspring also became known as Nephilim.

There is a perfectly natural confusion, which has sprung from the Book of Enoch. It is a relatively recent document by my standards, and I don't expect it to get the events of the distant past completely right.

Contrary to much contemporary speculation, the Nephilim cannot be considered true extraterrestrials, because they hailed from the Inner Worlds of the celestials. Their physical bodies had to be created specifically for them to indwell. Both the Prince's staff and the visitors' genetic structure, while evidently complementary with the human genome, was designed by Avalon surgeons to respond to specific spiritual energies. As I've already related, it was the withdrawal of these spiritual energies that led to the ultimate death of the staff.

In the generations following the death of the staff, the Nodite tribes had swollen in size through carefully arranged interbreeding between the different bloodlines. By the time the visitors' mission came along, the Nodites had largely settled in the mountains of eastern Lebanon and along the northern coastline of Syria. Their numbers had built up again after the atomic devastation that Caligastia had so directly instigated some thirty millennia earlier, which had devastated the Nodite population at the time when Caligastia's plans were starting to go terribly awry. Ironically, and sadly too, most of those who had been working on the development of atomic energy, and who were killed in their underground laboratories, had been of Nodite stock.

Caligastia and Caligastia alone had been responsible for that atomic war, yet he continued to deny it was his fault that matters had slipped so horribly out of his control. The few hundred Nodite survivors of the war had amalgamated with some of the smaller northern Nodite tribes who had escaped the worst of the devastation, and over the subsequent millennia the tribes had grown to become the dominant Mediterranean power. The blood of the Nephilim ran strong in their veins, largely undiluted by interbreeding with native women. Likewise, and in much the same way, Vanu and Amadon had been encouraging the procreation of the best and the brightest on the other side of the world in Lemuria, yet without the harsh strictures forbidding the exogamy imposed by the Nodites. The tribes and the people who sprung from Vanu's careful ministration would be long known for their creative intelligence and their peaceful ways.

As I observed that meeting transpiring around the massive table in the visitors' garden, the sea breezes were picking up with the approach of evening. It hadn't been an encouraging afternoon, and the faces around the table wore solemn expressions. Both Vanu and Amadon were trying in a number of ways to impress upon the visitors the imminent danger posed by the Nodites, but try as they might, they weren't able to convince the couple of the severity of the problems facing them.

"We are scientists," the male had said insistently. "We are highly trained biologists. We represent no threat to the Nodites whatsoever. We've come in peace."

Amadon had tried to prevail. "No, you really don't understand. It is nothing to do with who you are. It's enough that you aren't one of *them*. They'll see you as intruders."

"Ah! But we shall welcome them with open arms, Amadon."

This was from the female visitor, her arms stretched wide as if she were about to launch herself into the air. I smiled to myself—then masked off the thought just as quickly. I still wasn't sure how telepathically sensitive the off-world visitors were. Vanu, I knew had some elementary telepathic ability, but the frequencies at which he was operating made my thoughts opaque to him. If the visitors were capable of tuning in to my mind, I certainly didn't want them to hear me laughing at their antics. Remember, my presence is quite undetectable to normal mortals, but I wasn't at all sure whether the visitors were aware of my presence.

I needn't have worried. I don't believe the visitors even realized I was there. Although their psychic ability was more finely tuned than Vanu's, and they'd appeared to have an almost telepathic rapport with the higher animals, their range of available frequencies was still well below mine. However, I was intrigued to find that both of the visitors' minds were telepathically impenetrable—more like human minds than I would have expected from off-planet personnel. I didn't feel they were deliberately trying to mask their thoughts from me. It just seemed to be the way they were constructed.

While this apparently contradicted the general principle that the lower telepathic frequencies are automatically transparent to the higher, I could only assume this was a special situation; an exception created, I imagined, to render the visitors less vulnerable to Caligastia's telepathic influence.

The meeting was evidently drawing to a close.

Little had been accomplished. Vanu and Amadon still looked frustrated at the visitors' dismissive attitude to a threat that Vanu knew was very, very real. After all, he'd had to deal with the Nodite tribes for the previous seventy-five years while they were preparing the place for the visitors.

Apart from the few Nodite defectors Vanu and Amadon had come to know, Vanu was deeply suspicious of Nodite duplicity. Not only did the Nodites possess the very human capacity for cunning and cruelty, but their high intelligence gave them license to apply these capacities in ingeniously appalling ways. The most subtle of the physical tortures generally attributed to the Inquisition's dungeons had originated in the Nodite imagination and in the pleasure they took in other peoples' pain.

I could see from the state of Vanu's emotional body that he'd given up on trying to persuade the visitors of the danger he was convinced they would have to confront.

"Let's both return to the islands, Vanu!" I overheard Amadon whispering as he and Vanu walked through the house and out into the visitors' garden. "Our job here is finished," he'd continued. "This is out of our hands now." Amadon wasn't sounding particularly enthusiastic, and they both fell silent until they were well clear of the garden.

"Are you as concerned as I am?" Vanu broke the silence.

"Surely there's nothing we can do anymore, Vanu. They're going to have to learn for themselves, sad to say."

Vanu, walking with hands clasped behind his back, was nodding his head, which Amadon took as encouragement to go on; I could see he was bursting to talk freely again. "And to tell the truth, Vanu, by the end of the afternoon I was getting really angry at how blasé they both were . . . they weren't taking in a word you were saying. I'd have expected they'd be more open to what you had to say."

There was still no response from Vanu, and they walked on in silence to the place they'd left their fandors. The large passenger birds had been another constant bone of contention with the Nodites. Although their most ancient legends told of these magical creatures, no fandors had been seen in Caligastia's world since the birds had made the collective decision to follow Vanu and Amadon to Lemuria so many thousands of years earlier.

The Nodites were jealous of anything they didn't possess, and the news of the two fandors on the peninsula sent the tribal Elders into paroxysms of desire. While Vanu and Amadon had been preparing the garden for the visitors' arrival, the Nodites had made constant attempts to kidnap the birds. Fortunately, the birds' semi-telepathic sensitivity invariably alerted them to the approaching danger, and they'd flown off well before the kidnappers ever reached them.

Amadon was still angry. I didn't want to stop listening—this was starting to get rather intriguing.

"I wonder what they're showing them in the simulators these days! Are they ignorant, or are they just arrogant? It's hard to believe Lanaforge would deliberately hide anything from them, don't you think, Vanu? Would a System Sovereign really do that? Why would he want to hold back information?

"And all that stuff about doubting Lanaforge's good intentions . . . what about that? That was downright insulting, didn't you think? When they accused us of being infected—that was the word she used, right? When she said that, I could have punched her on her pretty nose . . . if only I could have reached up that high."

They were both laughing at this improbable image when Vanu stopped and turned to Amadon.

"There *is* something odd going on," Vanu said quietly, "but I think it goes deeper than those two."

Amadon protested angrily, "But they were completely unprepared! And they thought we didn't know what we were talking about! It was infuriating. And then to accuse us of . . ."

"Shush, Amadon, there's no point in getting angry with them. They'll find out the truth of it soon enough. The question we should be asking ourselves is, Why those two? Why them? Why were they, out of so many others of the same order, the ones selected for this planet? Material Sons and Daughters aren't novices . . . they're high beings, exquisitely trained for their functions . . ."

"Or so they say!"

"Do you think they were instructed to ignore us and our warnings?" Vanu mulled, ignoring his aide's jibe. Amadon evidently didn't feel it was his place to speculate on the motivation for the visitors' arrogance and thus the duo walked on in silence.

The fandors must have picked up on their approach, for they were making strange wailing calls of excitement. Vanu and Amadon increased their pace as they threaded their way through the trees.

Vanu was talking again, but more to himself than to his aide. "It wouldn't have been as crude as that," he murmured, answering his own earlier question. "I think it's simply the way they are. I can't believe they were following Lanaforge's orders. I don't want to believe that. Certainly taking over System Sovereignty from Lucifer after the rebellion was bound to be difficult for Lanaforge, but that shouldn't make a difference . . ." And with that Vanu lapsed into silence again. It was Amadon who seemed unable to put the issue aside.

"Perhaps Lanaforge has lost interest in us. That thing about us being infected by Caligastia? You think Lanaforge doesn't trust us?" Amadon was clearly rattled.

"Agreed; it was completely uncalled for. Infected by Caligastia, indeed! The damn cheek of it!" Vanu was evidently riled too, underneath his calm demeanor.

I hadn't seen Vanu express any real anger before, however, and it didn't last long. He'd released the emotion before he started speaking again. "You may have something there, Amadon, but I sincerely hope you're wrong. Yet there is definitely something happening at Lanaforge's court that doesn't smell quite right. It's almost as if they *want* us to fail . . ."

Vanu fell silent again as they emerged from the woods for their first glimpse of their fandors. Amadon's attention was now fixated on his bird, and he started running toward her. As he did so, he was greeted by a wild flapping of massive wings and her sonorous wail of pure friendship.

Watching Vanu hurrying after his aide to be welcomed with the same enthusiasm by his fandor, I couldn't help wondering whether fine, loyal Vanu, who'd thrown everything into trusting the legitimacy of the Multiverse Administration's Local System over Lucifer's revolution, might be entertaining some doubts about MA's sincerity.

Clambering on the two fandors' backs, Vanu and Amadon threw their arms around their bird's soft downy necks and bid their good-byes to the beautiful park that had been their home for almost a century as their fandors gathered themselves for flight.

A brief, and somewhat awkward jilting run, and the fandors were soaring up over the hillside, Vanu and Amadon clinging to their backs and whooping with the pure joy of being aloft and free of gravity.

I saw them taking one last swing over the peninsula, swooping low over the visitors' children playing in the orchards, before gaining enough height to catch the wind currents that would carry them on their long journey homeward.

Home to their beloved Islands of Mu.

It had been a long absence.

Far too long.

2

Reflections on the Visitors' Meeting

Off-World Arrogance, First Helianx Vision, and the Return of the One True God

All the copies of the Freedom of Expression issue of PROCESS magazine had sold out so quickly that work on the third issue was reaching a frantic pace. Mein Host and Andrew, the production manager, and Ewald, the photographic technical genie who was working in the darkroom, labored to finish it on time. No one was permitted to disturb their art department, except to bring them sustaining mugs of Ogmar, an apparently delicious power drink of their own concoction, from the Cavern just down the corridor. The trio stooped over their drawing boards until they dropped from exhaustion onto the floor, where they would sleep in a rather uncomfortable, albeit brief, fashion before clambering back onto their stools with coffee and cigarettes to launch them into the next grueling session.

As a consequence of the second issue's success, the print run for the third issue had leaped to 50,000—double the 25,000 copies that had been printed for the second. This third issue, featuring Mick Jagger on the cover, was devoted to the theme of mind-bending, which was what they'd previously been accused of in the Sunday rags. The word was featured prominently on the cover of the magazine in bold uppercase letters.

This cover was essentially a collage. Its background color was purple, and it featured five provocative little glyphs curling up into a white sky. One of these reads cryptically: "Just who is brainwashing who?" Another states flatly: "Rape of the mind," over a photo of brain surgery being performed. Elsewhere a batch of Processeans appear to be dancing—Lilliputian figures carefully cut and glued onto the tree-lined background, while the head and snout of a white German shepherd peers in from the right-hand side.

The cover also featured a full black-and-white head shot of Mick Jagger slanted back to the horizon as he looks directly and dispassionately out at the viewer. It is a striking photo of Jagger at his most serious, yet the perspective compressed and foreshortened his face, enlarging his already substantial lips to unlikely proportions and throwing them into the foreground.

Mein Host was elated. The entire art department had exhausted themselves completing this third issue and getting it to the printers in time. Now, he finally held the magazine in his hands and was excitedly paging through it with Andrew and Ewald. The printers had risen to the challenge in everyone's opinion, even expressing a lively interest in the magazine's content: not a reaction, said my ward, you'd expect from a hardworking jobbing printer. And I could see how happy and encouraged he was. The 50,000 copies were beautifully printed and were now stored in the extensive cellar running under the Balfour Place mansion.

Mein Host, as the magazine's designer, and Ewald, the photographic wizard, were evolving the most stimulating of creative relationships, which worked to bring out the best in both of them. It was my ward's approach to purposefully remain unaware of the limitations of the darkroom and various photographic techniques when designing the pages. This would challenge Ewald to apply his genius for innovation to replicate the required design. Ewald's technical brilliance at solving my ward's demanding design requirements then, in turn, inspired Mein Host to greater efforts to push the envelope of current graphic technology.

And so it went, upward and ever upward in a continuing creative spiral. And, although Mein Host hadn't yet acquired the sole attention of his two companion angels, Joy and Beauty—names he's given them when he finally made conscious contact later in his life—I could tell how delighted Beauty especially was with this flowering of his creative exuberance.

In retrospect, it's clear to see that the graphic design style seen in its mature form in the later issues of PROCESS first started manifesting in an incipient form in this third issue. (Only recently has the magazine been duly recognized for its advanced graphics and its provocative and controversial choice of content.)

With the second issue sold out, and Mick Jagger on the cover of the new one, sales projected for this third issue looked to be very promising indeed. Everyone loved the magazine. It was hip, it was cool, it was groovy, and it was *weird*.

Mein Host, as was true for everyone else in Balfour Place, hadn't the slightest clue as to what was going to happen next.

* * *

I knew I would have to report back to Prince Caligastia on what I'd observed in the visitors' new garden home, but I tried to delay doing so for as long as possible. Besides, I wanted to take some time to think through what I'd just heard—and what better place than a quiet corner of the peninsula that Vanu had prepared for the visitors?

Long since sunk beneath the waters of the Mediterranean, and now all but indiscernible from the seabed, the peninsula was something of an anomaly on the eastern end of the sea. Barely thirty miles across at the neck where it joined the mainland, it was a mountainous spit of land that projected about 130 miles into the sea.

I found my spot at the far western end of the peninsula. It was more arid than the central and eastern areas, which were well watered by the four rivers flowing down from the central mountain ranges. The aridity made no difference to me of course, so I settled down on a craggy cliffside overlooking the sea. It offered a good view of the long, thin peninsula, with the mountains on the mainland appearing like a sliver of clouds on the horizon.

It was a comfortable place for those of my kind; windy and stony and happily quite uninhabited by mortals. I relaxed amid a grove of scrubby nondescript trees as the sun was setting over the water. With what I'd heard recently in the garden, I'd been given a lot to think about. More, perhaps, than a simple Watcher deserves to know.

Frankly, I was as surprised as Vanu had been at the off-world visitors' apparent arrogance; it seemed incomprehensible to me that they didn't take better notice of Vanu's warning. Was it simply conceit? Or, did the visitors know something Vanu did not? Might they've been chosen deliberately because of their tendency for arrogance and impatience? Were they conveying, perhaps, some delicate subtextual message from MA? Or, was the choice of these two over the large number of volunteers initially well-intended, and it was only when they'd settled into their work here that the true dimensions of the opposition they faced became startlingly obvious? Perhaps it was thought that the visitors would be better prepared to handle the truth after they'd had a chance to experience it firsthand. And then again, perhaps these noble visitors were just shockingly naive.

I'm sure you can understand, dear reader, how confused my thinking was as I lay there on the hillside, with the sun breaking the horizon behind me. The ridge I'd taken for the tips of mountains on the mainland turned from rose-pink to lavender and then to the deepest violet before disappearing altogether. At this, I realized they weren't mountains, but clouds after all.

Writing in retrospect, I find it difficult to avoid the perfectly natural bias of knowing how situations are going to turn out. I know, for example, that the visitors' mission will come to a premature and ignominious end, so what most interests me now are my own personal reactions at the time. What was it that I missed? When did I start to feel that odd sense of inevitability, which was leading me to believe that everything of significance that was occurring on planet Earth was doomed to failure?

I also have to factor in the state of my mind at the time, and the degree to which my thinking was unwittingly colored by my alliance to Caligastia. As the behavior and thinking of mortals is, in part, shaped by their social affiliations in ways they are largely unaware, so also are we Watchers bound to be influenced by elements of which we are unaware. In this manner, for example, the narrative I am attempting here, and the state of mind I hope to represent in relating it, is colored by a spirit of reconciliation that is sweeping through the Local Universe.

We Watchers, in those days, still placed our hopes in Caligastia and his grand plan, despite all the difficulties and setbacks encountered. The revolution inspired by Lucifer was still going strong, with less troubled planets like Zandana thriving in revolutionary hands. Caligastia may have had his faults, but he sincerely believed in the revolution. Although he appeared almost entirely insensitive to the damage he'd inflicted on the human races, he would always point to his harsh measures as being a necessary means to a desired end, thoroughly justified, he'd claim, by the glorious utopian future he had in mind.

That's what he led us to believe, anyway. And why not believe him? Was it so inconceivable for a Planetary Prince to oversee his domain *without* the paternalistic blessings of MA?

And have I mentioned this? Prince Caligastia could be the most charming and persuasive of creatures when he wanted to be. I trust I'm not making an excuse for myself, or any other Watcher aligned with the Prince, when I say how convincing he could be: characteristics associated, at least in the modern mind, with psychopathology. Yet I believe that up to the time of the visitors' arrival, he was sure the revolt was still going his way. I knew their arrival had rattled him; he'd made no secret of that in my previous interview with him. He was all too aware that the coming of the visitors demonstrated MA's continued involvement with life on this planet, *his* planet, he would always emphasize, never wanting us to forget who was God around here. He knew it was going be the start of a long battle if he was to prove his primacy. And it was in that same interview that I'd also seen the depth of the villainy to which he was prepared to sink to achieve his aims.

I didn't know what to make of the entire scenario. From what I saw of the off-world visitors I felt that they didn't have a chance against Caligastia's wiles. I knew he would take many meetings with them and I worried at all the many ways the Prince might be able to derail the pair's good intentions. Certainly the visitors were beautiful and adored by their followers. They'd referred to themselves as botanists, so they had to be widely knowledgeable. Given the number of children I'd seen playing in the orchard, there was obviously no problem with fecundity. However, I'd little doubt that Caligastia would have no trouble corrupting the visitors' unnerving mixture of innocence and overconfidence. No trouble at all. It would just be a matter of time.

Then again, did I have the whole matter the wrong way around? The visitors had claimed they would greet the Nodites "with open arms." That they'd welcome them as friends! This was the plan? So, was what I'd taken as arrogance in fact the visitors' absolute confidence in the path of love? If that was the case then they would have been justified in dismissing Vanu's warnings about Nodite aggression as unnecessary fearmongering.

I can appreciate now the degree to which my thinking really *was* being influenced by my subtle-energy connection with the Prince. Was I therefore condemned forever to this dreadful ambivalence? There were just too many contradictions to think about, and, as I've already stated, Watchers are simple creatures who are not particularly good at complicated thinking.

As I've mentioned, I was required to report back to the Prince, but only what I'd observed, not what I thought or felt about it or, indeed, how I interpreted the information—which, under the circumstances I regarded as fortunate. Yet, I also had to get all my mental meandering under control so I could safely tuck away my ambivalence. I needed to be able to mask it sufficiently for Caligastia to be unable to read my conflicted thoughts.

I turned to face the sun just as the horizon rose to finally occlude it, and yes, to greet the green flash . . . and there it was! You should see a green flash from my dimension! It rippled softly toward and through me, like a tidal wave of beneficence. I love the experience and always feel rejuvenated by it. Whenever I have the opportunity to be in the right place at the right time to see this little optical miracle, I give myself entirely to it. For me, it always acts as a burst of restorative healing energy.

I relaxed into the green spiritual glow, and it seemed to me that I had entered a dream, except for the fact that I felt as awake as I am now. I was in the water—which for a Watcher is not exactly a wet experience! Initially I didn't know where in the vast sea I was, but I must have been close to the peninsula because the water wasn't that deep.

Before me and undulating gracefully past me was a creature that was strangely familiar, and yet I'd swear I'd never seen anything quite like it before. It was about the size of a small whale, but it moved more like a sea snake. A great multicolored plume streamed from behind its head, and when I caught a glimpse of its leonine head as it passed before me I could swear I saw eyes glowing with an ancient intelligence.

I sensed that the creature was telepathic, yet it appeared so unconcerned with my presence it was as if I wasn't there. Whether it was a creature of my dreams, or whether it existed in some reality of which I was unaware, I knew only that I'd been drawn into the creature's aura by the gravitational weight of its immense psychic power. It moved with a supreme ease and, somewhat in contrast to the increasingly distraught state of the visitors, appeared filled with purposeful intention. When it passed out of sight and I was no longer within its sphere of psychic influence, I unaccountably felt a new, deep sense of encouragement, as well as a much needed reminder that events of which I was only marginally aware were happening behind the scenes, and in which I simply needed to have faith.

Then I drifted into a curious meditative state in which faith, and what it meant to me, seemed to float up for my inspection. It came to me in those moments how much faith I'd lost as a consequence of the revolution; how much of a test of faith it had been. I saw how I'd confused faith with trust, and when I lost my trust in MA, I realized I'd also lost my faith in the Creator. I'd become so preoccupied with all the events occurring subsequent to the revolution that I'd lost sight of the underlying, benevolent purpose of the living Multiverse.

When I emerged from my reverie I felt cleansed by the lucidity of the dream, lovingly enfolded by the green flash, and finally ready to face the Prince.

The second interview with Prince Caligastia turned out better than I'd expected. Early on in the encounter I made sure to report on the apparent indifference MA's visitors had shown to Vanu's warnings about the Nodites. This delighted the Prince, as I knew it would. After that my report went swimmingly, interrupted only by Caligastia's intermittent bursts of laughter, which I assumed was him gloating on the many devious ways by which he was going to subvert the visitors' mission.

I thought he'd be furious when he heard how casually Vanu had dismissed him as a threat to the visitors ("Moi? the God of this World?"), but to my astonishment he'd greeted this with another roar of laughter.

"Vanu underestimates me," I heard between the laughter, "in the same way that the visitors underestimate the Nodites!"

I decided to do what I could to mask what I'd overheard of Vanu's doubts about the administration in Jerusem that he'd followed so loyally for so long. Apart from not wanting to hear the Prince crowing over it, with his "What did I tell him!" and his "I told him he couldn't trust MA!" I respected Vanu and what he'd accomplished with his Lemurian experiment. On the basis of an overheard conversation between Vanu and his closest aide, I didn't want to be the inadvertent cause of any misery Caligastia might vent on him. I also didn't want the Prince to try to capitalize on Vanu's doubts and mentally torture him with them. I rather surprised myself by thinking that it wouldn't have been fair to Vanu. We're all permitted our doubts—or so we should be.

Caligastia appeared to be reveling over what he had in mind for the arrogant visitors. He'd show them! Oh yes he would! After a while he seemed to have lost interest in me, so I slowly backed away. He'd become so entertained by his own malicious musings that I don't believe he gave the slightest further thought as to why the visitors might have acted in that surprisingly haughty manner.

I was happy to be out of his presence again, this time with no specific instructions.

I must have had Vanu on my mind, because in the next moment I was watching him and Amadon on their great flying mounts as they circled one of the Lemurian cities on the Peruvian coast.

It was early morning in Peru, and the sun glinted off the fandors' wings. Every movement threw off translucent shards of copper and violet light as they looped down and landed awkwardly on the pasture reserved for the birds behind the central temple buildings. Five other fandors who were quietly grazing in one corner of the field set up a wild cackling sound that must have been a greeting, because the pair just landing cackled happily back in response.

I found myself among the trees that lined the meadow, watching Vanu and his aide sliding off their mounts and taking a few moments, swaying slightly and laughing between them, to reorient themselves to life actually on the ground. It had been an exceptionally long trip all the way from the eastern end of the Mediterranean, and although the pair had made many stops, I could feel their exhaustion.

The two fandors stalked off contentedly to be with their sisters.

A number of people, some dressed ceremonially, ran forward to greet Vanu and Amadon, placing flowering leis around their necks and touching the ground before them in respect. I knew the small crowd couldn't perceive me so I followed it into one of the ancillary buildings on the temple grounds. Here the pair was fed a simple meal of fish that had been baked in a clay oven, together with a generous helping of what appeared to be a white pasty substance that I thought must be rice. Vanu clearly appreciated this sign of the high regard in which he and Amadon were held. He would have known how precious rice was, because it had to be imported from the other side of the Pacific. There it grew on the well-watered mountainside terraces that Vanu had originally organized and shaped before he and Amadon had left for the Islands of Mu. In this way, the Luzon area of the Philippines had been supplying the Lemurian islands with food grown on the mainland by following long-established navigational routes across the Pacific.

After Vanu and Amadon finished their meal and had enjoyed a brief rest, they returned to the temple. I discovered I was not permitted to enter. It was as though an invisible barrier prevented me from doing so. This was nothing physical on any level that I could perceive, but a horrible sense of feeling unclean and inadequate came over me when I tried to follow them in.

When I got over the shock of having all my sins thrown in my face—which summarized the feeling of hitting that barrier—I stopped outside to consider how puzzling this was. There had been something of the same sensation present in the Temple of the Invisible God, back in the days of Dalamatia, just after the revolution broke out. Then again, I recalled having the same emotional reaction when I had once approached a simple temple in one of Vanu's Eurasian settlements, prior to the Lemurian migration.

You might recall that Amadon had persuaded Vanu to substitute Father Sun and Mother Earth for the Invisible God, one that the people could not see but had to take on faith. Amadon had argued that the people needed more tangible, material gods to believe in and worship. And he had his way. This practice of worshipping Father Sun and Mother Earth continued to hold true during their long history and throughout the widespread Lemurian colonies.

Yet here I was, having this same unpleasant experience again. No temple devoted solely to Sun and Earth would ever have this horrible effect on me, so it could only mean one thing: Vanu must have been working to restore the old worship of the One True God. The First Source and Center. The transcendent Creator of All there is.

Caligastia wasn't going to like that development one little bit! In declaring himself God of this World, he had sought to obliterate any belief in a transcendent Godhead. This new change in religious emphasis, if indeed I'd read it correctly, was going to be a serious threat to the Prince's position and even more damaging to his exaggerated sense of self-worth. He prided himself on the guidance and inspiration he gave the midwayers who served him and, through them, the way he could bend the mortals' worship circuits to his end. There was no faith involved with this. Caligastia had no time for faith. Indeed, the concept of faith seemed entirely foreign to him. But, belief—now that was another matter altogether. I've even heard the Prince refer to himself as a "Master of Belief." I really hadn't seen this so clearly until I appreciated to what lengths Vanu had gone to protect his people from the pitfalls of mere belief. In Vanu's terms, he'd taken a real risk in allowing Amadon's plea for a physically real, material manifestation of the Godhead to be adopted. And here's the danger in that, something Prince Caligastia knew all too well. If you focus a people's innate religious impulses on believing in some aspect of nature, be it a sacred mountain, the moon, or the Earth and Sun, then they can be distracted and isolated from knowing the presence of the Indwelling Spirit, the Invisible God that Vanu was now evidently subtly reinserting into their religious practices. "You can *believe* anything you want," I've heard him say more than once. "But it is this God, the Father of All, in whom to place your faith."

With these thoughts on my mind, I moved slowly back to where the fandors were now sitting close to one another, looking like immense feathery bundles. They were so quiet and still I assumed they were absorbed in their own telepathic conversation. As I drifted toward the enormous birds I couldn't help laughing at the odd visual effect they created. Without some familiarity with fandors and without the momentary recall of their outlandish size, they appeared from a distance—as if in an optical trick—as a group of normal-size birds.

Then, as I drew smoothly closer, the fandors seemed to progressively expand in size, while the landscape around them behaved in the way I naturally would have expected a landscape to behave. Yet, suddenly, here were these enormous birds! Even sitting with their breasts on the grass and their legs tucked neatly beneath them, their heads atop long necks seemed to tower over mortals. From my dimension this was a rather dislocating vision.

Operating in the finer frequencies I could have eavesdropped on the fandors' silent interaction, but telepathic courtesy forbade it. However, I'm a rebel Watcher, and as such I can take some liberties—I'm almost expected to! So yes, I did take a quick listen and managed to quit the frequency before the fandors noticed my presence.

The birds were excited! Apparently this had been one of Vanu's first long trips on the back of a fandor. I'd wondered about that. I knew that normally the birds were only prepared to establish such intimate relationships with those of mortal stock. And even those who could ride fandors required an unusual psychic sensitivity, much initial training by the fandors, and a truly heroic courage.

At this point the fandors fell into amiably teasing Vanu's chosen bird for the airs she was putting on. Vanu, it seemed had fallen off five times while he was learning to ride the creature, and among the fandors this was regarded as a great joke (they could have quite a malicious sense of humor)! The joke, however, was not at Vanu's expense—it was directed at the fandor. It was expected that a mortal might fall off once or twice before acquiring the necessary grip and equilibrium—although the rider was never at fault in the fandors' eyes. It became something of a congenial game between the birds to compete in preventing this from happening. It was never easy . . . (I heard). But, five times! And Vanu's bird too! For the fandors that was too hilarious.

It was friendly teasing in which Vanu's fandor cackled right along with the others. To my surprise, I heard Onya's name mentioned in hushed tones as the only mortal who'd never once fallen from her fandor. Apparently Onya had achieved a legendary status among the birds. Young Onya, a mere slip of a girl, had been the first mortal in the fandors' memory to have "ridden the bird."

I was thrilled to have been present at that first auspicious encounter in which the young Onya, a local native girl, had leaped spontaneously onto the back of a fandor—despite all warnings of the bird's ferocious resistance to any physical contact. It was seen as a miracle and had initiated a whole new era of contact between mortals and fandors. Fandors were invaluable to the Lemurian migration—I've heard Amadon saying they couldn't have done it without the birds—and they had proved so reliable and effective in ferrying mortals around the islands that the Lemurians had no need to use any form of wheeled transport to achieve the same end. The fandors served the Lemurian cities and settlements throughout the Americas until the species made the decision to cease procreating and quietly died out. What would now be called a "species extinction" occurred some six thousand years later than the period I'm describing here. Fandors will have a progressively more important role to play when the Islands of Mu started sinking back into the ocean.

Soon after the last Fandor had disappeared, I recalled speaking with Astar, a sister Watcher with a characteristic acerbic turn of phrase, and she reckoned the poor old fandors most likely died off from a collective broken heart, saddened and horrified by Caligastia's blatant abuse of his powers. Fandor consciousness was always a delicate matter. They were a particularly tender and caring species so it wasn't altogether surprising when they chose to withdraw from the world stage. It spite of their large size, they were a timid lot and so averse to violence that their conceit was that not one of them had ever died in violent conflict. Whether true or not, I cannot say. The fandors were as prone to deluding themselves as any third-density species, and the more intelligent the species, the more inventive become the delusions.

They were extremely private creatures, these fandors, yet I recall thinking at the time that as a species they weren't bowed down by false pride. Perhaps, like dolphins, a fandor's lack of personal possessions obviated the need for prideful comparisons. Personally, I thought it was their humor that saved them: they were able to see the fun in everything.

"They're too good for this world," I recall thinking, as I quietly retired back into the woods behind the temple where I couldn't be distracted by the fandors' antics.

Deep inside me I found I had responded with something very much like gratitude to the knowledge that the old tradition of worshipping the Godhead continued. Like every other being in the Local Universe, I'd been expected to accept, on faith, the existence of the Invisible God. Then Lucifer, our System Sovereign, MA's High Son, in administrative charge of up to one thousand planets, was said to have come forward and announced that this so-called Invisible God was really a sham. A glorified fiction.

A fiction? A manipulative lie? Really? Could Lucifer really have claimed such a thing? I certainly have never witnessed or heard that he'd made such a statement. I wasn't present when this announcement was said to have occurred, so I can't be sure it wasn't part of MA's misinformation campaign. I suspected that it was MA's agents who had been spreading the rumor around that Lucifer claimed the transcendent Godhead was an invention concocted by all the Creator Sons as a way of maintaining their control over Multiverse affairs.

Naturally, for MA's loyalists this was the very worst allegation that could ever be made. In their minds not only was it a monstrous disavowal of the Creator they all held in such high esteem, but it was thought to be a particularly mean-spirited insult directed at Michael, the Creator Son of this Local Universe.

When I first heard this rumor being bruited around, it hadn't made any sense to me. It was simply not logical, and, surprising as it may sound, celestials of all ranks are nothing if not logical. If Lucifer had really announced that the Godhead was a deception fabricated by the Creator Sons, he would have had to explain away the obvious existence of the entire mortal ascension program for a start, as well as denying the validity of the personal encounters with the Godhead as related by those who have returned from such an experience. None of the 700,000 Creator Sons, as individuals or as a group, could have actually "created" the entire Multiverse—and would never claim to have done so. The hierarchical structure of the Inner Worlds clearly demonstrates that such a massive act as the creation of the Multiverse could only emanate from the very deepest and most fundamental source. Lucifer will have been aware of this. It makes little rational sense for him to assert the Creator Sons conspired to promote the fiction of an invisible, all-powerful Creator. Michael, our Creator Son, never claimed to be this fundamental omnipotent Deity: indeed, I'm sure no other Creator Son would ever consider making such an unlikely assertion. Powerful creator beings they may be in their own Local Universes, but Creator Sons are clearly not the original creators of the Multiverse.

Finally, it's hard to see what possible advantage the Creator Sons would gain from fabricating a fictional Deity when the mortal ascension program, as well as the subjective experience of ascending mortals, bear witness to the *reality* of the Indwelling God. Surely the logic of this would have prevented Lucifer from making such an irrational allegation. As I considered this, it seemed more likely that this was a propaganda slur, another false accusation promoted by the Local Administration to further discredit Lucifer.

I also hadn't aligned myself with the revolution because of any statement Lucifer may (or may not) have argued as to the existence of an ultimate Godhead. In fact, I didn't even hear about this—that it was all a plot by the Creator Sons—until a rumor circulated long after the revolution started. And it didn't feel true then, when I first heard it.

As I mentioned, I hadn't been present when this discussion was taking place on System HQ. These were simply my thoughts as I waited at the forest's edge for Vanu and Amadon to emerge from the temple. There was so much bad blood between the two factions it was hard to know quite what to make of it all. It seemed like MA, as well as the Local Universe administrations, thought they had every reason to malign Lucifer and Satan any way they could. Yet, underneath all of this mental conflict and confusion, I have to admit to having a renewed feeling of encouragement.

How long it would last remained to be seen.

3

In Disgrace Again

The Prince's Machinations, the Fandors' Flight, and Devic Telepathy Circuits

Mary Ann and Robert were traveling the world when the third issue of PROCESS hit the streets back in London. Being away from home base, their hold over the editorial policy of the magazine was, of necessity, far looser than it had been with the first two issues. There were a number of last-minute decisions Mein Host had to make that, due to long-distance communication problems, were impossible to have the Omega approve. The most important, as it would turn out, was the placement in the magazine of Robert's full-page portrait.

Mein Host was well aware that it was something of a coup for the new magazine to have scored an interview with Mick Jagger at the height of his notoriety, and to have also had a chance to photograph him. So obviously, the Jagger article needed to be placed in the front of the magazine, given that Mick's face had to be on the cover. Jagger was the draw; that was just common marketing sense.

So, what to do with the carefully posed, delicately air-brushed, professionally photographed portrait of Robert, the so-called Teacher of the Process? His gaze in the photo, as if over the viewer's left shoulder, is not a particularly welcoming gaze. His carefully positioned forelock framing his face, the grooming of his mustache and beard, and the oddly placid vacancy of his gaze seemed to draw its inspiration from, as my ward pointed out to

Andrew, "those silly idealized portraits of Jesus you'll find on the bedroom walls of motels owned by enthusiastic Christians." Frankly, I think he was embarrassed about the portrait. He'd known Robert well for three years before the Process. He was fond of the guy. But this wasn't a photo of the Robert he knew, and I could see that it annoyed him. He must have known this was Mary Ann's work, her idea of a holy man, her "messiah making" as I heard him call it some years later, when he wasn't so much under Mary Ann's influence. So here was the photo, just arrived from wherever the Omega were on their Middle East tour, and with the instruction to give it full prominence in the magazine.

With Mick Jagger at the front of the magazine, Mein Host had no doubt that the inside back cover would be the best place. "In the advertising world," he was telling Andrew, "inside back cover is primo . . . costs more to put an ad there, right? Much more. Robert is going to look just fine in that spot."

Andrew grunted in noncommittal agreement. It wasn't possible to check in with the Omega about this, and he was happy to leave the decision up to Mein Host.

"We've got two days left to get it to the printers in time," Andrew reminded my ward. "There's no time for indecision. You know how tight the printer's schedules are."

Two sleepless days later Andrew and my ward delivered the flats, with their acetate overlays, in a taxi to the printers, just making it for the deadline. I could feel Mein Host as happy and triumphant as I'd ever known him. This had been a long and devoted labor of love. Aided by Ewald's brilliantly inventive darkroom techniques, the third issue was the most innovative and adventurous one they'd yet attempted.

Mein Host was proud of the result, as well he should have been. It was the issue of PROCESS magazine that first started to demonstrate something of my ward's unique design sense, which blossomed into a fully developed and original graphic style over the next half a dozen issues.

Yes, I think he was proud of himself, perhaps a little too proud—and pride is a dangerous thing in a Mystery School.

In any event, Balfour Place had been running smoothly without the physical presence of the Oracle and the Teacher. The first copies of the magazine—fresh off the presses—were excitedly sent off to wherever in the Middle East Mary Ann and Robert were currently staying. Mein Host had appreciated the freedom to design the magazine as he wished, without any of their immediate oversight. Like most of the other members, he so seldom saw the Omega in person anymore that their being on a cruise in the Mediterranean made little difference to his life. They'd largely let him do what he wanted in the design of the first two issues when they were present at magazine meetings. He had no reason to doubt the Omega's approval. It was a fine magazine and a Herculean effort by the handful of those involved with its production.

As for what I observed? I had seen some previous signs of secrets developing between those favored by Mary Ann. I had seen aspects of it in Xtul when a separation developed between those who initially found Xtul and lived there with Mary Ann and Robert and those who had not yet plucked up their courage to make the long beach walk, only to find, when they did manage it, themselves rejected when they finally got to Xtul (and then having to walk exhausted the sixteen or so miles back to their hut in the village).

However, I believe the magazine fiasco was the first occasion in which a strict hierarchy was beginning to emerge. I also observed that it was no longer a coincidence that Mary Ann and Robert had once again chosen to be out of the country when critical headlines were appearing about them in the press. It was one thing, I thought at the time, to want to avoid being around when the going got tough and quite another to know in advance when to leave, or otherwise duck for cover.

However, fifty thousand copies of the Mind-bending issue of PROCESS magazine were now stacked in the basement ready to be sold. Excitement was running high in the community, bolstered, it seemed, by the opposition they'd been encountering from the establishment newspapers. Yet another article had appeared in the Sunday rags, and I could tell there was an edginess in the atmosphere at Balfour Place.

The brouhaha certainly suited Mein Host's rebellious nature. He obviously loved selling magazines on the street. He could break out of his shell and make a complete fool of himself if it sold the things. I've seen him hopping, one leg tucked up under his cloak, accosting young women shopping on Kings Road, as though he was a pirate.

Once the magazine hit the streets it sold even better than the previous two issues, helped along by Mick Jagger's popularity with just the people the Process hoped to attract.

And while they were doing this, they waited for a reaction from the Omega.

After a couple of weeks—the mail had apparently taken its time to track down the Omega—and when Mein Host appeared to have all but forgotten he'd sent the magazines off to Mary Ann and Robert, there came the furious telephone call from Mary Ann.

"Stop the presses! Immediately!" (Did she believe the magazine hadn't been printed yet?)

"Then, stop selling it! At once! Not one copy must be sold." (But, they'd been selling them for two weeks already!)

"Destroy all the copies. Throw them away!" (This is verging on craziness! What could be that wrong with it?)

And so it went, a tirade of bluster.

Mein Host wasn't enthusiastic about taking the call, so he had it relayed to him by one of the women standing in for Mary Ann. For her own reasons, this young woman took the opportunity to rub my ward's nose in his crime. It was a crime so serious, she told him, that every single copy of the magazine would have to be destroyed. Did he know how much money that represented? How much money he'd wasted? Had he any idea how deeply insulted and offended both Mary Ann and Robert were by his action? She added that he must have always been jealous of Robert, or he'd never have been able to do something so outright malicious.

And what was the terrible crime? An act so frightful that the Omega had ordered the entire print run destroyed? The insult that had so offended the sensibilities of the Goddess?

Mein Host had placed Robert at the back of the magazine and Mick Jagger—Mick "bloody" Jagger's!—photos at the front!

There was no explaining the logic of it . . . the weighing up of the two options . . . the obvious advantages . . . the importance of Robert's picture on the inside back cover. But the young matriarch must have had her instructions. The vitriolic tirade of accusations and blame continued until she finally ran dry.

Mein Host was in disgrace. Once again.

Overnight, almost all those in the community who had admired the magazine's design and layout and had so heartily congratulated him on it, now found reasons for renouncing the magazine and turning their backs on him. No one had previously noticed or commented critically about putting Robert in the back. Now, or so it appeared to Mein Host, *everybody* had thought about it. The atmosphere at Balfour Place turned from one of excitement to a dulled mist of depression that hung over all of them. Scarcely able to blame the Omega for their alarming decision to destroy the entire print run, the weight of the blame fell fully on my ward.

Nothing had been immediately done to organize moving and then destroying such a massive load. The instruction was so shocking, such a terrible setback, that nobody could quite take it in. Besides, there was a feeling I'd heard expressed a few times by some of the more experienced members: surely the Omega would never countenance such a colossal waste of *money*. Would they really sacrifice everything just to make a point? From what he knew of Mary Ann, Mein Host glumly told Andrew as they were sitting in the art department licking their wounds, he wasn't at all sure the Oracle wouldn't follow through on the threat.

Andrew had, in fact, been as much implicated in the decision to place the photo of Robert at the back as Mein Host had been, but as my ward was the art director, the responsibility was ultimately his. And it wasn't in Mein Host's nature to avoid his responsibility, even if he still felt entirely justified in the decision he had made.

"Destroy every single copy . . . she might do it just to put the boot in!" Mein Host was saying.

"She might do it, I agree, she's that headstrong. But I don't think Robert will let her. He's a lot more practical about things like that." Andrew was Robert's younger brother and tended to view him through rose-colored glasses.

"Practical? Robert? You really believe that, Andrew? I think he'll go along with whatever Mary Ann wants."

"Maybe not exactly practical, but more pragmatic, more reasonable, at least," Andrew replied. "He's too sensible to chuck 'em all away. He'll come up with something different, you'll see."

"Let's hope so, because it's really ridiculous. Think about it, Andrew. It means we'll have wasted the original cost, and then there'll be the cost of printing fifty thousand new magazines . . ."

"Plus there's the additional cost of *destroying* all those mags," Andrew chipped in, "and then there'll be no money coming in from sales during the time it'll take us to make a new mag and reprint it."

"*If* we get to do that!" Mein Host said. "You'll be okay, Andrew. Production manager, they'll always need you. Me? I don't think they'll ever let me near the magazine again!"

Their laughter must have seemed hollow to both of them.

It didn't pierce the gloom.

A week or so later Mary Ann and Robert must have come to their senses, because another call came through with orders to halt the destruction of all the magazines. And Andrew had been correct in his assessment of the situation. The Omega had indeed come up with an alternate solution.

Mein Host was instructed, as before, by the same self-satisfied young matriarch, to sell every single one of those thousands upon thousands of magazines all by himself.

Yes. By himself.

No one else was to go out selling. He had made the error. And now he had to sell every single one of those Mick "bloody" Jagger issues. Even selling an average of a hundred magazines a day, seven days a week, month after month . . . well! His swift calculation told him he'd be doing it for at least the next two years. Two years! And that was only if he kept those sales figures up!

"This I did *not* expect," he was telling Andrew, soon after they'd learned about it. "'Every damn one!' Mary Ann said. It's going to take me a lifetime."

Balfour Place had heaved a collective sigh of relief upon hearing the news. With one exception they were all off the hook. The sword had fallen, but not on them. And didn't Mein Host deserve it anyway? He thought it was his magazine, didn't he?! He was getting what he deserved.

"It's still a damn good magazine," Andrew had told him encouragingly.

"Know what, Andrew? I'm going for it. They want me to sell 50,000 magazines, I'll show them. I'm damn well going to sell all of them on my own."

"You're not!" said Ewald who'd just come into the drawing office. "You couldn't! It'll drive you crazy!"

"Oh yes I will!" replied Gabriel Stern with a surprising certainty. "And it certainly won't make me crazy."

Neither Mein Host nor anyone else in the community could have been aware that Gabriel Stern—my ward's subpersonality who had proved so helpful in the various crises they'd endured in Nassau and at Xtul—had reasserted himself in the shock of this directive from the Omega. Gabriel Stern, as the name implies, was a particularly hard and determined aspect of Mein Host's personality with a penchant for self-sacrifice.

And what of my ward? At that early stage of his life he only knew the as-yet unnamed Gabriel Stern to be another aspect of his personality. A "subtle shift of emphasis," or perhaps "a radical alteration of viewpoint," is how he might have tried to explain the feeling that came over him whenever this strong personality asserted itself. Mein Host was familiar enough with this "altered viewpoint" by now to trust it and go with it whenever it presented itself.

Gabriel Stern apparently was not under my ward's conscious control, as this aspect seemed to appear whenever he decided to do so. All my ward really knew in this, his twenty-seventh year, was when Gabriel Stern came a-knocking, it was wise to let him in. This Mr. Stern (his other preferred name) had taken a lot of punishment. Whether simply a shift of viewpoint or a well-developed subpersonality, Gabriel Stern had earned his time in the sun.

And if anyone could sell all those 50,000 magazines, I recall thinking in the moment, it is going to be old Gabriel Stern.

* * *

I was in a most unsettled state of mind when Vanu and Amadon finally emerged from the Lemurian temple. As a result of my having been rebuffed by the temple entrance, I'd been more disturbed by my thoughts than I was prepared to admit to myself. It threw me back to those early days of Dalamatia before the uprising, when we were aligned in a common cause and were functioning in synchrony with one another. Sure there were some problems, some frustration with slow progress, but at least back then we were all moving steadily forward together.

That had disappeared. Everyone, great and small, seemed to be going in their own direction now. The constant conflicts between Prince Caligastia's various proxies, which characterized his ruling strategy, was echoed by the gulf separating Vanu and the Prince. It felt as though the interplanetary isolation, imposed by MA as a result of the angelic revolution, had filtered down to every being on this world. Whether mortal or immortal, everyone seemed isolated from one another. There was no longer any central underlying sense of purpose that we all could share.

That memory of the good old days had flooded in so unexpectedly that I was shocked to the core. I'd really hoped I'd left that sentimentality behind. This was in stark contrast to what I was experiencing and to what I'd observed when I looked around and saw the terrifying inevitability of the global situation simply getting progressively worse. After the Prince's ambitions for a planetary utopia—a world completely dominated, of course, by *him*—had crumbled, Caligastia made it clear that the well-being of his indigenous subjects was a matter of complete indifference to him. They were merely tools to be used for his own purposes.

It has only become more and more obvious over the millennia that what this really meant was that Prince Caligastia was in it entirely for himself. Vanu and Amadon, with the exception of their recent episode organizing the habitation of the visitors, had spent their time almost exclusively circulating between the Islands of Mu and the extensive Lemurian colonies throughout Asia and Central and South America. Considering there were only two of them to do the work that the entire Prince's mission would have taken on had there been no revolution meant that they had to spread their visits far wider than they would have desired. This had also led them to be stuck over on the other side of the world for almost a hundred years. One of the results of this long absence was the stress this laid on their midwayers. On their return, Amadon especially was horrified to find out how exhausted the midwayers had become. Somewhat dispirited too. It appeared that Caligastia, hoping to take advantage of Vanu's absence, had been sending teams of his own midwayers over to the Pacific islands to infiltrate Lemurian life and sow discord among the placid islanders. It had been shaping up to be a full-scale assault, and although I never heard any midwayer claim it, it was clearly them with their diminished numbers (if you recall, only one out of every five of the fifty thousand midwayers chose to stay loyal to Vanu and MA's ways) who managed to forestall the potential invasion by Caligastia's proxies that was sure to follow the initial disruption created by the rebel midwayers. It was a close thing, by all accounts. And as it was a confrontation taking place almost entirely within the domain of the midwayers, it was thus imperceptible to most islanders. I did hear it described by one particularly sensitive Lemurian fisherman as an "invisible storm raging in Dreamtime." He couldn't really perceive it, of course. There was no tempestuous rain and the wind was barely blowing. Yet as sure as the drop in barometric pressure signifies an approaching thunderstorm, so did the fisherman experience a similar drop in what he described as his "psychic skin." He said he had stayed in that state of mind, unable to fish or carry out his spiritual duties, and only found relief when Vanu's midwayers had succeeded in driving the opposition away and clearing the islands of any who had successfully infiltrated the lives and consciousness of the good people of Mu.

Vanu's approach to dealing with the Prince was to leave Caligastia's territories well enough alone. He was not aggressive and had never invaded another tribe's land during that long trek halfway across the world prior to moving his people to the Pacific islands. I suspect Vanu may have been secretly glad he wasn't present when the Prince's midwayers had launched their attack. His principle of passively letting the opposition be on the principle that corruption will sooner or later end up by corrupting and destroying itself would have had little value under the circumstances. It was action that was needed, and it was the courageous midwayers who stepped up to the plate.

After that piece of Caligastia's skullduggery the Prince had retreated back to his magnificent citadel to lick his wounds and regroup. As far as I'm aware, that was the last time he attempted such a frontal attack on the loyalists. Thus, the overall global situation settled back into what was essentially a Mexican standoff.

Caligastia seemed to have given up his dreams of invading Lemuria and finally humiliating and ridding himself of the pesky Vanu. Yet, I knew that every century Vanu was on the planet would become a knife in the Prince's gizzard. Caligastia must have felt his presence as a constant irritant and an open insult to his self-proclaimed godhood. But there was even worse news for the Prince. Astar had told me Caligastia had worked himself into a fury that seemed never to stop when he heard that Lemurian temple worship was reverting back to all that he most detested! Back to the Invisible Father God! To that ridiculous conceit! To this so-called God that no one could see or know, when here *he* was, the great Caligastia, the God of this World! It must have been downright infuriating.

Prince Caligastia, for reasons that weren't to emerge until well after the revolution, turned out to have his own motives for supporting Lucifer's rumored accusations. He'd claimed that he too had always believed this so-called Invisible Godhead was a fabrication. Indeed, I've heard Watchers gossiping that it was actually the Prince himself who spread the rumor for his own ends—but I can't be sure of this. It would mean that he was merely voicing the accusations of MA, his sworn enemy, in its campaign to discredit Lucifer. Yet, by then, I felt I understood the Prince's duplicity somewhat better; I'd little doubt he derived a malicious pleasure from playing both sides so effectively.

I also reminded myself that with the arrival of the off-world visitors, Prince Caligastia was going to have his hands full for quite a while. The visitors had no intention of leaving, and their assigned mission of refining the human genome should have kept them on the planet for the long-term.

I could tell that Vanu and Amadon were anxious to get back to the islands. After hearing all the news from Lemuria and resting for the night, they declined their host's offer of a ceremonial visit of their capital city, and they set off to find their fandors, who were already preparing for the next leg of their long journey home. Now more than halfway there, with only the island-hopping journey across the Pacific to come, the fandors, with a great clacking of beaks and little shrill shrieks, were obviously as exhilarated to get back to their communities as their riders were to return to theirs.

A small crowd had gathered to watch Vanu and Amadon mount their fandors amid a sonorous clattering chorus of the other birds. Then there were those comically awkward, stiff, jerky steps as the two birds picked up enough speed to make it worthwhile flapping their massive wings. The pasture they took off from dipped down toward the coast and a sudden updraft must have caught beneath their wings, because in the next moment they were circling overhead, their riders waving at the wildly cheering crowd below.

The city, with its broad avenues, its stepped pyramids, and its monumental stone buildings, lay in the shadow of the mountains rising behind it. As the fandors spiraled ever higher, there was a point when they seemed to explode with color. One moment the birds were dark, wheeling forms etched against a cerulean sky, and in the next, the early-morning sun, breaking over the jagged mountain peaks, was illuminating the giant birds in bursts of color.

A gasp of delight went up from the crowd as everyone tilted their heads back to watch the fandors until they were nothing more than tiny flashes of brilliance in an endless sky.

I had the strong sense I'd be ending up on the islands myself so I saw no harm in accompanying Vanu and the fandors for part of their journey. Besides, I was curious as to how the birds could fly such long distances without tiring. I knew they would have worked out a plan that allowed them, in most cases, to rest overnight, but there were still islands they were bound for that were very far apart and well beyond their normal range. Setting off from the Peruvian coast and taking the southern route was one such plan, so I was intrigued to observe how the birds would manage that initial long stretch before reaching Easter Island. They'd been flying for almost a day when I spotted the first clue—although I didn't know its meaning for a while. The fandors had gradually been reducing altitude for some time now, so I was clearly able to see a small school of whales below us moving in a stately procession in the same direction as we were traveling.

Dusk was falling. Still on the surface, the whales were continuing to plow through the ocean, and now I could see that their pod was surrounded by dolphins. The dolphins kept pace with the school, looking like little leaping toys next to the enormous bulk of the sperm whales.

Then I understood what was about to happen. Both of the fandors were circling lower and lower, their riders peering down at the great flat backs of the whales below. Three large males closed ranks so that their flanks pressed against one another as the school slowed down.

Of course! I realized that both species, fandors and cetaceans, must possess an active telepathic ability. They must have been using devic telepathic circuitry for communication because I was unaware of it occurring. Although I'm capable of tapping in to this circuit if absolutely necessary, it requires considerable focus to discern signal from noise at those lower frequencies, so I generally leave it alone. As you'll discover in pursuing this narrative, however, there'll be a time when I will have no choice but to dive deeper into the devic circuit.

Incidentally, my ward believes that what I've called the "devic telepathic circuit" is the same as the matrix a small group of U.S. Naval researchers stumbled upon while investigating dolphin communication. It appeared that by placing two dolphins in tanks hundreds of miles apart, they were able, through testing, to establish that the dolphins were in some sort of contact with one another. From this, the scientists further postulated what they called a "telepathic matrix," which instantaneously connected marine mammals over long distances in a way the researchers were unable to explain through any contemporary theory of physics. News of this unusual insight was shared with some in the loose-knit community of those concerned with dolphins and whales, but according to my ward, the experiment and its profound implications had never made the headlines. There was a brief report in one of the technical journals that Mein Host found, before it was quietly removed, presumably suppressed by the military, subsequently disappearing from the discussion.

I noticed then the whole school of whales slowly turning in to the wind while the fandors were continuing to wheel soundlessly overhead. There was a long pause in which I imagined both the fandors and the whales were telepathically making their last-moment adjustments to what must surely be an extremely tricky process. Perhaps, if I was a fighter pilot seeking to land my plane on the deck of an aircraft carrier in a heavy swell I would better appreciate the skill involved in a maneuver such as this one. However, the fandors had managed it with such an unexpected grace that it was obvious they'd done it many times before.

Initially, one of the birds swooped low—far too fast I thought at the time—yet at the last moment those great wings spread out and down, catching the wind and bringing the bird to a sudden standstill in the air. For one long moment the colossal bulk of the fandor, wings outstretched wide, appeared to hang in the air, free of gravity's pull, before settling down the last few feet to land gently on the broad back of one of the whales. The second fandor followed moments later with equal elegance. Well, of course they would. These were two of the finest, strongest, and most experienced of all the fandors. They had to be the best; they were transporting Vanu and Amadon, who, though graced with eternally long lives, were nevertheless vulnerable to injury and possibly even physical death were a fandor to fail them when over the open ocean.

However, Vanu and Amadon were obviously familiar with this routine, and they slipped off their fandors' backs as the birds crouched, tucking their long legs under them for the night's rest. Amadon slid himself down the side of the whale on which he'd alighted and then clambered awkwardly up to join Vanu as he was unhitching a satchel, from which he then removed small bags of food. After they'd eaten, Vanu's fandor fluffed up the soft feathers on her chest and formed the most comfortable of beds for the pair.

The whales changed course again, reverting to their original direction. They swam slowly on through the night, their modest bow wave throwing glistening streams of bioluminescence down their flanks. With no need to dive, the quiet splashing of the waves was only broken by the sibilant hiss of the whales' exhalation, followed by a long in-breath, which was kept deliberately even and slow out of consideration for their sleeping passengers.

The dolphins continued to swim around this massive, slow-moving platform, playing games with each other yet always maintaining their circling pattern. The two fandors, with their long necks tucked under their wings, were swaying with the gentle movement of the whales as though bonded to them. Vanu and Amadon slept side by side, cushioned on their feathered bed, with Vanu, I noticed, on his back and lightly snoring.

It was a tender sight, representatives of the three most highly developed species on this world working in close contact with one another. This was a vision I would hold in my mind for a long time. In all the millennia I've been on Earth I've not witnessed such a profound harmony manifested between three such different sentient species.

This unusual little flotilla swam on through the night.

As the sky lightened and the stars flickered out, strips of clouds appeared on the horizon, their grayed undersides stained by streaks of rose, lavender, and duck-egg blue. The fandors uncoiled their long necks from under their wings, clacking their beaks to welcome the sun. Amadon stretched his limbs and prodded Vanu awake. They shared some food and sips of freshwater from a gourd before remounting their fandors.

The sun was breaking the horizon when the whales turned once again into the wind and picked up speed. I'm always astonished how fast these enormous creatures can move through the water. It wasn't even necessary for the birds to run before lifting off; the combination of stiff breeze and the speed of the whales allowed the fandors, their wings fully extended, to waft gently up into the air as though they were weightless. These huge creatures, their wingspans the width of the Supermarine Spitfires that Mein Host had watched soaring overhead in the Second World War, appeared first to hang over the whales, kept aloft by the cushion of air washing over the whales' backs.

Then the fandors broke away with a powerful flapping of wings beating the air to gain height, while below them the whales were turning back toward the sun.

The Earth fell away, revealing now the beet-red orb of the sun.

The very moment the horizon tipped the bottom curve of the sun, I saw the whales breaching as one. They then positioned themselves so a good third of their immense bodies stuck vertically out of the water, each surrounded by expanding ripples spreading out on the surface as though, for a moment, they might have been wearing summer dresses. Holding that position and facing the new sun for far longer than I expected, it came to me that the whales were not only greeting the sun but that their action had something infinitely holy about it. Then, in unison again, they were hurling themselves up into golden-red arcs, rainbows of spray following from their flanks, leaping, once, twice, three times, before diving and disappearing into the deeps.

I knew it was an act of joyful worship.

It was as if the ocean had exploded in a synchronized triplet of prodigious gray waves each time the whales had crashed back into the water. These were glorious creatures. They took no part in the angelic revolution as far as I was aware. Perhaps they didn't know about it, their attention on higher matters. And even if they knew of the uprising, maybe they simply didn't care. After all, Caligastia's ambitions seemed entirely focused on attempting to control the human races.

I could see to my surprise then that there were far more whales in the school than I'd previously realized. They had evidently kept their distance throughout the night, forming the first barrier a curious predator might encounter if they had hungry eyes on the defenseless whales who cradled the sleeping pair.

It was also clear to me from observing this whole encounter just how revered were Vanu and Amadon, and by creatures who were other than human.

I have to admit it unsettled me.

It reminded me of what the world might have been.

It saddened me too while it also seemed to give me hope.

And it just confused me all the more.

4

The Subpersonality Returns

The Benefits of Radical Change, Finding the "Right Place," and Reincarnational Hints

Mein Host was as surprised as anyone else when his subpersonality, Gabriel Stern, stepped forward to help sell those 50,000 copies of the magazine. It was perhaps the most assertive display of dominance by this alternate personality that Mein Host had experienced to date. And although my ward was starting to appreciate the difference between himself and the Stern subpersonality, as of yet he had no real framework to understand what was, in truth, actually happening to him.

There came a couple of months in early 1967 when a number of small incidents occurred that could have prompted him to investigate this more closely at the time. Perhaps the closest he came to stumbling on the truth was when I watched him prepare for sleep each night for at least a month. Before going to bed, he would position his few simple possessions with great care on the floor around the head of the mattress on which he slept.

Four men of the Process community slept in the same room, their sleeping bags and mattresses parallel with each other and separated by a couple of feet of carpeted floor. Mein Host's mattress was in the far corner, the farthest from the door on the other side of the room, with the three others sleeping to his right. His roommates would watch with amusement as my ward laid out his wallet (empty), together with his watch, his passport, a manila envelope with his identification papers in it, and various personal items that otherwise would have been hard to locate in the morning. I had no idea what he was doing or why he was taking such care with articles that wouldn't seem relevant to a sleeping man.

This is what I heard him explain to the long-suffering Juliette, a colleague and good friend of his from a time before joining the Processean community. Although Juliette was by now familiar with his odd quirks, it was still also the case that she never quite knew what to expect from him. "I keep getting this feeling," he was trying to explain, "that I'm going to wake up tomorrow a different person. That's why I'm laying my stuff out, so whomever it is that wakes up will be able to find it and, and . . ."

". . . and continue *your* life happily uninterrupted?" Juliette said, humoring him.

"Come on, Juliette, it really isn't that funny. It's such a weird feeling . . . never quite knowing if I'm going to be there when I open my eyes."

I believe this strange impulse came from the stress building up in his psyche as a result of having to go out every day for up to twelve hours, regardless of the weather, to sell all those magazines. Gabriel Stern was making himself progressively more felt ever since my ward had to be out for those long hours on end. I suspect the month during which my ward was wrestling with his identity was when Gabriel Stern was pushing for more autonomy. I doubt if Stern really wanted to take over the primary position—he would have done so already had that been his aim—but rather that Mein Host was reacting to an unaccustomed psychic sensation.

It seemed to be a time for new psychic sensations; some were trivial, some prescient, and others more relevant for my ward's spiritual growth.

Mein Host woke up one morning in mid-January with the Beatles singing "Strawberry Fields Forever," followed by "Penny Lane," playing loudly in his head—or, this is how he described it later that day. This would scarcely be worth mentioning if the record had already been released. It hadn't. He first actually heard the songs when they came out on an EP disc (extended play!) a month later in mid-February and remembered them well enough to sing along with them at that point.

This odd phenomenon has happened on a number of subsequent

occasions over the course of my ward's life when his telepathic sensitivity was being adjusted by one of his companion angels. Mein Host is by now more familiar with this awkward sensation, which in almost all cases has been remarkable only for their lack of any real consequence.

Within this same period another event occurred that had considerable consequences for my ward. I've already touched on it because it was his first significant fully conscious out-of-body experience without the aid of entheogens. I should add here that since joining the Process my ward had ceased any experimentation with entheogens, preferring to explore what can be experienced of the transcendent realms without the aid of power plants.

This next event occurred in the same room I described before, when Mein Host was sleeping and his three companions were fast asleep on their mattresses. Sadly, I wasn't there to witness what happened, so I will let him relay how he was introduced to this out-of-body experience.

He writes, "It seemed to start, although I didn't know it at the time, when I woke up. It was dark outside, yet I recall being able to see the other guys asleep, so there must have been some light in the room.

"Anyway, I woke up and sat up. So far so good. I looked around the room. The others were fast asleep, a couple of them snoring quietly. I twisted my torso to see the bookshelves behind me. Yes, they were there. Then, still twisted around, I looked down. And there was my body, lying flat on the mattress and as fast asleep as the others. I twisted hurriedly back to find myself sitting from the waist up, my legs still where they should be. What the hell was going on? But, strangely enough, I didn't freak out. It was actually rather exciting.

"I realized in those moments that I must be half out of my body. It was easy to get up. I kind of rose up out of my physical legs and was floating toward the door. I can't remember . . . I think I actually opened the door, but I might have just gone through it . . . that bit's fuzzy. Next I was going down the stairs . . . the bedroom was on the fourth floor. I'm pretty sure I was floating down, but I definitely followed the curved contours of the staircase.

"I was in the lobby and through the front door before I knew it. The street was suffused with a sort of crepuscular half-light and seemed longer than Balfour Place was in reality. I was moving steadily down the street when I looked down and saw that I was naked . . . I prefer to sleep without clothes on. And then I freaked out. Oh! Lord! I'm naked in public!

"Next I knew, I was slamming back into my body. But I was amazed. It had never happened like that before. This was no lucid dream. It wasn't an acid flashback—I've never had one of those in my life!

"Now I absolutely knew for sure that I existed free of my body. And as if to confirm it, I had another brief and somewhat inconsequential out-of-body experience a few weeks later."

Mein Host believes it was what he witnessed in one of the community's group meditations that has had the most long-standing effect on his creative life. This last event would prove to be the final one of its kind.

The community had kept up their practice of regularly meditating together first thing in the morning and last thing at night—with the exception that now the Oracle and the Teacher no longer attended them. Most of the group's meditations involved directed intention or creative visualization, but occasionally they opened up the meditation to whatever people came up with.

It was during one of these unguided meditations that my ward caught his first glimpse of the Helianx, although he wasn't to know that name, or indeed what it was that he'd seen in his vision, until some years later. I should add that Mein Host himself says that he is not given to visions or hallucinations as a general rule (although it might sometimes seem like that from this narrative). But, of course, I'm cherry-picking those events in his life that I feel are significant to his spiritual development, or those on which I can throw some insight on what has previously puzzled him.

Here again I will ask him to describe what he saw, as this was an internal experience that I wasn't able to share.

He writes, "It's about five minutes into the meditation, and I've gone through the process of grounding myself and clearing my mind, when I chance to look upward. Of course I have my eyes shut, but I recall my whole head tilting back. This is unusual, as any meditator will tell you; normally it's best to face straight-ahead.

"So, my head is back, I'm fully conscious but doubtless in a mildly altered state, and I'm looking upward into the darkness. But it isn't all darkness, is it?! There's an enormous object—and I mean enormous! It must have been several miles in length—and here I'd no idea what to call it, or make of it.

"It isn't a craft—I've no doubt about that. Perhaps calling it a gargantuan crystalline bowl would be the closest I can get to describing it. But I'm only seeing it from below; I can't see what is on top of the bowl, or whether it *has* a top. The object is glowing with a soft white light, and it's translucent enough for me to be able to make out that there's something alive inside the bowl. Whatever it is appears to be larger than the bowl itself, because I can just make out that the creature is coiled back around on itself.

"And it must be a creature of some sort because I can see its slight movements. There's absolutely no sense of threat—rather the opposite: I'm transfixed with fascination and yet I feel comfortably detached.

"Somehow, in some unexplainable way, it's deeply familiar. Yet I've no idea what I'm seeing. Even if it's an illusion, or a hallucination—which I sense it's not—the question would still be raised as to why on earth I would be faced with this particular, utterly strange vision.

"It doesn't last for more than ten seconds, which nonetheless is somehow long enough for me to be able to glimpse this enormous, gelatinous, multisegmented creature curled up in its crystal bowl. The surface of its milky-white, semitranslucent body, or what I can see of it, appears to have an iridescent sheen.

"I am struck with the utter beauty of what I'm looking at, even if it is incomprehensible to me. I'd never seen anything like it, nor had I ever imagined or conceived of such an extraordinary image. If I had preconceived it, I would have known what it was. Yet, perhaps the biggest mystery I was left with was the question of why the object felt so strangely familiar to me. That's what really caught my attention."

Indeed it was a mystery, and one that has gradually been unraveling itself bit by bit over the course of Mein Host's life. These were early days, however, and while he clearly never doubted the essential authenticity of the vision, that it had some ontological reality outside of his imaginative capacity, he must have found it so strange that he tucked it away and spoke to no one about it—not even Juliette. He obviously felt intuitively protective of his vision and feared she'd dismiss it as mere imagination.

Mein Host's main focus at this time was to get rid of all the magazines he'd been instructed to sell. A typical day featured him arising with the rest of the community, keeping their collective, agreed-upon silence, and entering into morning meditation with them. Their silence would be broken only when they sat down to their communal breakfast. After that my ward set off on his own, into the London streets, with an armful of PROCESS magazines—the Mind-bending issue.

Balfour Place was a short street running parallel to Park Lane and somewhat off the main pedestrian areas, yet within easy walking distance of Marble Arch, Oxford Street, Regent Street, Piccadilly, Knightsbridge, and Bond Street; in short, all those places in Central London that were generally crowded with tourists and shoppers.

I watch my ward hurrying along Park Lane, a freezing wind whipping across the barren waste of Hyde Park in winter and blowing his long hair behind him as he strides along. He is dressed entirely in black: black shoes, black trousers, a black top, and a thick black sweater. However, swinging from his shoulders and reaching down to mid-calf is a violet-colored cape that, like his hair, is streaming out behind him.

As he approaches Marble Arch and spots his first prospective buyer walking toward him on the sidewalk, I watch him go through an interesting change. He slows down and his shoulders pull back so he seems even taller than his normal height of six-foot-two. As the woman—and it's most frequently a woman—draws closer I see he's starting to do a curious little dance with his feet, nothing too conspicuous but clearly directed at the approaching target. I can see she's curious and rather amused at this odd sight. It's not threatening, so she doesn't break eye contact with him as he dances nearer. He's smiling inoffensively; she can't help smiling back. Is he tap dancing? Whoever is it? Does she know him? And that violet cape?! He looks clean and smart, even if his hair . . . Well!

And before she knows it she's safely in his aura, gazing up at him and probably marveling at how remarkably blue his eyes are. She likes the lilting tone of his voice. It's deeper than she would have expected and he speaks well; he was "obviously a well-educated young man" as she'd later say to a friend when she was justifying why she bought her copy of this weird magazine.

She would never know, of course, that she had bought the magazine because she'd been entranced, or more specifically, she'd been induced into a light hypnotic trance by a certain Gabriel Stern and had therefore found it almost impossible to refuse.

In this way, and without Mein Host's knowing quite how it was happening, the numbers of magazines that he was selling increased steadily as day followed day. Seventy-five magazines a day soon became one hundred, then two hundred, until he was regularly selling between two hundred and fifty and three hundred magazines a day—sometimes even more. These were astonishingly high numbers. On a good day on Carnaby Street, or Kings Road, Gabriel Stern was selling a magazine on average every two minutes and bringing back hundreds of pounds when he returned to Balfour Place each night to count the change that bloated his pockets.

However exhausted his body was from this physical exertion on the streets, I watched him make sure he always came back into the house singing to himself and appearing obviously happy—which he genuinely was. And he wanted people to see it. He wanted all those people, who'd originally raved about the magazine and then suddenly changed their opinion when they heard Mary Ann's condemnation, to eat their words. He took a quiet (but malicious) glee in counting out the money he made as other members came and went, peering over his shoulder in awe at the ever-growing stacks of pound notes.

It was the same spirit of defiance that had risen to the surface so many other key times in his life. When he was at his English Public School it had been his defiant act of will in refusing to make a sound while being formally thrashed by an increasingly furious and out-of-control senior monitor. Likewise, it was my ward's determination to push the boundaries that created such a division between the staff of his architectural college; and it was this very same spirit of rebellion that dictated his sitting outside Xtul for as long as it took to be invited back in.

Yet he was still unaware of Gabriel Stern's part in all this, only that some other part of him would take over whenever he went out magazine selling. He was conscious of it to that degree. I would hazard that Mein Host's primary personality shared the experience to the extent he believed that it was him, only a different, amped-up him. With the recent understanding of brain waves emerging from neuroscience—of beta waves manifesting during normal everyday conditions; alpha waves, a little slower and signifying a more creative state of mind; and theta waves, slower still and manifesting in deep meditation or sleep—he decided to call the change of consciousness he experienced as "deliberately moving his brain into the alpha waves."

Gabriel Stern will continue to make a few more appearances in my ward's life until such time as he will finally become integrated into Mein Host's primary personality and my ward will have no further need to split off an alter ego to cope with this kind of pressure in his life. Although Gabriel Stern might have thought differently (subpersonalities tend to have exaggerated ideas of themselves), his role in Mein Host's life is a relatively minor one. His position, if I call it that, in my ward's life will soon be replaced by yet another of these buried personalities, split off from my ward as a small child in his terror and confusion of the bombs of the Second World War. (*And* those dreadful "doodlebugs," he makes sure I add—the V.1 German rocket bombs that so terrified him as a child. They were the worst.) And it's true, it was those wretched contraptions that created the most damage, both on peoples' houses but less obviously on the psyche of those, especially the children, who suffered under them.

Micah, the name of the subpersonality who will subsume Gabriel Stern in my ward's life, has something of Stern's grit and determination to make something of himself. He has charm and guile, which he uses to mask his flinty hardness. Interesting for me is that it will be Mary Ann who recognizes this personality and will be the one who names him Micah Ludovic.

Needless to say, within a couple of months the evident pleasure and the extraordinary success Mein Host was receiving from his "punishment" must have reached Mary Ann's ears. A punishment enjoyed is scarcely a punishment. Additionally, the lure of radically amplified profits was just too powerful for Mary Ann not to take advantage of. If she could get everyone out on the streets making the same amount of money! Well, then. So I wasn't altogether surprised when the order came down from the Omega for *everybody,* not just Mein Host, but everybody, to go out daily to sell magazines. Mein Host was clearly amused at this turn of events, although the four hours daily required of everyone—including him—would never match his twelve-hour stints.

The consequence of this mandate served to complete Mein Host's revenge. Those who had rejected him were now required to go out on the streets too. Most often these individuals would return with nothing more than a handful of change and a really bad attitude, as compared with Mein Host, who would continue to count out scores of pounds. In addition, the good news was his time out selling was reduced from the ten to twelve hours he'd been doing back to four hours a day, like everyone else.

With the Mind-bending issue selling fast, it was time to start working on the next issue of PROCESS; this one was to have the theme of Sex.

Mein Host was back in favor again with his Goddess.

Striving to make a success of Balfour Place while the Omega was away, many of the community's senior members were hard-hit emotionally when the message came down from the top that it was time for their organization to uproot and move. This was made even more pointed in Mein Host's case. He'd been chosen to be one of the half a dozen members who would be sent out in pairs ranging through Europe to find this ultimate center that Mary Ann had conjured up in her ambitious imagination.

In this endeavor Mein Host was paired up with Nicholas, a street kid from San Francisco, barely twenty years old. They were a most unlikely pair: Mein Host was twenty-eight, tall and slim, blue eyed with fair hair, sensitive under a hard exterior, artistic, cerebral, and massively overeducated. Nick, on the other hand, was as tall as my ward, yet thick around the shoulders with the body and scars of a street fighter—which was what he had been back in the Bay Area. He was as dark as Mein Host was light; his black beard and long, unruly hair made him a twin to Che Guevara.

Nothing concrete came of their months of hitchhiking around France,

Germany, and Italy, nor from all of the meandering trails they took trying to find their new center. I could see it was a pointless quest. Finding
a place that would comfortably house forty to fifty people, together with
an assembly hall and the ancillary rooms required to service such a place,
was never going to be a straightforward task. Expecting not to have to pay
for it was a challenge of quite a different order. This idea that the "right
place" was out there just waiting for the Process to come along, and they'd
be recognized and the "right place" would somehow be gifted to them,
was one of Mary Ann's more grandiose conceits, an arrogance that proved
over time to be as unrealistic as I'm sure it must seem to the reader.

The Process would move around a great deal over the ensuing nine
years, and Mein Host was frequently the one sent ahead to locate one of
these "right places," so he was in a good position to see how this concept
actually played out in real time. There were some rare occasions when the
"right place" was found, but far more frequently the place found became
the "right place."

This brief European trip, however, would yield neither option.

I won't speak for the other two pairs of location scouts, but for Mein
Host and Nicholas the trip was an eye-opener. It will probably come as
no surprise to my ward to hear that Nick was one of the incarnate rebel
angels he encountered over the course of his life, without being aware of
it at the time. Nick was a natural rebel who appeared to need to defy—
to an almost obsessive degree—any authority he came across. Mein Host
wasn't aware of it, but Nick had spent time in juvenile detention back in
the United States for a violent crime, something he'd told no one until
he started attending Process activities in London. Although his natural
urge was to rebel against the Process—it represented everything Nick
must have instinctively hated—he was courageous enough to try to face
his fears and demons by throwing himself as wholeheartedly as he could
into the community and its various endeavors.

Every day was a battle for Nick. His inner wisdom as a reincarnate
must have encouraged him to submit to the authority of the Process,
although his reactive emotional intelligence caused him to fight against
it with all his strength. This was made more complicated because, as frequently happened to people drawn to the community, Nick had fallen in

love with Wendy, one of the attractive young matriarchs of the group (as they were now formally calling themselves).

Wendy has already appeared briefly as perhaps Mary Ann's most committed young proxy. As articulated in a previous volume (*Confessions of a Rebel Angel*), she'd been one of those who, along with Mary Ann, Robert, and "Canadian Dave," had made that first midnight trip to Xtul—and from where they had run in terror on that first night. Wendy was no great beauty, but she had a vivacious quality I've observed in certain women who are not confident about their looks. Yet she would have been rendered all the more alluring to Nick (and others) by her very unavailability. She, like the other members of the community, had agreed to lead a celibate life—at least for now.

Nick had been hanging around the Cavern for months trying to engage Wendy's attention before finally being allowed to join the community as a full-time member. Living in Balfour Place with the rest of the group and having given up everything—money, personal possessions, sexual freedom, and personal autonomy—Nick had somehow found himself no nearer to satisfying his carnal desires than he was before becoming a member.

However, when Wendy approached my ward and told him to take Nick on the European trip, she said she'd hoped Nick would find his sexual desire for her transformed into something deeper.

"Like a fourteenth-century troubadour," Mein Host suggested, "sublimating his passion into a pure love for his lady?"

"It's making him a complete bore to be around," Wendy confessed. "He clings to me whenever he can. Wherever I turn, there he is, gawking at me . . . wants to be around me all the time, with his great cow eyes."

"I thought *you* fancied him?" Mein Host evidently caught the pride in her voice underneath her implicit denial. I could see he was not relishing carting a love-sick youth around Europe with him.

"Well, I do a bit!" she grinned with a tad more enthusiasm than seemly for a celibate. "He is gorgeous. But you know as well as I do that if I let him seduce me, which I'd never do anyway, we'd lose him. He'd have got what he wanted. He'd leave the community . . . of course, he'd just walk out." Wendy was being unexpectedly open.

Mein Host was nodding; all of them could justify this sort of sexual manipulation as baiting the hook, becoming the proverbial "fishers of men." They had no qualms about it—they were doing it for a higher purpose.

"But now he's becoming an awful nuisance," Wendy felt free to complain. "I just want him out of my hair for a while. Please take him with you. It would do him good."

As you'll have gathered from this narrative, Wendy had known my ward since college; they'd shared an apartment together with five others, but they'd never shared a bed—much to Wendy's chagrin. She'd long set her sights on my ward, to be met by his continuing lack of interest. I say this because he seemed unaware that her next statement carried a subtle subtext implying that, celibate or not, she was still hoping to engage his passions. I'd guess it had become a matter of personal pride for her by this time. She was a matriarch, after all, and used to getting what she wanted.

"Nick's jealous, you know, of anyone else getting close to me." She was nibbling the end of one of her long curls while she spoke. "Really! It's becoming a nightmare. Either he's all over me, or he's moping around throwing me horrid, sulky looks."

Mein Host didn't seem to be aware of how much pleasure Wendy was deriving from her protestations. Like other sexually insecure people I've observed, she relished the power of being passionately desired, with the additional bonus, in Wendy's case, of a legitimate spiritual reason to keep him on the hook.

"Sometimes he's like a thug . . . a beautiful thug, but a thug nonetheless," she went on complaining. "I think he's going to lash out at any moment. No, no, not at me. Anyone else I spend any time with."

With Nick's increasing attachment, Wendy, under Mary Ann's tutelage, saw that by sending Nick off with Mein Host, she was getting Nick away from her and at the same time she was giving my ward an almost impossible challenge.

"Look, just take care of him, will you? For me? He's never had a real man he could look up to. He hated his dad. So see what you can do with him." Wendy had a small, freckled face with very blue eyes and a crinkly smile. She was now the picture of pretty persuasion, and her challenge for Mein Host to become the "man Nick could look up to" (a line that had been suggested by Mary Ann) had, in fact, been the hook that flattered my ward into going along with the plan. It was only after talking with Wendy that I heard him musing with one of his friends, it was Juliette, I believe, about Wendy's curious manner in almost pleading with him to take Nicholas with him when her normal behavior would have been to simply instruct him to take the lad. Juliette was somewhat noncommittal but agreed that it sounded like something else was going on behind the scenes.

As for my ward's thoughts about Nick, I could tell he hadn't given much consideration to just what this trip might entail.

Nick and Mein Host set off on their mission, traveling with no money and only a few magazines to sell in an emergency. They hitchhiked from place to place, with no plans except to move as their intuitions took them. And, of course, there was Ishmael, my ward's beloved German shepherd, traveling with them.

Coming into small European towns at sundown they learned to follow their inner guidance so as to arrive at the one hotel in town that would be happy to feed and provide beds for two self-described "wandering missionaries." Day after day they discovered the kindness of strangers. Drivers went miles out of their own way to deliver the pair to some obscure villa, which may or may not have been suitable or even available to be the next headquarters of the Process community. People fed them, gave them money for their mission, bought their magazines, and even appeared to be interested in the organization's message regarding humanity's dire plight . . . or as much as the language barrier allowed them to understand it. And, as Nick was fond of pointing out, "A whole heap can be lost in translation!"

One of the more significant encounters for Mein Host occurred one evening in a Bavarian monastery. It was an enormous building that had once housed more than six hundred monks yet now had less than a dozen full-time trainees in residence. It was the clearest example they'd yet seen of the progressive irrelevance of the Catholic Church. They'd been delivered to the remote monastery by a helpful Italian who was sure the monks would put them up. And indeed they did, and quite enthusiastically too, telling them how rare it was to receive visitors.

After a splendid dinner, all of them sitting at long wooden tables at one end of the vast refectory, the small group of monks clustered around the visitors. It was at this point that one of the young monks told my ward about the doctorate he was currently working to obtain. He kept saying that he couldn't believe his good fortune at having an Englishman right there; at last a brain he could pick.

Now here I have to be a little enigmatic for the sake of Mein Host's perfectly reasonable reticence. As I've previously articulated in some detail, Mein Host's previous incarnation was that of soldier in the First World War who achieved a certain level of controversial recognition. It so happened that this young German monk in the monastery happened to be writing his dissertation on this particular soldier.

I should emphasize that, at this point in time, as they sat around those ancient wooden tables, Mein Host had no idea of his connection to this soldier. He'd had some vague hints of particular incarnations, and after his revelation in Nassau he understood that he was a reincarnate, but it was by no means anything to which he seemed to have given much serious attention. He appeared to take the idea of reincarnation in stride, as perhaps should be natural for someone who'd had previous lives.

The soldier had made enough of a reputation that English schoolboys knew his name and something of what he'd accomplished, so when the monk started asking his questions, my ward was able to answer his first questions from what he'd learned in school. The monk continued, his questions about the soldier and his life becoming more detailed, more personal. And the answers just kept on coming.

The next morning, as Mein Host and Nick, with Ishmael slinking along between them, were walking back to the road, my ward was trying to explain what had happened the night before. "It was the strangest thing, Nick. As you heard, the guy just went on asking me questions, question after question, and I just went on answering them. How would I know what his mother's name was?! Or how many brothers he had? Or where he'd lived? And all that stuff about his life? Where on earth did all that come from?"

"Yeah! He was scribbling away," Nick said. "I watched his face while you were answering. It was like he couldn't believe it . . . he'd hit the jackpot. Then he'd start wondering how the hell you knew so much and his face dropped . . ."

They were both laughing by now. No cars had yet passed them, so they headed for the crossroads they could see in the distance.

Nick was talking. "Then I swear he'd ask you something he knew the answer to and you'd answer right and his face would light up all over again."

"I'd no idea that was happening, Nick. I was kind of listening to myself answering . . . telling him stuff I'd never even thought of before . . . it was weird. But the monk just went on and on; he wouldn't stop. So I just went on and on answering."

"Yeah, but how did you know all that? Were you bullshitting the guy?"

"Didn't feel like that. I was as surprised as anybody when it started coming out. It wasn't like guessing either. If anything, it was like getting information. You know what that feels like, when the words appear in your mind. Here, it was like speaking them, not writing them down. That's the nearest I can get . . . nothing like that's ever happened to me before. Not exactly like that, anyway."

They walked on in silence, Ishmael now tugging on his chain. It had been a strange night for both of them.

That day they had arisen before dawn with the monks for a breakfast so large and rich that Nick claimed happily that it would last them for days. Nothing much was said by the monks during the meal, and when my ward and Nick bid their farewells the monks' attitudes seemed so much more abrupt than they had been the evening before.

I happened to know why this was because I was prowling around the monastery after the pair had retired for the night. The senior monk had called a meeting to discuss what had occurred. Apparently he and a couple of others in their order had felt something unnerving about the young Englishman. They too had noticed how fluidly Mein Host slipped into answering obscure questions with correct answers, which he'd have no way of knowing. It had to be the work of the devil. Without a basic belief in, or acceptance of, reincarnation, Roman Catholics would have had no option but to reject Mein Host's information as unnatural—and possibly even demonic. In the authoritarian structure of the monastery, the opinion of the senior monk was final. The strangers were to be moved along as quickly as possible before they could do any real harm.

Nick and Mein Host took to the road again, and, as they neared the crossroads after a short hike, a car finally appeared, puttering out of the morning mist. It slowed down briefly for the pair, the driver craning his neck to look them over—in their black clothes and cloaks and their long hair blowing in the wind—and that huge dog! He accelerated wildly, spurting dirt and pebbles in the car's wake.

Nick ran after the car shouting obscenities, vigorously trying to kick its rear bumper, and slipping and sliding and coughing in the cloud of black exhaust fumes. He was furious. My ward stood shaking with laughter at the incongruous sight. He tried telling Nick how absurd he looked trying to drop-kick a Volkswagen Beetle when he didn't have a chance of stopping it.

This hadn't made Nick feel any better, and he settled into a long and bitter sulk that didn't lift until they had reached the dangerous, windblown, rubbish-strewn streets of Palermo, the old capital city of Sicily.

5

Dreams of the Divine Twins

The Star People, Lessons in Courage, the Abbey of Thelema, and Georgia on Aleister Crowley

Astride their faithful fandors, Vanu and Amadon flew on, bound for their island home. On five occasions different schools of whales, together with their accompanying pods of dolphins, came forward to serve as nocturnal landing pads for the fandors. The birds also stopped off at several of the islands colonized by the Lemurians before finally arriving home on one of the larger southern Islands of Mu.

Little appeared to have changed in the now nearly a hundred years since Vanu and Amadon had been away, so they relaxed, ate their fill, and slept with their fitful dreams. Having been flying on their fandors for the past few weeks—which, I'm told, is not as comfortable as it sounds—I heard them comparing their dreams the next day. They broke out laughing loudly when they discovered they'd both had frightening dreams in which they'd fallen off their birds from a great height.

"So? Did you hit bottom, Vanu? I've heard tell that if you dream of hitting the ground, you'll be dead when you wake up."

"Amadon, that's the talk of children." There was sometimes a note of condescension in Vanu's voice when speaking with Amadon. Vanu had lived his mortal life on another world altogether before moving up through the next levels to Jerusem, where he volunteered and was chosen as one of the one hundred in the Prince's staff to take MA's mission to Earth. Amadon, on the other hand, was originally one of the indigenous tribesmen chosen for their superior physical and mental qualities to contribute their DNA and for the surgeons of Avalon to fashion a physical body for Vanu to occupy while serving on Earth. Although it's not altogether accurate, you might think of Vanu as being Amadon's clone, except in the case of the Prince's staff, it was these so-called clones who were the prime movers in their ongoing relationships with their donors. Vanu and Amadon had drawn particularly close as they'd labored together for so many millennia. Even I, who both would have written off as a rebel, found I admired Amadon for the easygoing manner with which he overlooked Vanu's tendency to occasionally try to lord it over him. Fortunately these moments were rare, and, as far as I've been able to observe, Amadon has benefitted greatly from all he has learned from the older and wiser Vanu.

"My dear Amadon, you must learn to separate your dream of life and your nightly dreams." Amadon was listening intently. "Never allow your night dreams to frighten you during the day. Better to learn from them and understand why you dream such things."

There was a long silence while Amadon's fine brow furrowed in thought. In spite of his superb genetic pedigree and the gift of an immensely long life he'd received as a reward for donating the bioplasm that would form Vanu's physical vehicle, despite all this, Amadon was still essentially very much a human being—and dreams have always confused and frightened humans. Indeed, there were some tribes they'd encountered who had created a religion devoted to placating or pleading with the gods and demons that plagued their dreams.

"But then, why *do* we dream of falling?" It seemed that Amadon wasn't going to let it go. "When I'm actually on my fandor I've never felt like that. I never even *think* of falling off."

"Well, it *is* a long way down. Your body can't help knowing that. It's merely your body that's reacting, not you, Amadon. It's an instinct inherited from your distant simian forebears."

At this, Amadon was quiet again. He'd identified so closely with

Vanu that he sometimes believed they were the same person, with the same thoughts and experiences. It always surprised him when Vanu reminded him of his humanity.

As Vanu's physical body was originally cloned from Amadon's, they'd looked very similar for a long time, much like twins—and they were even worshipped as the "Divine Twins" in some quarters, although they did their best to discourage it. Human beings, as I'm sure I've already stated (but it can't be stated enough), were, and still are in some cases, unfortunately prone to making a god, or a devil, out of anything seemingly mysterious and more powerful than them.

As the millennia passed, the "twins" grew gradually less alike as their individual personal experiences shaped their features. Amadon still limped from a nasty fall he'd taken a couple of centuries back. Yet in his mind—as mirrored surfaces were a rarity—he continued to believe he looked just like the Vanu who'd stepped out of the temple in Dalamatia for the first time in his new body, whole and complete unto himself. It felt to Amadon then, or so I heard later when he was talking to Vanu, that he was seeing in front of him a more perfect version of himself.

"I still don't understand, Vanu, why we dream of falling? If I'm not afraid when I'm actually flying, why am I so fearful when I dream? It doesn't make sense!" I thought it was an astute question and wondered how Vanu might answer it.

"Amadon!" Vanu said firmly, interrupting his aide and cutting him off before he could start creating a thoughtform of denial, upon which further fears could find a home.

"Amadon, Amadon, my dear old brother," Vanu continued, his voice softening when he saw he had his aide's full attention. "Has it never occurred to you that I have all the same feelings of terror in my falling dreams as you do? It's hardwired into us . . . into *your* brain. When I took on this vehicle, it came along with your mental circuitry and some of your instinctive reactions. I've needed to deal with and master very much the same fears and passions as you. Does that surprise you?"

This, evidently, had not occurred to Amadon.

"I'm not trying to make you feel bad, Amadon. You know me too well for that, my brother, I'm telling you this to get across to you that if I go through the same fears as you, then there's nothing to be ashamed of! Is there? If I have to face them too."

"Do you ever get over it? Over the fear?"

Vanu paused before replying, and I could see the ambivalence playing across his honest face.

"Well, yes, I have learned to master the fear. That doesn't mean I don't experience it, but I've transformed it from fear to excitement. And anyway, fear has its purposes. It teaches us humility as it also challenges us to keep our nerve. Don't try to avoid fear, just feel it, feel the fear. Know you're stronger than the fear. You don't want to lose your edge, do you? *I* don't want you to lose your edge.

"And, Amadon," he said with a rueful smile and terminating the conversation, "you *really* wouldn't want to be me!"

After the pair returned on their exhausted fandors, the Lemurian Elders had been courteous enough to leave Vanu alone until such time as he was rested and refreshed. Although they were obviously anxious to hear his news about the visitor's arrival, they also wanted to tell their chief how they foiled the attempted invasion by Caligastia's midwayers. A couple of days later that time arrived, and the Elders were called together. I could sense their impatience as well as their nervousness as they whispered among themselves in the council chamber while awaiting Vanu's appearance.

Another thing was noteworthy: there was something new in Vanu's aura that I hadn't noticed before. I realized how long it had been since I had seen Vanu actually excited. I observed this as I watched him straighten his robes and run a carved bone comb through his long hair before making for the chamber. One of the Elders scuttled ahead of him to apprise the others of Vanu's imminent arrival. Apart from the few who'd greeted Vanu and Amadon on their return, none of them had seen their beloved Vanu for almost a century. Most Elders carried enough of Vanu or Amadon's exalted genes, permitting them exceptionally long lives, but a few of the youngest ones had never even met Vanu before. To them, he had become virtually a mythic figure.

It was these young ones who first leaped to their feet, while many of the others were struggling to haul themselves up, bowing deeply to

Vanu as he entered. Cautious as ever of being an object of devotion—Vanu wasn't one to stand on ceremony—he quickly took his seat and gestured for the Elders to quell their enthusiastic greeting. Then he started to speak of his time with the visitors, and I was impressed, being so much more familiar with Caligastia's duplicitous tricks, by how open and frank was his account.

It was obvious he could feel the excitement in the room. The Elders were squirming in their seats in their impatience to tell him what had happened while he was away. Still Vanu spoke on. I could see he knew perfectly well what was happening in the chamber. He wasn't stupid. He was enjoying making them wait. It soon became a form of friendly torture . . . a wake-up call . . . a signal that old Vanu was back. He had his tricks too. But they were never malicious, and I don't believe I'd ever seen Vanu trying to deceive his followers—although he certainly enjoyed pricking their bubbles of self-importance.

I was starting to really appreciate this guy!

As the hours passed and on and on Vanu spoke, the Elders relaxed and settled in for the long haul. I imagined they were remembering how unrelenting Vanu could be when he was making a point.

Once again I was surprised at how openly he talked about his disappointment on witnessing the visitors' cavalier dismissal of his warnings of the serious threat from the Nodite people. However, in my opinion, he did downplay the importance of the visitors' presence and warned his listeners not to expect any immediate improvement in their ongoing conflict with the rebel faction. I noticed, for example, that he didn't once mention the visitor's genetic importance or the part they would play in MA's plans for the world.

Vanu was known to be close-lipped about the subject of the Multiverse and what he knew. Thus, the Elders had no prior knowledge of MA's second mission and didn't know how much weight to give Vanu's casual reference to the visitors. Besides, I could see the Elders thought their news was far more interesting. By this point they were fidgeting again, trying to be patient while Vanu was finally closing his monologue.

There was so much clamoring to speak as Vanu was completing his report that I was sure he'd finally concede the floor, but no! The old trickster must have noticed Amadon coming in at the rear of the chamber. He was gesturing for his loyal aide to come forward and join him on the platform. The Elders quieted back down as they too spotted the impressive figure of Amadon striding regally down the aisle to join Vanu in the center of the bowl-shaped space.

Amadon, perhaps even more than Vanu, was venerated by all generations of the Lemurian culture. He was more approachable than Vanu; "more human" was how I'd heard him described. By this I reckoned that people meant he was more pliable, more anxious to please and be liked for who he was; more easily manipulated, perhaps. And there was a certain truth to this. I'd seen how Amadon struggled with his pride, with his innate superiority, especially when the rest of the loyalist staff and their companions were lifted off back to Jerusem, leaving just him and Vanu, sole remnants of the days when the Prince's staff still had physical bodies.

Amadon's immense longevity had allowed him to make observations of natural phenomena over exceedingly long time periods. His vigorous fertility had fathered many of the prime bloodlines. He possessed a physique that appeared eternally youthful, as well as a deep well of information drawn from his many millennia of practical experience.

In short, he had much to tempt his pride.

There were a couple of occasions when Vanu was away, leaving Amadon to keep an eye on the islands, when the people rose up in a collective spasm of worshipful devotion for Amadon that, apparently, he'd done little to discourage. The Watcher who'd passed this along told me there had been a terrible row between them after Vanu had returned to Lemuria. There were accusations that Amadon had thrown away centuries of patient religious engineering, of disobedience, of disloyalty, and of his vanity and pride. There were additional accusations from a clearly distraught Vanu that soon morphed into how terribly disappointed he had felt after all the warnings he'd given about the perils of allowing either of them to be worshipped as gods. I was told that among his most vicious and hurtful comments, Vanu had actually used Caligastia as an example of the horrific consequences of this sort of hubris.

The second time this occurred it was admittedly some tens of thousands of years later, and in Amadon's defense, the Watcher said that, in this case, Amadon had tried hard to prevent the people from worshipping him. Quite how hard, the Watcher added with a knowing smirk, wasn't for her to say. Regardless, and not really surprisingly, Vanu was so appalled at his aide's second indiscretion that he threatened to send Amadon away for good, back to System HQ on Jerusem. Only an intervention from the Seraphic Over-government, which was a rarity in and of itself, managed to persuade Vanu to take his aide's long and loyal service into account—and that was what saved Amadon.

Just as Amadon was sometimes inclined to identify too much with Vanu, Vanu in turn was liable to lapse into an excess of empathy, believing that he and Amadon were much the same, that there was really no difference in what they knew, or where they came from. Vanu, I'd noticed, could forget his long personal history prior to being accepted for the Prince's mission and his arrival on this world 500,000 years ago. I'm sure the seraphic agents will have reminded Vanu of his own first lifetime so long ago on the planet of his mortal birth and of his subsequent experiences that had led him to Jerusem.

And what of Amadon? He'd been living for a mere 455,000 years at the time of his second infraction. Yet he knew almost nothing of the Multiverse. "Vanu! Amadon is a child," I imagined those seraphic agents telling him. "See him clearly for who he is. And never forget he's a human being first. He may be a very fine specimen, but Amadon has failings that you won't be able to really understand. Irrational failings to you, of course. There's no point in trying to make sense of his silliness; just forgive him and love him the more."

As a consequence of this intervention, the cult of Amadon that had been growing around him was soon dissolved with some firm words from Vanu and his removal from the center of Lemurian political life. He was quietly transferred to one of the smaller islands, where he was given a magnificent residence and asked to record his memories from the earliest days of the Prince's arrival. The seraphic agents had advised on this course of action as having a threefold benefit: it would provide a valuable personal record of that key period of human history; it would keep Amadon beyond the reach of peoples' need to make a god out of him; and most important, they guaranteed that an honest survey by Amadon of his long life would be sobering enough to bring him back down to Earth once and for all.

Amadon's exile had ended long ago. He had delved into the past so thoroughly and had become so involved with his narrative that he'd taken the time to bring it up-to-date. At this point Vanu had invited a much humbled Amadon to join him back in the mainstream of Lemurian life. Although these troubles had occurred at least two thousand years before Amadon and Vanu's recent trip to prepare the peninsula for the visitors, some of the complexity of these various different tensions still hung unexpressed in the group mind as all eyes in the council chamber turned to Amadon.

Ignoring the troubled atmosphere, Vanu greeted his aide with a warm embrace and finally invited the Elders to tell them what they were so excited about. What had happened on Lemuria while they were away? This broke the tension, and the Elders' spokeswoman stepped forward to address them.

"Well, Your Kindness," she said, using Vanu's formal title, "you'll never guess what's just happened. We've had some visitors too. Just as the legends tell us. These ones . . . they say they've returned. They say they were here once and that you will know them, Vanu. They spoke of you but didn't know you'd be away, and they had no wish to enter in to Caligastia's territories . . ."

"Slow down, Grandmother, slow down. Now tell me what happened. Who are these visitors of yours? And everybody else calm down!" Vanu motioned to the animated Elders, extending his right arm and slowly lowering it with the palm of his hand flat to the ground. This was clearly a powerfully hypnotic gesture that the Elders were instantly silent and seemed to be lowered back into their seats by some gentle, invisible force.

"Give Grandmother a chance to speak!" Vanu said again when the Elders were seated.

"They tell us they come from the stars . . . these visitors . . . that they came here once before, long long ago . . ."

I noticed Amadon look sharply at Vanu in surprise.

"Grandmother," Vanu said firmly, looking into her eyes, "you are sure these visitors are from the stars? How can you be certain?"

"Because, Kindness, they arrived from the sky in a silver ship. They say they come from a world lying in a region far behind the Seven Sisters. They seem good and kind. How could they be otherwise but from the stars?"

"And you have tested these star visitors?"

"There has been no need, Kindness. We have seen no signs of enmity. They desire nothing from us."

It was only then that it came to me what Vanu's caution was about. He knew that soon after our revolution this world had been placed in what amounted to an interplanetary quarantine. This applied to all extra-terrestrial races with potential access to third-density frequency domains. It was also one of the functions of the midwayers to warn away any off-world races that showed any interest in this planet. In almost all cases the quarantine could be made to hold, because the midwayers would inter-vene and demonstrate to the star visitors just how depleting the subtle energies were on this planet. They would also be sure to impress on them that they'd become mentally unbalanced, or even perish, if they spent any time on this world.

"And the microbial life!" the midwayers would tell the horror-struck Star People. "It's way out of control! You've never seen anything like it!"

This was invariably frightening enough to send curious interstellar travelers on their way. Yet, with Caligastia running rogue on the other side of the world and prepared to flout every law in the book, who knew what he'd commanded his midwayers to do.

To add to this worry, Vanu had recently been told—by the two off-world visitors that afternoon during their meeting in their garden—of a large exodus of survivors from a planet in the Zeta Reticuli System of worlds. The Zetas were believed to be surveying this sector in the lower frequencies of the Multiverse for a genetically compatible species with whom they might interbreed. There'd been some talk of their heading in this direction. "Only rumors at this stage," the visitors had told Vanu breezily. "Nothing to be concerned about."

I didn't have to read Vanu's mind—which I'm not able to do anyway—to know that he felt that the visitors' opinions were not to be trusted, given their arrogant disregard of his warnings about the Nodite threat to the north.

"Grandmother," Vanu said, breaking the long silence, "these star visitors, they are still here?"

"Yes, Kindness, and anxious to see you."

"Then, Grandmother, have one of your people bring them to me. We will see what they have to say for themselves."

The tone of finality in his voice marked the end of the session. Chairs squealed loudly on the tile floor as the Elders pushed themselves to their feet and began to leave the chamber.

"Gather here again at sundown! With the Star People," Amadon intoned loudly over the din.

Then both he and Vanu retired to the central temple to meditate and reflect on this new and unexpected turn of events. Whoever these Star people were, Vanu would have been aware it must be something out of the ordinary for them to have broken the quarantine.

* * *

The conversation between Nick and Mein Host after they left the Bavarian monastery was one of the last occasions that they'd managed to maintain amiable contact with one another as they were hitchhiking down Italy. None of the places they saw were even halfway appropriate for a new Process headquarters, which wasn't helping Nick's mood any. He seemed unable to stop blaming my ward for taking him away from his ladylove, unaware, of course, that his ladylove was the one who had sent him away. I could read the tension in my ward's aura during one of these rows as he struggled to resist telling Nick the truth about his ladylove.

Nick was a man on the edge. He had the hair-trigger anger of someone whose self-esteem was constantly in doubt. His fury erupted violently and unpredictably at anything he could interpret as being disrespectful to his person. This would happen for the most absurd reasons, and often occurred when he and my ward were standing at the roadside trying to get a ride. And traveling with a large German shepherd wasn't making it any easier.

Hitchhiking in Italy, Mein Host tells me, was never easy. If you were two large men, dressed entirely in black, clad in black capes and having hair down to your waist, you wouldn't find it any easier. If you were two large men, dressed entirely in black, clad in black capes and having hair down to your waist, and you were seething with anger, you might have to wait six hours with your thumb out before a driver would summon the nerve to stop and pick you up.

And then there was the language issue.

Mein Host had never shown much proficiency for languages. He spoke schoolboy French and, in spite of years of Latin lessons, had only just squeezed through his final exams, and then promptly forgot everything he'd learned. When he was in school he'd relied more on his skill at cheating in subjects he considered irrelevant than he did on his memory; thus he'd retained nothing of the language he'd been taught in class.

However, in light of Nick's emotional volatility, his general dislike of any foreigner, and his refusal to speak Italian, Mein Host had to be the one to sit in the front seat and engage the driver in casual conversation. Nick would sit smoldering in the back, seething with fury and disappointment at the world and everyone in it.

Mein Host, to his surprise, picked up workable Italian within two weeks of his earnest attempts to engage with the drivers who picked them up. He'd made it clear to Nick, who appeared to care little about "being nice" to anybody, that because it took an open-minded person to pick them up, the drivers deserved to be treated as well as possible. And if that meant speaking ridiculously inadequate Italian to them, then that's what had to be done.

Nick, in turn, ignoring his own lack of initiative in learning the language, would take this as a personal insult to his education (or lack of it) and his intelligence. This would kick off another roadside row with Mein Host. In this way, their journey down the length of Italy came to resemble a juddering series of stops and starts. The picture looked like this: long stationary quarrels interspersed by short trips with a sullen, silent Nick in the backseat and my ward in the front, beside the driver, haltingly trying to make cheerful banter.

Obviously this situation was far too volatile to continue for long. My ward and Nick were such opposite personalities it was almost as though they'd been thrown together for the express purpose of pushing each other's buttons. Nick's explosions of anger and his reactivity to every assumed slight taxed my ward's patience to the limit. At that point, however, rather than express his anger, Mein Host would suppress it under a cool, detached exterior, as he'd learned to do in response to the abuse he'd suffered at public school. This, naturally, was interpreted as "limey arrogance" and angered Nick all the more.

And so it went.

There were, of course, a few occasions during which Nick's macho, inflammatory personality came in useful, even if it was his own behavior that had caused the crisis to begin with. The most pointed example of this occurred as dusk was falling one evening on an isolated country road in Sicily.

It had been a hot and sticky day and the unhappy pair had been waiting hours for a ride. Cars on these country roads were a rarity, so when one came along and puttered past, the driver indifferent to hitchhikers or, more often, with a passenger throwing an Italian insult out the window, Nick's anger would ratchet up uncontrollably. He'd run at full speed after the car, shouting and screaming at the driver. If there was more than one person in the car, their jeering laughter at Nick's ridiculous behavior only served to further stoke his fury. Then, like a dog who'd once again failed to bite the tires of a passing car, he'd come limping back, cursing and exhausted, to where Mein Host stood, doing his best not to laugh.

All in all, this was not the most offensive behavior to be expected in a country where every driver had a shotgun or revolver beside him in the car. But Nick had seen guns before, and he wasn't afraid of them; he claimed he'd grown up with them. So when a small Fiat—most of the cars in Italy and Sicily were small Fiats—approached and slowed down, making as if to pull over but then suddenly picking up speed again, Nick became possessed with rage. He leaped at the car, oblivious to the four young, large country lads taunting him from the car's open windows, and delivered a brutal kick to the car's rear bumper. The Fiat lurched off, with Nick chasing behind it. He was still screaming at it, his limbs flailing wildly while trying for a second kick, before hobbling back to Mein Host with a triumphant look on his face.

The pair trudged on, the deepening gloom matching their mood. No more cars passed. Topping a small hill about a hundred yards ahead they set eyes on the lights of a broken-down shed of a gas station with a single pump in front. Beside the shed sat the Fiat. In the light streaming from the shed's window, Mein Host and Nick could see four large men standing in a line, each one with their arms crossed—obviously waiting for our two hapless missionaries.

The imminent and inevitable conflict didn't appear to faze Nick for a moment. Now, at last, he was in his element.

"Do exactly what I do," he told Mein Host out of the side of his mouth as he picked up speed and strode, with my ward at his side, down the incline and straight for where the four men stood motionless and menacing. They were not tall men, not nearly as tall as the two black-cloaked figures marching toward them.

"I'll take the largest, you take the second," Nick hissed as they closed the distance. Now they could see the men more clearly. Although they were young, their skin was deeply tanned from a life of working the fields. They were broad in girth and appeared to lack necks, with powerful chests and muscles bulging under their rough work shirts. Two of them wore caps over their black hair, and all of them sported vigorous dark mustaches at different stages of growth.

Without hesitating, Nick marched straight up to the largest and most threatening of the men and, with my ward beside him, stopped within inches of the astonished man. There was a tense silence as the six of them sized up the encounter. Nick then started spewing a stream of American street invective right in the man's face. Mein Host, watching Nick out of the corner of his eye, had picked the second largest man. Emulating Nick's example, he discharged the full force of his pent-up fury—consisting of all of his frustration with sadistic drivers as well as his unexpressed anger toward Nick—directly in this second man's face.

I watched the surprise on the men's faces change to fear and then to what I took to be an animal respect for alpha males—a clearly unanticipated reaction. I'd warrant they'd been looking forward to teaching "those long-haired weirdoes" a lesson by which to remember Sicily. Yet for all their tough and intimidating exteriors, they'd been outmaneuvered by the old master/servant routine. The situation had unexpectedly flipped on them, so much so that the only thing they could do was back down as respectfully as possible, with some nervous gestures toward caps and forelocks.

"Never back down," Nick told Mein Host as they walked off, leaving the four men standing around, shuffling their feet, lighting cigarettes, and laughing a little too loudly to cover their embarrassment.

"On the street, you never show fear," Nick summed up after a few more steps. "If you bully a bully right back at 'em, right in their faces, most of 'em will back down."

"Most of them, Nick?"

"Yeah . . . most." He paused. "But we sure were lucky that time! And Ishmael wasn't much help!"

It was not a situation, or a piece of valuable advice, that Mein Host was likely to ever forget.

The exhilaration and adrenaline rush Mein Host felt during the course of the encounter did not last long as the pair continued toward Palermo, and by the next morning Nick was as morose and infuriating as ever. Like many people I've observed who think poorly of themselves, Nick was unable to take any pleasure in doing things that interested other people.

And so it was that they came to Cefalù, an ancient and exhausted Sicilian town halfway along the island's northern coast on the Tyrrhenian Sea. Mein Host had insisted, over Nick's inevitable resistance, on seeing if they could find Aleister Crowley's Abbey of Thelema, which he'd read was somewhere in the hills near the town.

Clambering up through the undergrowth, they found the abbey tucked into a hillside. It was in an appalling state. Wild vegetation had broken through the floor and rubbish was strewn all over. One of Crowley's sexually evocative murals was still visible amid water stains and moldering plaster.

"You call this dump an abbey?" Nick couldn't understand what the fuss was about.

"Does seem a bit pretentious, doesn't it?" With his finger, Mein Host was trying to trace the vague outline of the painted mural. "But then Crowley was a pretentious man—what d'you expect?"

Nick, who didn't seem quite sure who Aleister Crowley was but I imagined didn't want to show his ignorance by asking, went on idly kicking a piece of broken plaster around the debris-strewn floor before stating the obvious.

"The place hasn't been touched for years . . ." Nick said, before beginning to laugh. "It sure must have spooked out the locals. Look at it!"

"The whole idea was absurd." Both of them were chuckling now. "Plonking his abbey down in the middle of the enemy camp! He was trying to create a magical community here, you know that, Nick? The Catholics had to love that!"

"You mean like *we're* trying to do?" Nick snorted, without missing a beat.

Mein Host was trying not to laugh because, of course, it *was* ridiculous. They didn't know the territory any better than poor old Crowley had. If the mage and his tiny group of followers hadn't been expelled by Mussolini after living for a mere three years at the abbey, they more than likely would have been condemned to a far worse fate at the hands of the locals.

"You couldn't shout them down so easily," Nick said, voicing what I'm sure both of them were thinking. "Let's get outta here. Tell you the truth, it's givin' me the creeps." Nick was evidently more sensitive than he liked to admit. He was also right. The abbey was a dank, dilapidated place, the stones dark with imprinted licentiousness, and now quite devoid of spirit. Besides, there was nothing more to see.

I don't believe Mein Host knew what to expect when the idea to visit the abbey came to him. He certainly wasn't planning to go there, and he'd received no instructions to do so. Like most people who have experience with entheogens, he was aware of Aleister Crowley but hadn't read any of his books. Nor did he know much about him. Crowley was a man from a different age and little of what he left behind when he died in 1947 has proved to have much continuing value to any but the most devoted (and patient) follower. That the old trickster had died dissolute and addicted to heroin in an English boardinghouse, Mein Host had remarked to Nick, "wasn't exactly a ringing endorsement for the Great Beast's chosen path."

It was only many years later, after Mein Host had read Crowley's autobiography, *The Confessions of Aleister Crowley*, that his opinion of the man softened somewhat. The Great Beast was essentially a product of the

Victorian age. Although his poetry has a distinctly Victorian tone, his life can be viewed as one long rebellion against conventional social mores. Whether his psychic and magical investigations can be considered truly authentic in light of his need to impress and shock is a matter that people must decide for themselves.

When Mein Host was writing *Ask Your Angels,* the book he coauthored in the late 1980s, he researched the magical workings that Crowley had undertaken with his wife Rose in Egypt in 1904. After Crowley had experienced some intriguing synchronicities following a magical rite invoking Thoth, for which he was doubtless well stocked with excellent hashish, he came to believe he was hearing the disembodied voice of his "Holy Guardian Angel," Aiwass. He spent the next few days taking dictation from Aiwass, and from this emerged his most seminal work, *The Book of the Law.*

There's an interesting contrast here that demonstrates how much matters have changed since the struggles that Crowley went through to make initial contact with Aiwass. Although it will take my ward about two years of focused meditations to make contact with his own companion (guardian) angels in the early 1980s, he discovered that the impulse to make the connection, an impulse he believed was his, was actually coming from the angels themselves. It was his angels who were waiting for *him*! It was they who considered that a fully conscious contact might lead to a more valuable connection. And I have to add that I, Georgia, am particularly grateful to both Joy and Beauty for their patience and dedication over those two years, as it made my advent into Mein Host's consciousness almost twenty years later a far more fluid process.

Aleister Crowley has probably become best known in popular culture for such maxims as "Do what thou wilt shall be the whole of the law," "Love is the law, love under will," and "Every man and woman is a star." Crowley's channeled book is erudite and puzzling and may be viewed as a manifesto promoting Aleister Crowley (or Prince Chioa Khan, the name he used in Egypt) as prophet of the New Aeon. The content of the book shocked Crowley sufficiently to have put it aside. Yet, over time, he came to think of *The Book of the Law* as the seminal text of what was becoming his complex and magical belief system.

I'm sure Mein Host will appreciate my clearing up one of his perennial questions about Aleister Crowley. How could a man who claimed contact with his guardian angel, and seemed to have an authentic commitment to spiritual exploration, end up in such a sad and terrible mess?

The short answer is that Aiwass was not a true guardian angel but a mishmash of thoughtforms and Crowley's own subconscious. Although Crowley had used mediums before, this was the first time he'd personally been on the receiving end of a constant stream of material. He was sadly ill-equipped to assess the authenticity of the source of it, or the value of the information received. The level of his spiritual immaturity is well illustrated by his identification with the Beast of the Apocalypse. Despite admitting that as a six-year-old his strictly devout Puritan mother would accuse him of being the Beast when he misbehaved, he never released what a debilitating thoughtform his mother had hurled at him and the effects this negative imprint had on a young mind. While it's hard to know whether by adopting the title of the Great Beast he was hoping to defuse its impact in his subconscious mind or whether it was merely his desire to shock, but regardless this emotional block would continue to distort his character, his influence, and his writings for the rest of his life.

But to take Crowley's work at face value would be to misunderstand his more fundamental function. While many writers choose to disappear behind their words, others become more significant for the manner in which they've lived their lives. Whether or not they are aware of it at the time, they will likely become known in posterity for how authentically they lived the truths of what they wrote; how well, or badly, did the beliefs they espoused in their books serve them over the course of their lives. Aleister Crowley was a man who believed implicitly in his channeling ability. He always asserted that Aiwass was the author of *The Book of the Law* and he merely the scribe. He lived with an enormous passion. He was a fearless mountain climber; an erudite, if somewhat overwrought, poet; a spy, it seems, for all sides in the Great War; a great traveler and organizer of secret magical societies; as well as a prolific author of books, some channeled, some not, that became required reading for all serious students of magic.

His writings, however, fade in light of his real function as a social engineer. While he may have never resolved the personal issues he had with his demented mother, the trauma she caused him as a child helped mold his character in preparation for the tasks ahead. Crowley was never consciously aware of it, but he was among a small vanguard of rebel angels who chose to incarnate toward the end of the Victorian age. Their given intention was to dissolve—and in some cases smash open—the social strictures and restrictions of a rigidly stratified and increasingly materialistic culture.

As a Watcher—though not yet embodied—I can be forgiven for noting that those early rebel angel incarnates had some rough edges to them, which they needed. They were known for their arrogance and their commitment to change. They were bold, courageous, and frequently foolish. Many of them behaved appallingly in their efforts to tear down the structure and conventions of Victorian and Edwardian society.

I've known Watchers who believed that this group of rebel angel incarnates were actually premature, brought forward on instructions from MA to accelerate the speed of social disruption. That their efforts bore fruit can be appreciated from a dispassionate assessment of the twentieth century, which saw the most massive social upheavals that humanity has undergone in the modern era.

Aleister Crowley was a good example of someone who helped demolish some of the sexual, metaphysical, and religious social imprints that had held the Western world in thrall for so long. His chosen function would always condemn him to be hated and discredited by conventional society, yet his intellectual superiority and overweening pride made him all but impervious to the vilification he received throughout his life.

Few people set out to dismantle their society in a direct way. Those who do are generally tyrants or terrorists, whose brutal methods invariably belie the credibility of their regimes and the beliefs they impose on their people. Yet, facing the impenetrable religiosity of late-nineteenth-century Europe, Crowley—like others of his radical ilk—had no choice but to use harsh and brutal, if more subtle than a terrorist, methods of his own.

The paintings of Paul Cézanne, to give another example, were harshly rejected by a horrified Paris salon for eighteen years before his first and only painting was accepted for exhibition—and only then through the intervention of another, more celebrated, artist.

Sergei Prokofiev, the Russian composer and a contemporary of

Crowley's, who was also known for his eccentricity and arrogance, provoked much the same hysterical reaction to his dissonant harmonies as Cézanne had created in the world of art, and Crowley in the field of metaphysics and religion.

To give Crowley and others their due, their tasks were formidable, and they took their toll. Most of these individuals died disappointed and penniless, despised or unrecognized. Few saw their revolutionary contributions accepted in their lifetime. Some were persecuted to death. And even if, like Prokofiev, they were celebrated when alive, their death was frequently overshadowed by an event deemed more significant. The Russian composer, for example, happened to die on the day Stalin's death was announced, and Stalin's mass of mourners thronging outside of Prokofiev's house made it impossible to remove Prokofiev's body for three days.

Lest you conclude that all rebel angel incarnates are well known, or become so later for their contributions, the above-mentioned individuals are among the few who have been recognized. The overwhelming majority of angelic incarnates live far more private lives, facing their own demons and working for their own redemption.

While it's true that a few rebel angels have been incarnating over the course of recent human history, those who lived through the second half of the nineteenth and the early twentieth centuries shouldered the most challenging tasks. They blazed the way for the wave of incarnates who started arriving in large numbers after the Second World War.

So, even though Mein Host found Crowley's magical methodology for invoking Aiwass both laborious and unnecessary, he needs to know he owes a debt to the old mage for taking the brunt of the cruelty and cynicism of an uncaring public.

As I write these words, Mein Host is two years shy of the age that Crowley died. Despite my ward's turbulent life, he has never had to suffer the humiliation or the cruel indifference that was heaped on those courageous rebellious souls who were in the vanguard of the approaching global transformation.

6

Lemurian Technology

Pleiadean Visitors, Christ and Satan, and a Warning from the Star People

The sunset meditations were over when Vanu and Amadon left the temple and made their way thoughtfully toward the great central plaza. Word of the upcoming formal meeting with the Star People had got around and other Lemurians were streaming into the square to behold what promised to be a most significant event.

The four Star People, two males and two females, had apparently arrived in their silver craft only three days earlier. After initially making themselves known to the Elders of the city, they'd retired back to their craft to await Vanu's return. My source, another Watcher present on Mu at the time, told me the only thing the off-worlders told the Elders was that they weren't strangers to this planet and that they wished to see Vanu.

Dusk was falling over the city when columns of light, initially dim and golden hued and then gradually becoming brighter as the evening grew darker, served to outline the limits of the plaza. This I had never seen before. I couldn't tell what the light source was—whether it was contained in something, or it was simply a beam of light—until I saw millions of tiny flying creatures fluttering freely in the glowing columns. Then, as the light brightened, more and more insects—brightly colored ones—joined the whirling throngs of fireflies, so much so that soon the columns appeared to be almost solid.

The columns stood in constant multicolored movement against the darkening sky. Then, below the line of columns, I could see light of a warmer, more consistent nature flowing like water around the far limits of the immense plaza. It had none of the constant flickering of all those millions of fireflies, but the light surged and dimmed as if some hand was controlling a rheostat.

I was watching this splendid spectacle when I sensed the presence of one of my colleagues, Astar, a Watcher who'd been specifically appointed to Vanu's Lemurian mission and with whom I'd established a warm, if sometimes prickly, friendship.

"They're doing it with eels," I heard her say in my mind. I must have seemed surprised—which I was—so she took this as her reason to continue.

"You'll see. They'll dim soon. Beautiful, isn't it!"

"But how?" I have an innate curiosity for what humans have come up with themselves.

"Can't tell you the details, but they've got hundreds of electric eels in those stepped pools behind the temple. They've been bringing them in from South America! Risky business, though. I've seen men die trying to catch them. It takes awhile to get the hang of it."

Frankly, I was disinclined to take Astar seriously, she was known to be mischievous. Yet, that ribbon of light *was* gradually burning dimmer, just as she'd said it would.

The light was undeniable. Some new energy was being used.

"You ask what can it be?" she whispered on. "You are surprised? No, it's not atomics. Vanu wouldn't dream of that—especially after Caligastia's disastrous wars."

Now that was interesting. She was the first Watcher I'd come across who seemed to have developed sufficient psychic and psychological distance from the revolution to openly criticize Prince Caligastia. I've deliberately kept out of the way of the few Watchers on the planet, as I haven't wanted any of my growing ambivalence about Caligastia's brutal ways to leak into the telepathic circuitry.

Yet here was Astar, who had approached me. I knew she'd have needed to let down her shield long enough to read me, which meant she must have trusted me. This is one of the unwritten laws of telepathic interchanges—we only perceive in another to the extent we're prepared to reveal of ourselves. There can be no invasive probing without our own motives being equally apparent. It works on the basic principle of like attracting like, of subtle correspondences, and it keeps us all honest.

At that moment I saw Vanu, with Amadon at his side, entering the far side of the plaza and starting to climb to the top platform. All attention was now fixed on them and what was about to happen.

A central plaza was to be found in every Lemurian city of any substantial size, with smaller versions acting as the central gathering places for the more far-flung settlements. These plazas were essentially flattened step pyramids—massive rock platforms, piled one on top of another in a series of shallow steps that rose to a smaller flat space at the top. Here, closer to the gods, the ceremonies took place, surrounded by thousands of worshippers filling the steps below, all of whom were presently craning their necks upward.

Astar and I were still hovering some hundred feet above the plaza, and I have to admit it's always an odd feeling when a mass of humanity looks directly at me. I know they can't see me, but it always sends a shiver through me anyway.

I could hear Astar's laughing tones again. "Silly you!"

She'd been around large crowds before in Lemuria and was more familiar with the sensation, or perhaps she simply felt less guilty than I did.

"Clever that," I heard her say, "the way the platforms function."

Platforms? Function? All I could see were those upturned faces.

"You don't know much about human physiology, do you?!" It wasn't really a question, so I ignored her condescension while she continued to surprise me. "When human beings crane their necks back in that way it shifts their consciousness . . . this can make them shift into a mildly altered state. You didn't know that, did you?! They can almost, almost see us!"

Fascinating, I thought to myself. I'll have to be more careful. But, really! Did she have to be so patronizing?! Apparently she hadn't liked that thought because she moved away from me.

Beneath me I could see the platforms had filled up. A quiet buzz of anticipation rose from the crowd. Vanu and Amadon had almost reached the top platform when a unified gasp rippled up from the people. Heads turned to watch a small, silvery craft wafting down from the night sky in a series of gentle loops.

As if supported by an invisible hand, the craft settled down gingerly and hovered a few feet above the platform. It bobbed gently on a cushion of electromagnetism for a few minutes before an opening appeared in the craft's smooth skin and a ramp unfurled, the end of which flopped down onto the platform's edge. With an animal-like motion, the ramp seemed to shrug before straightening itself out and settling into place just as Vanu, with Amadon right behind him, stepped up onto the platform.

A soft, almost tangible silence fell over the crowd as the two Divine Twins, Vanu and Amadon—tall, magnificent, and beloved of their people—stood side by side, waiting for the Star People to emerge. The columns of light were dimming around the perimeter of the plaza and now were replaced only by a gentle glow emanating from the craft.

The glow grew brighter as if the craft itself were made of light. Out of this radiance stepped two humanoid forms: a male and a female. Their silvery one-piece suits reflected the light. They wore no helmets. When they emerged I saw them pause briefly to take in deep intakes of fresh air before walking side by side down the ramp to step onto the platform for the first time.

The female extraterrestrial stepped forward, and moments later Vanu separated from Amadon and moved to face her. The silence was deafening. Although she was probably a little over five feet tall, she appeared astonishingly small opposite Vanu's tall, spare frame. Her silver-blond hair was long and tucked in to the back of her tunic. It framed a broad, unlined face, which was recognizably human, with large blue eyes and a narrow little nose above an appropriately small, yet remarkably generous, lips and mouth.

It was only the quality of her skin, when seen under a harsh light, that might have distinguished her from being more obviously human. The skin on her face and hands was translucent without being transparent— that's the only way I can describe it. She seemed to exude a gentle light of her own as her aura spread wide around her in a soft lavender glow. As I watched, her aura expanded to include those standing on the platforms beneath her.

Vanu and the extraterrestrial stood facing one another and spoke in silence, a slight smile of amusement flickering over the alien's open face. Although Vanu's face was hidden from me, I imagined he was overjoyed to see her. I watched the colors swirling with delight in his emotional and spiritual subtle energy bodies. His physical shoulders relaxed from the tension that seemed to be perpetually stretching him to the limit, as though he was carrying the world on his shoulders—which, of course, from MA's perspective, he was.

This encounter was clearly having a profound effect on Vanu, and I felt it courteous to refrain from eavesdropping telepathically on them. However, reminding myself that I'm a Watcher by nature, I couldn't resist tuning in to the occasional phrase, hopefully unobserved by them.

Telepathic dialogue is inherently difficult to render in the words of any language. So much of the communication is conducted in images, in holographic shards, in monads of multilevel information, and in silent sounds and snatches of music. So, dear reader, I apologize for the fragmentary nature of what I overheard and hope you'll discern a coherent meaning from the scraps.

The information appeared to be flowing almost entirely from the extra-terrestrial to Vanu. The information I received, and can put into words, is as follows: Pictures of a world somewhere in a frequency domain behind the Pleiades cluster . . . Their infrequent visits here . . . Provided craft for Avalon surgeons . . . Vested interest in third-density life-forms . . . Continuing respect for interplanetary nonintervention agreements . . . Two references to a "DAL Universe" . . . Their teaching race . . .

At this, Vanu interrupted and the flow of telepathic glyphs slowed down sufficiently for me to perceive another more ancient frequency domain within the lower octaves of the fifth dimension. This must be what she meant by the DAL Universe; a region within the material Multiverse in which various teaching races live out their long lives on idyllic worlds. Next, I was being invited to think of DAL as a parallel universe, one just as material to its inhabitants as this one is to you and yet one that is slightly out of synch with yours. DAL was being characterized as far more ancient than this universe, with many of its planets inhabited by beings whose wisdom and counsel is highly valued by other races. It is these advanced species who are considered the Mentor Races.

I'd been informed in general terms about these parallel worlds in my training sessions. But as they weren't considered strictly relevant for my given mission—which was to be grounded in my observation of third-density activities—no particular importance was given to them by our tutors. As a consequence, I was aware that this event had to be an exception to MA's directives, because meetings across such a vast gulf of experience and knowledge were extremely rare; on par perhaps to offering a squirrel an iPhone. It's an unprofitable encounter for both species—and it will really annoy the squirrel.

But, of course, if this race had brought in the Avalon surgeons—the off-world medical team who originally cloned the physical bodies for the Prince's staff and watched over their growth to maturity—they would have a vested interest in seeing how the surgeons' creations were holding up. Wouldn't they?

I thought that Vanu and the extraterrestrial may have been becoming aware of my intrusion, so I withdrew, and in so doing I lost the train of their thoughts. The meeting was not a long one, and I caught the impression that the female was rapidly losing her energy. Her smile was becoming more fixed, and I sensed she was starting to feel some pain. As the Prince's staff had discovered, the emotional density of a three-dimensional world such as Earth can be extremely dispiriting for a more finely tuned and sensitive species.

Amadon stepped forward and both he and Vanu bowed their heads to the female. I quickly tuned in to the telepathic circuits and caught a brief reference to an upcoming event that would have a significant impact . . . and then I lost the train again.

The female inclined her head slightly to Vanu and turned to the crowd, spreading her arms out wide and delivering a blessing to the four directions in ringing telepathic tones that touched every heart on the Islands of Mu. The extraterrestrial couple then turned and entered their craft, the ramp curled up behind them, and the opening in the side of the craft rearranged itself closed. For a brief moment the disc seemed once again to hang in the air, bobbing very slightly while its glow dimmed and different colors were starting to whirl around its outer rim. Then, soundlessly, the craft took off straight upward at a speed that took the breath out of the awestruck crowd.

Vanu and Amadon turned and slowly made their way down the steps and across the plaza to their sleeping quarters. They walked slowly with heads bowed, seeming not to notice the crowds parting the way before them.

Everyone was aware, each to the extent that they were capable of appreciating it, of having just witnessed a rare and wonderful event. And yet I could feel from Vanu's solemnity that far more was revealed in his interaction with the Star People than I picked up in my eavesdropping, and it was evidently having a profound effect on him.

* * *

Nick and Mein Host left Crowley's Abbey and stumbled down the hill through the long, dry grass to the road. After climbing over the stone wall, they started to make their way in a series of short hitches toward the city of Palermo.

As the capital of Sicily, Palermo is commonly believed to be three thousand years old, but naturally its history stretches much further back than that. We'll encounter the city again later in this narrative when, during the Antediluvian period, before the great rise of the seal levels, there was a land bridge to the toe of Italy, and the Italian peninsula played its part as one of the lesser Atlantean colonies.

As their driver puttered slowly through the dilapidated streets before dropping them off in the center of town, Mein Host's first impression of Palermo was of a city in a constant state of ruin. He understood little of its ancient history, and had someone mentioned Atlantis to him at that point of his life he had as a reference only his one conversation with Xtul's owner in Merida and the man's talk of the Maya being survivors of the Atlantean catastrophe. Regardless, what was unavoidable about Palermo was the exhausted, weary atmosphere of a place that had been ravaged and ransacked over the millennia by every invading army of the Middle East.

Mein Host had already commented on this sense of apathetic indifference that they'd seen everywhere in Sicily. At one point they traveled through a region that must have suffered an earthquake many years earlier. The landscape was dotted with piles of rocks, the debris that had once been small stone cottages, while around them in the fields the trees were standing firm and unbroken. Nothing had been rebuilt, and even Nick remarked on how spooked he was by the atmosphere of complete social and physical decay.

Palermo had something of the same atmospheric quality as those broken piles of rock: an eternal ennui that seemed to seep from the very ground of its being. It was as though the rocks and bricks from which the buildings were made, whether ornate or decrepit, had absorbed the suffering of a population beaten down and ill used, millennia after millennia, by foreign invaders, by kings and emperors, by strange beliefs and a religion of death, and now by organized crime.

Palermo by the 1960s was almost entirely in the hands of the Sicilian Mafia. This was most clearly discernible in its shoddy buildings, financed and held under Mafia control, that were thrown up willy-nilly to cater to the ongoing mass migration of country folk to the city. Due to frequent Earth tremors, most of these poorly built apartment blocks were already crumbling as if in slow motion for the timber, the cement blocks, and the rubble to be reused yet again to make shacks for the poor, as must have been done over and over down through the centuries. The psychic atmosphere was as thick and dull as the buildings, and depression seemed to leach from the dry and unloved ground.

The pair was now walking through the haphazard expansion of the old city that was now little more than slums. Young Sicilian men, flat caps aslant and pulled down over their eyes, hung around shiftlessly on unpaved street corners, posturing for one another—and for the girls who giggled from balconies that were almost obscured by the lines of wash strung out on clotheslines between the buildings. With the Mafia so firmly in control, Mein Host commented that it wasn't altogether surprising nothing much had been done even to repair the ravages of the Second World War.

"Crazy to build here anyway," Nick said with some authority. Having grown up in San Francisco, he knew about earthquakes.

They were plodding up what may have been the main street when they saw a cluster of magnificently pretentious-looking buildings ahead. There was evidently a cathedral in among all that extravagant religiosity. My ward remarked that it looked like such a mishmash of architectural styles—the original medieval basilica appeared endlessly added to by centuries of religious ambition—that it seemed to echo the soul of the tragic island.

In my own opinion—and I do try to avoid opinions—for all its opulent magnificence, there was very little of the sacred left in this prideful place. Mein Host, as one who was deeply suspicious of organized religion, would have agreed with me. His was a distrust that sprung as much from his disgust at the cruelty and profligacy of the Roman Catholic Church as from the hostility he'd felt from the priest at his school when he was thrown out of confirmation class for asking questions the priest couldn't answer. His experiences with entheogens had changed all that. It was only then, when he'd had a direct experience of the Divine, that he became truly appalled at what had been done in God's name. Robert and Mary Ann may well have been concocting their own arcane religion with its "four Great Gods of the Universe," but it will mean little to my ward *because* of his entheogenic encounters with the Godhead prior to his joining the community.

I've already made it clear, I hope, that Mein Host didn't place much credence in the Omega's religious dogma, and, as a consequence, he seemed to take in his stride the transition the group was gradually making from a psychotherapy to a religion. Given his previous aversion to organized religion of any sort, the ease with which he accepted this shift of emphasis surprised me. He has stated that he'd joined the group for the different experiences it promised and with the intention of developing more self-knowledge. Then, when he encountered the Goddess in the form of Mary Ann, he stayed for the deeper matters of heart and spirit. Yet, his experiential contact with the Godhead remained with him as a living memory throughout his time in the Process and continues to stain him to this day.

Mein Host and Nick stood gazing up at the main facade of Palermo's cathedral with its unsettling mixture of styles ranging from Gothic to early Renaissance. There was also architectural evidence of its ancient incarnation as a mosque. Nick and he started discussing their spiritual beliefs, and my ward was talking about the one theological principle being stressed by the Omega was the basic concept of unification.

"The unity of Christ and Satan," he was saying, "that's the one concept which really gets through to me. I can feel it . . . like bringing together the parts inside of me that are at war. I don't really give a toss that they call these opposing elements Christ and Satan . . . they're just words . . .

"Sure are buzz words, though!" Nick said. "Gets people all riled up. Christians hate Satan! Satanists hate Christ!"

"Part of the fun of it, right Nick? It gets everybody steamed up."

Two great arches, high on the facade and at right angles to it, reached over the street to connect to an improbably tall bell tower and a cluster of other equally muddled and portentous buildings. There were other towers, square ones on either side of the facade with delicate arcades around their tops. There were also domes of many different sizes and profiles, all of them appearing just a little too tall and slim and delicate to survive the slightest tremor, let alone resist the powerful earthquakes that regularly rumble through the region.

"And yet there they stand, defiant . . ." mused Mein Host, head craned back. "Like they're boasting of God's protection from the natural world . . ."

But Nick wasn't listening.

"Let's do it then! Come on!" Nick was calling over his shoulder as he strode across the road to catch up with a priest who was just emerging through the Gothic doorway, under a weatherworn Madonna mounted at the doorway's apex.

"He says it's that way," Nick called out, pointing over Mein Host's shoulder. "And he's a new archbishop. The priest said he may be open to seeing us."

Perhaps it had been all the talk about uniting extremes as they'd been walking toward the cathedral that brought up the idea of telling the Archbishop of Palermo about the Unity. Of course, he'd want to hear about it! Well, wouldn't he?!

They found the archbishop's offices after traipsing through dusty, windblown forecourts and under arched arcades, and then by threading their way through corridors as wide as the Channel Tunnel. The cor-

ridors featured dark wood and polished marble and lots of brass orna-
ments. Statuaries of every shape and size filled innumerable alcoves, and
it seemed everywhere they turned they faced yet more opulence steeped in
an ornate vulgarity—as offensive to a returned messiah, my ward had said
dryly, as the moneychangers in the temple.

Another priest appeared from out of the darkness and guided them
to where the Archbishop of Palermo, the recently appointed Cardinal
Francesco Carpino, had his suite of offices. His secretary, a harried, portly
priest with the red-veined nose of an alcoholic, signaled for them to wait
and then showed them to two overstuffed, seriously ragged armchairs,
complete with their greasy antimacassars.

While the secretary was out of the room Mein Host whispered to
Nick that the poor creature was probably carrying the entire burden of
the change in archbishopric. He looked like someone on the verge of his
nineteenth nervous breakdown, and they were still chuckling at the reference when the harried secretary returned.

Whatever reason the archbishop gave himself for his willingness to
see these two self-styled missionaries of another church, I've no doubt he
had second thoughts after the meeting as to whatever might have possessed him to do it.

Archbishop Cardinal Carpino was in his early sixties at the time, yet
he appeared somewhat older. He had a thin, aesthetic face, but his features were unexpectedly heavy: a large nose hung over a wide mouth with
deep smile lines. The sprigs of white hair poking out from under his little
red cap contrasted with his dark eyebrows, and although his overall air
was professorial, I could see that his eyes were smiling behind his glasses.

Neither Mein Host nor Nick appeared to know how to formally
greet an archbishop of the Roman Catholic Church, and I was relieved
to see the dignitary hesitate and then draw back his ring hand. Frankly I
feared what Nick—who was ruggedly democratic and independent in the
American fashion—might do if he'd been expected to kiss another man's
ring, however exalted that man's ring was.

Mein Host, as we know, was no great admirer of the Roman Catholic
Church. Even though he did not believe in Jesus Christ, he'd frequently
made the point in his discussions with Christians that he was quite

certain it wasn't such lavish opulence that their Jesus Christ had in mind, when a religion came to be founded in his name.

It was an irony that amused me. You see, I knew something that my ward wasn't to know for another twenty years. It was the fact that his mother, Diana, although herself a lifetime agnostic, finally confessed to having bent to her Catholic mother's demand that her infant son be baptized in the Catholic Church. As Diana had matured she'd found the act increasingly hard to justify by claiming her religious indifference, or by attesting it had been done merely to placate her mother. So guilty had she ended up feeling about this personal betrayal of her principles that she'd resisted telling her son that he'd been officially baptized a Catholic until he was well into his forties. I've heard him say, not entirely humorously, that after hearing his mother's action, he'd spent the rest of his life trying to get excommunicated.

Without rising, the archbishop gestured for the two lads to sit in two of the three richly upholstered chairs in front of his desk. The heavy wooden doors closed behind them as the secretary silently removed himself.

There was an awkward silence during which I imagined both parties wondered why they were there. The archbishop hadn't yet spoken but was sitting with his arms on the desk leaning forward slightly with a bemused expression on his face.

Mein Host spoke first, more, I suspect, to stop Nick from leaping in with his customary bluntness. This had to be handled gently. My ward went on to quote liberally from the Bible, emphasizing Christ's admonition "to love your enemies." He then developed that to its rational conclusion, that we should love and forgive Satan—I saw the archbishop flinch at the terrifying name, but if my ward noticed the grimace it didn't stop him—and continued by telling the archbishop that surely this was what Jesus Christ would want us all to do as good Christians.

Cardinal Francesco Carpino settled back into his throne. The bemused look was back on his face, but this time it was mixed with a tinge of fear. The smile had left his eyes, and his expression was as hard to read as that of a professional poker player. Mein Host waded on in his incomprehensible Italian, the picture of earnest candor, peppering his sentences with English words spoken with an Italian accent. He appeared engagingly sincere in his desire to make himself understood.

I won't try to reproduce his diatribe, except to say it was delivered in a reasonable tone and followed the logical path of Christ's admonition. He spoke about archetypes and Jung; about resolution and reconciliation; about alchemy and the sacred marriage; about responsibility and the need to find the Satan within; and about coming to peace by resolving conflicts within the self.

My ward became more animated, insisting the church needed to take responsibility for creating a monster—for turning Satan (another flinch) into an unredeemable devil figure. He demonstrated how this had produced a level of intolerance and violence in Christian societies, justifying the most terrible of crimes in Christ's name. He talked about the ready temptation of blaming a convenient devil for human failings; how this fiction has perverted the thinking of entire cultures; and how this fallacy had been promoted by the church for its own purposes—to make people feel guilty and fearful and dependent on that religious institution.

It really was a splendid speech. Awkward yes, and it would have been laughably inept in a less sober situation, but I could see from my ward's face that he believed he was hitting all the important points.

No one spoke. The look on Nick's face was almost as bemused as that of the old primate. Mein Host took the silence as an encouragement to continue.

This time he stood up to talk—he was getting the hang of this.

Still in a quiet, measured, and unthreatening tone, Mein Host pointed around to the gold-leafed magnificence, to the vast and unshared wealth of the church, which had been gathered at the expense of a population held down by poverty and ignorance. He described walking through the palace with Nick, and all of its ostentation. While he well understood that those were the de rigueur trappings of a long religious tradition, he said it really demonstrated just how long corruption had been eating away at the heart of the church. It was by learning to love our enemies that we could heal this wound. Only by doing this could the church reestablish its authenticity and its relevance to modern life.

Inflammatory though this might appear when laid out on paper, it was said with a gentle intensity that was devoid of the slightest tone of accusation. He could have gone on, but he clearly felt that what had needed to be said had been said. And, moreover, Nick had been prevented from losing his cool and attacking the priest.

The Archbishop of Palermo continued to sit perfectly still, although I could see his hands under the desk. They were making motions of washing each other. His face remained passive, though not obviously unfriendly. He hadn't yet spoken, but clearly the interview was over.

Nick stood, and both he and Mein Host shuffled their feet in the awkward silence. They could hear the priest coming in behind them, presumably in response to a hidden bell.

The archbishop's features broke into a friendly smile.

"Bene . . . bene signori . . . no Inglesi . . . I spika no Inglesi," said Cardinal Francesco Carpino, as the pair were led away by the secretary. The last Mein Host and Nick saw of the archbishop, he seemed to be waving his right hand in what might have been a blessing but was more likely a gesture of benign, uncomprehending dismissal.

It was only a few minutes later, when they were back on the street, that it occurred to Mein Host that the archbishop's mastery of language may well have been far superior to what he'd let on. An archbishop would have to be a diplomat. Had the wily old cleric been humoring them from the start and just let him rant and rumble on?

"They've been avoiding those issues for two thousand years— what d'ya expect?!" Nick chortled. "Lucky they didn't lock you up for blasphemy!"

"That bad, huh?"

"I was ready to make a run for it," Nick admitted. "I thought the church police were going to burst in any moment and drag us away. 'Specially when you went on 'n' on about Satan this, Satan that. Geez man! You see his face?"

"It felt a bit odd, Nick. Like I wasn't really there. I'm not even sure what I said . . . no, what do you mean, his face?"

"Like whenever you said Satan his face tightened up around the side of his mouth. Then he covered it up with that weird look . . . happened a few times. I didn't think you'd spotted it, the way you went on and on.

It was cool, though. From what I could make out, you laid it right on the line. Couldn't have done it better myself."

Rare praise indeed. But Mein Host was shaking his head, still bewildered by what had just occurred. They walked on in silence, cars and trucks spewing black smoke juddering along the road beside them.

"Know what, Nick? It was more like someone else speaking through me. Like I was listening to myself say those words. And some of that stuff I'd never even thought of before. Weird."

And so it was that another, as of yet unexpressed, subpersonality made his first appearance in Mein Host's life. He is a minor character who will make several appearances in my ward's development until he finally becomes fully integrated into my ward's primary personality.

* * *

I stayed on the islands long enough to see the populace settle down again after their brief visit from the friendly extraterrestrials.

The people probably hadn't appreciated the emotional pain that the ETs had willingly undergone in order to drop into the third-density frequencies required to meet face-to-face with those of native stock. And although the people of Mu couldn't have understood how acutely uncomfortable it had been for the extraterrestrials, they would have had no doubt as to the unique privilege of the visit.

Their legends still spoke of Star People and of a time before the troubles (the rebellion), when visitors from other worlds had been a more familiar sight. But there hadn't been an actual encounter with an extraterrestrial race, or a face-to-face meeting like this one, for almost 165,000 years. Thus this event acted as a profound confirmation that they were not alone in the universe.

If it's a surprise that a civilization forty thousand years ago might have the same yearnings that move so many contemporary minds, it's only recently that I've stumbled on what I suspect may be the underlying reason for this. As I say, I did not know this at the time, but it deserves a short digression, because ultimately it should be deeply encouraging to everyone reading these words.

Know that you humans are regarded as a truly special people. Not necessarily for who you are as individuals, but for where you are living out your mortal lives. This is not idle flattery, but a truth to which all human beings will awaken sooner or later. Many people will die to this life and pass over before they understand how deeply they are loved and respected for having lived on a planet as isolated from the Multiverse as the Earth.

A world like Earth, quarantined and isolated from the general interplanetary trading routes, will always discourage explorers or tourists. Planets such as these are inhabited by mortals who are largely unaware of the angelic realms and who are either irrationally susceptible to superstition, or worse, are rationally contemptuous of the paranormal. These are the planets that present the greatest challenge to incarnates, whether they are Watchers or Wanderers. Living on a world amid a people who, throughout the course of their history, have been deprived of their rightful spiritual heritage by an angelic revolution not of their own making—all this serves to create an arena for the toughest of spiritual paths.

As an angel I've come to accept that we Watchers once betrayed what our faith knew to be true. I know now that's why I'm here: to regain and renew my faith.

Before the revolution, our faith—no, *my* faith (I'm learning self-responsibility from Mein Host)—had grown habitual. I can see that now. I simply took for granted that the Multiverse was a benign Creation; that the Creators were loving and good; and that nothing could ever go awry in such a magnificent affair. And because there were so many of us who followed Lucifer, I have to assume I was not alone in this habitual state.

Had we angels, therefore, become too complacent? Too easily moved by clever rhetoric? Too willing to mindlessly follow our leaders? Were we, in fact, fertile turf for an angelic revolution?

Perhaps we all needed to be jolted awake.

Of course this wouldn't in and of itself justify Lucifer's revolution. But I do wish to state that one of the most valued positive outcomes these quarantined worlds provide is the most demanding of spiritual challenges: the opportunity to acquire faith without the benefit of convincing physical evidence. For me this underscores the fact that it's the spiritual and emotional intelligences that each individual needs to activate and develop.

Here I speak to my fellow rebel angels, incarnate or not. We are the ones who most need to learn to trust our deepest intuitive insights in the face of a cynical and materialist age. Wanderers, those advanced souls who have willingly volunteered for their current incarnation and who haven't suffered under the stain of the revolution, seldom lose contact with their Source. While rebel angels incarnate to learn and redeem themselves, Wanderers incarnate or, in rare cases, walk-in to teach and inspire others. There are exceptions to this that my ward will encounter later in his life.

Small numbers of Wanderers have been present here operating quietly behind the scenes throughout human history, yet over the previous couple of centuries I've observed their numbers are increasing. They need to be hardy and courageous souls who volunteer for their postings on a world known to be sorely troubled. They need the wisdom to live alongside people considerably less developed than them without drawing unnecessary attention to themselves, and with the compassion to know when and how to intervene. Wanderers tend not to value any particular ideology or theological principle but will lay their emphasis on the principle of kindness. Unlike incarnated rebel angels, Wanderers are generally aware of who they are and why they are here. Wanderers don't seek the limelight, and you'll rarely find them playing significant roles in the public domain. Their intentions are more modest and personal. The general state of the world with its deteriorating biosphere will generally hold lesser threat for Wanderers than for others because, I can only imagine, their intuitive awareness drawn from who they truly are will reassure them as to the larger picture. They know they're not here to deprive humans of the opportunity to learn from their experiences and from their errors, so it is often through personal example that Wanderers most effectively operate.

Thus, while the original reason for isolating this planetary System was to keep the rebellion from spreading to other sectors, the quarantined worlds can now more significantly be seen as serving to provide appropriate arenas for accelerating the individual spiritual growth of their populations.

It's not within my purview to know how many rebel angels are currently incarnated in human bodies, but my ward was informed by one of his other angelic sources in the early 1990s that the number was "about sixty million—with more coming in every day." These are the incarnates who will most need to rise to the challenge of "believing without seeing."

It is likely by this stage—in the second decade of the twenty-first century—that the majority of those individuals who are under the age of thirty and living on Earth are embodied rebel angels or Wanderers, or those who have chosen to incarnate to witness and facilitate the upcoming global transformation.

It was sometime after the Star People had left and the people of Mu had settled back into their regular lives that I chanced to overhear Vanu and Amadon discussing the extraterrestrials' visit and what it might hold for the future.

"Why now?" I heard Amadon asking. "After all that time, why did they come back right now?"

There was a long pause before Vanu responded. I realized they hadn't yet discussed the ETs and why they might have come visiting. Since Amadon hadn't been included in the telepathic interaction with the alien, he had taken the hint and refrained from pestering Vanu for more details than his chief had been inclined to share.

"The information they told me is quite startling, Amadon. You'll understand if I've had to consider it closely in my mind before coming to terms with what to do about it."

They were sitting on the balcony of Vanu's simple dwelling. The house was set on a slight incline at the base of one of the island's three dormant volcanoes, where the grassy plain swept down to the sea. The house was small, barely larger than a couple of monks' cells placed side by side. It was cut into the cliffside so as to give those on the balcony a clear view of the bay below and the Pacific swell beating against the coral reef at the bay's outermost limits.

Vanu had resisted the Elders' pleas that their esteemed leader should live in a palace as befitted his station. Instead, Vanu had chosen to live in a humble abode, and it had taken all of his considerable powers to insist on such modesty. This brought up a tension that had been following Vanu and Amadon from the very start of their long trek east. Yet it had only become a serious problem after the islanders of Mu had started to construct buildings as a coherent and settled culture.

In spite of everything he'd done to discourage these attempts to deify him, Vanu had recently become aware that both he and Amadon were being talked about as god-kings by the common folk of Lemuria. This belief had sprung up again while the pair had been away on the other side of the world and would have to be snuffed out quickly. In fact, Vanu's insistence on living in the most modest of dwellings was a strategy created specifically to help deflate any popular impulse to make him a god.

A light breeze rustled the palm trees hugging the black sand beach, which curved away beneath where they sat. The sky was an unblemished azure, sweetening to a duck-egg blue where it touched the horizon before turning indistinguishably into a misty aquamarine. A pod of dolphins swam lazily across the bay just inside the reef; sleek dark wheels rolling and disappearing, rolling and disappearing.

It was a perfect day. Yet here was Vanu, who seemed to be in a curious mood. I could see that Amadon was nervous; he clearly hated it whenever his beloved chief folded into himself, as he had now. From the state of Amadon's emotional body, he must have been biting back his questions until they became too much for him to hold back.

"Vanu, ever since you met with the Star People," Amadon finally stammered out, "I don't know how to say it, but you've drawn away from me . . . from all of us. I know we've been busy, but you've been different than usual . . ."

"I know . . . I know, Amadon. Have patience. When I tell you what I learned, you too will be silent." I could hear the exhaustion in Vanu's voice. "How long do you think we've been on the islands, my brother?"

Amadon was quietly pensive. "You mean since we got back from the visitors?"

Vanu shook his head and made a rolling motion with his right hand and arm. "No, no, back when we first came here."

Amadon's big, open face was flushed, and his broad forehead furrowed with thought. I could tell he wasn't quite sure whether the question was purely rhetorical. He was not a complicated creature, in spite of his extreme longevity. He appeared content to live in Vanu's shadow and with few exceptions deferred the important decisions to his chief. With the exception of the shameful time he'd allowed himself to be venerated, Amadon was loyal to MA's principles and would have died for Vanu—the last remaining member of the Prince's staff—if he'd been capable of dying, that is.

I'd observed on several previous occasions Vanu's irritation with Amadon's dependence on him, as well as how hard he tried to hide his annoyance from his aide. I'm sure Vanu had to frequently remind himself that although he and Amadon looked physically similar, he, Vanu, carried a depth of knowledge within himself that his aide did not. This clearly rendered Amadon an entirely different person. And, as a highly trained member of the Prince's staff, Vanu was a being of a totally different order than his aide. I could appreciate how easy it was for Vanu to forget this.

"Some say there've been more seasons, Oh great Vanu, than there are numbers to count them."

Vanu grimaced slightly. Amadon must have noticed this because he shrank back into his chair. Vanu was always trying to stop his aide from referring to him as "Great" and from putting him up on a pedestal. Others were far too quick to emulate him, and before long the people were back to calling them god-kings again. No reprimand came this time, however. Vanu had other things on his mind.

"Indeed, Amadon. Countless seasons. And so much to remember . . ."

Vanu drifted into silence again. A seabird called from the beach. The distant thunder of the waves rolling in for thousands of miles and breaking on the reef seemed to be having a soporific effect on Vanu.

"But Vanu . . . the Star People . . . you promised . . ." Amadon blurted out impatiently.

"You asked 'Why now?'" Vanu said. "'Why, after all that time, would they come back now?'" Another long pause followed while he must have been wondering how to share the news with Amadon. Then he leaned forward, speaking quietly.

"I want you to keep this to yourself for the moment, my friend. You'll understand why when I tell you."

Amadon's open face lit up. He was proud, I assumed, to receive such a confidence from his chief.

"You may not like what I have to say . . . anyway, this much I can tell you. There are some terrible times ahead. It will seem like the world is ending—not once, nor twice, but three times. Our islands will disappear, say the Star People; they will be swallowed up by the ocean."

He stopped on seeing Amadon's happy smile freeze in shock. Amadon, for all his exceptional life and the knowledge acquired from his service to Vanu, was still very much a human being. He identified himself with this world in a way that Vanu never could. Indeed, I've heard it said of ascendant mortals that long after they've passed from mortal coil and have had other lives they will often refer to their planet of origination as "home."

"They said the world will end?" Amadon finally squeezed out, his voice rising in horrified panic.

"No, no . . . not really the world. That'll go on. No, they meant our world will end."

"That's even worse, Vanu. What do they mean, *our world*?"

"Our world . . . the islands . . . Lemuria. All we've built here. Everything we've worked for. All this will disappear. That's what the Star Woman showed me. She said fire will come from the sky and tear our islands apart."

"But that's not fair, Vanu! That's not right! And how do they know, anyway?" Amadon's anger changed to incredulity.

"They're Star People, Amadon, they know what's going on in the depths of space. I've told you about the sun and the planets and how everything you can see when you look out there—how all this is whirling around in space."

Amadon looked puzzled. I doubted if he'd ever really understood Vanu's astronomy lectures.

Vanu continued. "Yes, even us. Doesn't feel like it, though. But that's not the point. We can see the planets and stars—it's what we *can't* see that's going to cause the disaster. There are rocks the size of temples; there are chunks of ice as large as mountains. They too are hurtling around in space. When something that large gets too close to a planet . . . it doesn't even have to hit it . . . if it just gets too close, it'll pull the Earth apart.

"That's what the Star Woman showed me. It's not going to happen soon, but it *is* going to happen. And not just once, as I said. It's going to swing by three times, and each time it'll get closer and the damage will be worse . . ."

"And Mu? We'll lose Mu?" Amadon still couldn't quite believe it.

"There is more, Amadon, but have no concern, my brother. We'll have time to make arrangements."

"Arrangements?"

"The Star People have made us an offer. They will take those who wish to leave to another world. They have prepared a place, a safe home for our people. Lemuria will live on after the islands have long sunk beneath the oceans."

"There will be many who will not believe this, Vanu. We can't see these mountains in space, you said. So how will you make it real to them?"

"I may not be able to, but the Star People are prepared to return once more—after the first devastation. They'll take those who've survived, if they wish to leave at that point," Vanu solemnly replied.

"How long did they say we have before . . . what did you say? When's the first of these events . . . these space mountains?"

"We've ample time, if we can keep the people together. This is what I've been considering. We'll reach out from Lemuria and search the world for its highest places, for the places where the seas won't reach. Some of us will be sure to settle there and continue our ways."

I could see that Amadon had been severely shaken by the news. The concept of such a massive rise in sea level, which would cover their islands, seemed to be quite beyond his ability to comprehend.

"These will be difficult times, my brother. There's no avoiding that. Some will believe; some not. And I fear this might split the people."

"Some will want to stay—whatever you tell them," Amadon murmured.

"Yes, there will be people too old or too frail . . . some perhaps will put their faith in Mother Earth . . . we can't force anyone to do anything against their will."

Now it was Amadon's turn to flinch. It had been he who had prevailed on Vanu to permit the people to worship Father Sun and Mother Earth instead of worshipping an invisible God.

I have previously narrated how long and hard Vanu had resisted this compromise. He'd insisted that the development of faith in a supreme, if invisible, God was far more critical to the mortal experience than a spurious belief in the divinity of natural elements like Earth and Sun. In the end, though, Vanu had to give in or see the people, his people, fracturing into smaller groups and reverting to their more primitive superstitious impulses.

"Amadon!" Vanu said sharply. "I need you right here with me. The past's the past; let it go. I need you to understand the importance of what I'm telling you before I address the Elders. I want you with me. It's not going to be easy."

"But, you say we have time, yes?"

"MA has been generous with us, my brother. We've been given ample time. Let's keep this between ourselves, as I said. We'll discuss the changes we need to make, and we'll take things slowly. We cannot risk a general panic."

The tropical sun had sunk low in the sky as the two sat quietly contemplating (how could they not?) the imminent devastation of all they'd built together for the past 27,000 years in what had been their great Lemurian experiment.

I'm sure they were also giving serious thought to their own eventual destinies.

"And Amadon," Vanu said with a mischievous grin, saving the best till last. "After we've seen to this, I'm told that MA is calling us back to Jerusem. Our task here will have come to an end. It will be the visitors who'll replace us. It'll be them who'll be responsible for keeping the light of truth alive in this world. So, cheer up, old friend. We'll soon be home!"

7

Catharsis in Palermo

Amadon's Crisis of Faith, the Mystery Voice, and Empathy Sessions

It was midafternoon when Nick and Mein Host emerged from the grounds of the Cathedral of Palermo and started along the busy main street, back the way they'd come.

The heat rose in rippling waves from the sidewalk, and filth and rubbish filled every nook and cranny of the busy streets of the city. The traffic was thick with ancient trucks, their open backs piled with rocks towering ominously over tiny Fiats, every motor belching black smoke and every driver leaning on his or her horn. Young men on motor scooters, their girls sitting sidesaddle behind them and waving and shouting to their friends, puttered and looped carelessly through the jammed traffic.

It was hot and dirty, and Nick and my ward clearly felt let down by their interview with the Archbishop of Palermo. Their feet hurt. They were exhausted. Their black clothes absorbed the sun's rays, and they were frying in the great orb's fierce rays.

Whether or not the old cardinal had understood what Mein Host had said, the whole episode ended up being both inconsequential and potentially humiliating. However, they tried to bolster themselves with their magical thinking, but they were unable to convince themselves that the great truth they carried—that of the Unity of Christ and Satan—had truly been heard in the halls of the high church.

I don't think either of them could have stated with any surety afterward quite how the row started, or who might have set it off. The only certainty was that it had been boiling under the surface for much of their journey through Europe.

The words exchanged were unimportant. The two men were from very different worlds, and consequently they argued in different ways. Nick, coming from the street, quickly resorted to curses and insults of a peculiarly American nature involving mothers. Mein Host's way was to become increasingly cold and analytic, making his points with an icy logic, which naturally infuriated Nick all the more. There were more curses and then there was more shouting, which precipitated more cold and caustic responses from my ward.

And so forth.

They're walking more slowly now; Nick's arms are gesticulating wildly. He's getting angrier and angrier.

Mein Host . . . or, I should say Gabriel Stern—because an imminent threat of violence by this point seems to bring this subpersonality through—continues to remain irritatingly cool. The pair has had their disagreements before, but nothing like this potential eruption of violence from Nick.

Now they are stopping. Nick is muscling my ward against a boarded up shop window. He is still spitting insults as he steps back a pace. Mein Host's arms are by his side; his left hand holds a couple of Robert's books that he'd waved around in the archbishop's face; his right hand clutches timid Ishmael's chain.

I can see Nick's hands are curling into tight balls, his knuckles whitening as he shouts at my ward to put up his fists and fight. Unaware, of course, that he's now addressing Gabriel Stern—a far cooler customer than Mein Host—Nick's fury explodes at the lack of the emotional response he so badly needs.

The younger man throws his first blow, a solid right-hander to the side of my ward's face. It appears to make no impression. My ward scarcely moves. The second blow hits him on the jaw. He rocks slightly on his feet, and for some reason he is now smiling. This is Gabriel Stern's province—he seems to know precisely what to do.

The calm smile drives Nick into a renewed frenzy. I'm sure this shouldn't be happening. They seem unaware of the small crowd gathering and watching the dust-up with much the same bemusement as had the cardinal and, like him again, making no attempt to stop the show.

The third blow, the hardest yet, catches my ward once again on the left side of his head. Still there is no physical response. Nick is shaking with fury; he's on the verge of going berserk.

The smile doesn't leave my ward's face, and now Gabriel Stern is inviting Nick to do his worst—to get it all out if that's what he needs to do. He says this without a trace of guile. It's obvious now, even to Nick, that he's not going to get the response he'd demanded.

"C'mon, Nick! It's what you want to do," Gabriel Stern says again, with a quiet insistence. I felt that this was taking self-sacrifice a bit too far, but it's Mr. Stern's gig, and he seems to know what he's doing.

This last invitation is having a most interesting effect on Nick. His anger is falling away, and he appears to implode psychically. His body physically relaxes, his eyes blur with tears, and he's throwing his arms around a surprised Mein Host's neck, sobbing his apologies loudly in my ward's ear.

Life on the Palermo street has been continuing unfazed throughout this violent encounter. No one has intervened, and passing drivers barely bothered to look twice before thumping their horns and accelerating in bursts of black smoke.

Yet some deep gulf of misunderstanding between the two young men had been bridged, although neither of them could put words to it. They'd both taken their chosen course of action to the limit. They'd seen beneath the surface of one another, and they had understood and forgiven what they'd seen. They were two strong-willed men from quite different backgrounds who needed this violent catharsis to form the basis of a friendship that would last until Nick left the Process a few years later.

My ward and Nick arrived back from the Continent a week or so later, as did the other two pairs of scouts, with nothing of substance to show for their efforts to find a new center for the community. One of the pairs related their experience of being shown around one of Hermann Göring's hunting lodges, which might have tempted Mary Ann but turned out to be a hopelessly impractical option, to say nothing of an expensive one. At this lack of suitable locales, the Omega gave up on trying to relocate the community's base from London, which its members were all secretly pleased about.

Mein Host, although happy to be back home in England, was still energetically engrossed in the cathartic exchange he and Nick had undergone together in Sicily. One afternoon, over a cup of coffee, he tried to articulate his feelings to Juliette, his confidante in most things. "When he and I were fighting, I was present, but I wasn't . . . at the same time. I could watch it playing out, but, like . . . it wasn't me speaking."

"Didn't you say something like this had happened before? Remember?" Juliette asked. "In Xtul . . . when you were flagellating yourself?"

"No. Well, yes. That was different, though I see what you mean. That hurt like hell until I was up and out of my body. Thing is, Juliette, this *didn't* hurt. When Nick was hitting me, it was like I wasn't feeling it. Not afterward either. No bruises, nothing. It was all very odd."

"So? You ended up friends? You and Nick?"

"Yeah, that was fine. Who knows what really happened between us!" Mein Host was thoughtful for a few moments as they both sipped their coffees in the Cavern.

"He never hit you again?" Juliette must intuitively have felt there was more to the story.

"Never. We're fine with each other now. I delivered him back to Wendy safe and sound. No, it's not that. I hadn't thought of this until now, but something like this has happened before—a couple of times, but with women. The first one attacked me with a hammer. For no reason I could understand. She was up a stepladder fixing a curtain, I think it was . . . came down at me swinging the thing at my head. I must have really pissed her off, but I've no idea what I did. Didn't know it then, and don't know it now!"

"Did she get you?"

"No, no, I managed to dodge her and get out of the house. But she chased me up the street waiving the hammer around for a whole block! At night! In a nightie, for God's sake!" Juliette was laughing at the image.

"Thing is, Juliette, to this day, I'd no idea I'd provoked it. I must have said or done something to make her attack me . . . she *was* my girlfriend after all. But God knows what it was. Second time was even weirder. With a different girlfriend: Jean . . . you must have met her. She came around a few times before we left for Nassau. She hated Mary Ann . . ."

"Tall blond girl; quite a looker," remembered Juliette.

"One moment we were peacefully lying on her bed talking . . . can't remember what about. Next moment she's flailing at me with her fists. Hitting me with all her might."

"She was a big girl, I remember. You didn't hit her back, did you?"

"No, of course not. I don't think I could ever hit a woman. I curled up in a ball and let her hit me until she tired out. And yeah, that did hurt. Nothing like with Nick. Point is, Juliette, the attacks seemed to come out of the blue. I'd no idea what I'd done to set them off . . . all three of them."

"You can be pretty sarcastic. No one likes that."

"Yeah, but I'm fairly sure I know when I'm doing it."

"Fairly sure? Just fairly? Doesn't much sound like it."

Mein Host hadn't much to say to that, so they sat in silence, finishing their drinks, before getting up and going about their tasks. My ward wasn't to know it then, but part of the puzzle of what lay behind these apparently unprovoked fits of violence would reveal itself over time. It will be challenging, and there will be a few other incidents before he will get to the bottom of what triggered these violent outbursts, and how, finally, he'll come to resolve this troubling personal problem. I'd like to believe that my ward, as his younger self, would have drawn some confidence in knowing that as I write in 2014, he himself had never lashed out in this way in his life up to this point, and, in the few times that he did, it was in the face of extreme provocation. But then, he wouldn't have needed to actually start the fight himself if Gabriel Stern was ready to step in and absorb the violence. But, as we'll discover, my ward is going to have to confront this issue of the violence he can unwittingly provoke in others and what that reveals about himself.

* * *

Amadon made his way down to the beach, a puzzled and confused being. He'd left Vanu at the house catching up on the official business he'd set aside before leaving Lemuria nearly a century earlier.

Amadon wasn't hard to read. To paraphrase his thoughts: "How could this be happening? We were doing everything right . . . and now it's all going to be taken away! How can we trust those Star People? Are they plotting with Caligastia? Is this just another of the Prince's tricks to frighten us? Why would MA let this happen to us? It hasn't been easy. We've been fighting off Caligastia's influence every day—don't they know that? And what's all this about going home?! *This* is my home, the islands of Mu, and they're telling us these are the islands that are going to vanish!"

Inside the reef the water was calm, with small waves lapping softly on the black sand, leaving a frothy white stain in the sand that dissolved moments later. The dolphins were long gone, off on their afternoon patrol along the coastline. Ostensibly, the pod would be feeding, but Amadon was close enough to the dolphins to understand that their more basic mission was to keep the waters safe for the fishermen in their small boats. This tradition had continued for so long that it was a rare and dull-witted shark that ever ventured near the shore. Schools of smaller fish guided by their devas took advantage of this safe zone surrounding the islands, thus providing both fishermen and dolphins with a richer and more plentiful fare.

Amadon, who was gazing out to sea from his perch on a block of lava worn smooth by the waves, knew this. He was a being of nature, of a sort that is hard for the modern mind to grasp. He felt no separation between himself and the land. He knew intuitively the meaning of a flight of birds; he could talk to the animals; he knew the phases of the moon and the precession of the solstices; he worshipped both Father Sun and Mother Earth with an engaging sincerity and loved his world as if it was part of him.

His mind wouldn't stop turning. "Is all this beauty to disappear under the waves? Are Father Sun and Mother Earth turning against their people? Why are we being punished so? What have we done to deserve it? Was it because I insisted the people needed physical representations of Father God? Is this a punishment for something I did?"

Amadon was clearly not immune to self-pity, but at least he knew enough to keep it to himself and not express it too freely around Vanu and especially never around the people of Mu. He knew better than that.

The sky was darkening. Storm clouds were gathering behind the island. Outside the reef, the water was starting to get choppy. The waves were pitching sheets of spray over the coral ridges—curtains of foam that glowed momentarily in the setting sun.

Amadon sat unmoving on his rock while the horizon rose to obscure the sun. Darkness fell with an equatorial suddenness as Amadon slowly scrambled up through the lush forest to reach the house and the security of Vanu's presence. I knew how much he disliked being separated from his beloved chief. He really didn't possess the inner resources to handle the conflicting emotions that were arising within him as a result of the recent horrifying news.

I was interested to observe that Vanu made no move toward Amadon when his aide climbed up onto the balcony and entered the dwelling. I reckoned he was going to leave Amadon on his own to work things out for himself.

It's about time, I remember thinking, somewhat uncharitably. Then again, perhaps it was time for all of us to wake up! Life was on the move whether we liked it or not.

I wondered then whether there might be something about this world that dragged everything into failure and death? Something we'd missed, even before the revolution; something endemic to the planet itself that conditioned us all to expect disaster? Was even the good, the true, and the beautiful guaranteed to tarnish, grow old, and become corrupted?

And perhaps more relevantly, was this inevitable spiral into disorder and chaos an unavoidable result of the angelic revolution? Or was the angelic revolution itself a result of what the world needed to ensure a certain level of disorder and chaos?

Although I believe I now know the answer to this, at the time I was just starting to struggle with the deeper and more occulted motives behind the angelic revolution. As I've previously stated, the only description the world currently possesses of Lucifer's activities has been scripted from MA's point of view, and no administration—human or angelic— likes a revolution. I've no doubt it's why they call it a "rebellion" and not, as we knew our uprising to be, a revolution. We weren't seeking to overthrow MA, no, I don't believe even Lucifer had that intention. All we wanted was a change in policy, a loosening of MA's rigid hold on developing third-density worlds and the opportunity to make our own decisions, even if they're not the right ones in MA's judgment.

I found myself left with the question that I still ponder: However painful a revolution was for MA's bureaucracy, might it be so that a revolution is one of the most natural ways of introducing change into a benign, if somewhat ossified, administrative system?

I'd seen enough of Lemuria for the moment. I observed how painful it was for the immortal Amadon to come to terms with the Star Peoples' distressing message. I really didn't want to be around when the news became more general knowledge. Vanu's fear that the information might split the people was not unfounded. Whatever was going to occur, even if nothing were to happen, the Lemurian civilization would forever be changed. Changed, or extinguished.

It was time to see how life on Zandana was progressing. I wondered if they were facing the same issues.

I thought myself across the Pacific and worked my way slowly up the western coast of the great American continent. There were a few scattered Lemurian settlements in the southerly regions, but as I moved farther northward they became more of a rarity. I began to see a different race of men and women streaming down from the north. They were a smaller people, with black hair, copper-colored skin, and Asian eyes, all bundled up in furs and moving across the continent. Some settled down in one spot, but most of them continued to live their nomadic existence as they crossed over the Bering land bridge to a new world so recently covered in ice.

The long ice age that rendered most of the northern landmasses uninhabitable had been and done its worst, and glaciers were already grinding their slow retreat when the immigrants arrived in their clans and moved steadily south.

I found the Seraphic Transport Center in the sequoia forest with no difficulty. Since the ice had withdrawn, this location had taken over from Salem as the main portal used by the Transport Seraphims. No one wanted to mention that the real reason was Caligastia's presence in the Salem area, where he'd created his magnificent palace. No loyalist wanted to risk being anywhere near the Prince, so distasteful had his reputation become.

Was it a coincidence, I wondered, that my friendly Transport Seraphim was available when I arrived? Her smile of greeting was as enigmatic as ever, and this time I didn't make the mistake of asking her whether she was waiting for me. Perhaps I was changing and letting in some more light, but I had a distinct sense she felt warmer and more open toward me.

We exchanged some thoughts as I was going through the laborious bureaucratic process of leaving the world for even the briefest of trips. It was slightly easier on this occasion than it had been on others, because I'd made the voyage a sufficient number of times before, which established that I'd always return. This was invariably the transport authority's main concern: that Watchers always return to the world on which we'd originally been posted. I used to think this was a punishment, pushing us back into the mess we'd all made. By now, however, I was beginning to grasp the wisdom of ensuring we were present to observe the consequences of our choices being acted out in front of us.

I've been grateful for these brief excursions. They've helped clear my mind and have allowed me a broader perspective on what is happening on Earth. I was surprised when my Transport Seraphim told me that I was one of the few Watchers making these trips. The main traffic, she showed me, was composed of MA's loyalist angels, who were periodically given spells of rest and recreation on worlds of their choice. However, the one function that Transport Seraphs take most seriously is when they carry the souls of dead mortals from their planets back to Jerusem, from where they embark on the next stages of their ascension. Or, in the case of rebel angels, return them to their planet of origin—or indeed, a similar world deemed appropriate for the next stage of their education—for yet another lifetime as a mortal of the realm.

In a Watcher's case travel is restricted to planets within our System of Satania, which allows for a fair amount of differentiation. I can't speak to the degree of seraphic travel permitted in Systems not subject to quarantine, as I've never traveled outside Satania. I should also add I've never ventured to any of the more than six hundred worlds where the Planetary Princes remained loyal to MA by rejecting Lucifer's ambitions. I'd heard via the circuits that the cautious administrators of those planets do nothing to welcome any Watchers to their worlds. While they can't forbid us from traveling to them, because that would be to curtail our freedom to assert a perfectly legitimate choice, they can make it excruciatingly uncomfortable for Watchers to be on their worlds.

Once ensconced in the embrace of my Transport Seraphim, the trip to Zandana passed as quickly as ever, but this time I came to really enjoy the subtlety of the music my seraphim created as an electromagnetogravitic artifact of her speed through subspace. Truth is, I suspect I might have drifted off, I was that comfortable.

On arriving on Zandana, I was able to spend some of the long afternoon with my Transport Seraphim, because her services wouldn't be required again until sunsdown later that day. (Zandana exists in a two-star system, thus the patterns of day and night are different from worlds such as Earth and together with the rotation of the planet can seem disconcertingly random until the newly arrived traveler has been on the planet long enough to appreciate its odd diurnal rhythms.)

I never did find out my Transport Seraph's name (names tend to be more stringently protected in the telepathic realms), so I'll call her "Eleena" and trust she won't mind. It turned out that she was extremely interested in my experiences on Earth. There were few enough Watchers permitted to undertake these short off-planet trips, and I was the only one, she'd confessed, with whom she'd gathered the courage to engage. Wasn't it on one of my previous trips that Eleena came straight out with how bad I smelled to her?! That we could now converse more easily, without Eleena wrinkling what I took to be her delicate breathing mechanism, was a small sign that reconciliation will ultimately be found between Lucifer and the MA.

"You've changed since I last saw you," Eleena told me as we took our refreshments in the transport lounge. "You're softer . . . I can feel you better."

She was equally direct when she spoke again. "Why? Why did you do it? That's what I can't understand. None of us can. Why did you rebel when everything seemed to be going along just fine?" Eleena's words came through in a jumble of images and a confusion of feelings ranging from fear to excitement to a hint of envy, followed immediately by a flicker of guilt, a splash of shame, and then back to fear and more fascination. There were more shifts in color and tone than I'll bore you with, but that should give an idea of the quality of a passionate telepathic exchange.

The realization came to me then that Eleena was an innocent, a simple creature who would probably never understand the inspiration and excitement we all felt at the prospect of our new freedoms. She had her function—it wasn't a complicated one. It was matched, I imagined, by a suitably uncomplicated intelligence. (Over time and as I came to know Eleena better, I understood how wrong I was. It was simply a very different intelligence.)

"I've been to many worlds," I felt her calmer tone, "and I've transported the finest in the System, yet I've found no one willing to open up about the rebellion. It's a closed subject. Everyone just masks it off. I transport so few Watchers, anyway."

Well, of course they were all going to keep quiet about the revolution. But why can't we be proud of our revolution? With what we stood for? Why the reticence? I took some time before replying.

"It was a *revolution,* Eleena, a genuine revolution—at least it was to begin with. Rebellion is just what MA likes to call a revolution. They're not going to want it bruited around, are they? A rebellion . . . a revolution, whatever it's called, is going to reflect poorly on them!"

"Yes, but what I want to know is why some of you chose to follow Lucifer, and others didn't. Can you answer me that?" I felt her gentle insistence redoubling.

Before I could mask it off I was thinking of that tender and mysterious female "voice," who seemed to make what we were doing at the time of the revolution all the more holy and right.

Eleena jumped on the thought. "What do you mean, a voice? A *female* voice? It was nothing I ever heard! No one else did either. Not that I was aware of, anyway."

"That's just it, Eleena. It seems that only those of us who heard this voice joined the revolutionaries. Whether some heard the voice and ignored it, I can't say. I do know that every Watcher I've ever shared this with also heard her in their minds."

"So? You think you're special? You were specially chosen? Is that what you believe?"

"No, no, no, Eleena. I thought that everyone heard the voice. *All* of us." I wanted to make sure I got this across firmly to Eleena. "It turned out we all thought that . . . all of us Watchers . . . we'd no reason to believe otherwise. And I've certainly never heard any Watcher or rebel angel claim to be particularly superior . . . well, outside Prince Caligastia's circle, anyway. In all seriousness Eleena, I don't think I would have been nearly as keen to join the revolution if I hadn't heard the voice's encouragement and assurances of a final reconciliation in which both MA and the Lucifer faction will grow in spirit and advance in understanding. I'm being as open as I can with you. Is it answering your question?"

I could feel the protest in her rising to the surface, an almost desperate need to understand why she wasn't one of the chosen. I wasn't going to be of much help.

"It turned out that we Watchers were all masking the instances we heard the voice from one another! We didn't know we'd all been hearing her . . . not until soon after we were quarantined. By that time no loyalist angels would come anywhere near us, near me, so I never knew whether they'd heard her voice too."

"Not only haven't I personally heard this . . . this . . . voice of yours," Eleena assured me, "I'm not aware of anyone else in the System ever talking about such a thing!"

This made me thoughtful. If Eleena hadn't heard this voice, and as she said no other loyalists were aware of it, then what did it say about those of us who did? And acted on it.

"So, you rebels *were* special," she broke into my train of thought. "That's what you're saying, even if you didn't know it at the time. You were selected by the voice, even though you believed it was your choice to follow Lucifer into rebel . . . into a revolution," she trailed off after correcting herself. Was that just the tiniest hint of respect I heard in her changing tone? This could be getting a little close to the mark. I'd no wish to stir up any trouble with MA's loyalists, which might prejudice my ability to travel to Zandana.

"No, no," I thought quickly, "it wasn't like that, not like that at all. I don't think any of us felt particularly special, or if we were, then for what? And the voice never told us to follow Lucifer. She simply supported us in our choices with her reassurances. What was it she called it? 'The Long Road Home,' that's right."

I felt the Transport Seraphim melting somewhat, and I realized what courage it must have taken for her to broach such a delicate subject. I was glad I'd been cautious as I hadn't known that Eleena and her kind were unaware of this voice and the effect it had on us who heard her until she'd just picked it out of my mind.

"Perhaps you didn't need it," I thought encouragingly. "Maybe it wasn't your function. Then again, it could have been that some of us just happened to possess the right sort of characteristics for more independent thinking. But, as I said, it doesn't feel particularly special. There's nothing to envy—unless you like being ostracized and derive pleasure from vilification!"

We sat in telepathic silence for a while. Dusk was falling, and I could see the lights of Zandan, the city on the other side of the bay, glittering between the trunks of the nearby trees. Music and the sound of a girl's laughter drifted up from the beach far below us. A water fowl chimed out nearby, its call harmonizing pleasantly with the distant music. I was struck again at how similar were these third-density worlds. Modern mortals, contemporaneous with the time of writing, were they to give any credence to intelligent life on other planets, would be astonished after a heady diet of Hollywood monsters to find such correspondences existing on third-density worlds.

I wondered if we'd taken our unlikely friendship too far. I'd not intended to display such intimate thoughts to a loyalist seraph, even if our contact explained something I hadn't previously understood.

The source of this special voice has always been a mystery. She would never identify herself. She told me only that her authenticity lay in the truth I'd find in her words. Although I considered that this may have been some Luciferic telepathic trick, that idea hadn't held up to closer scrutiny. I've mooted the possibility it might have been the Mother Spirit, but some of my sister Watchers have made the case as to why this was unlikely. It would require a level of deception, they told me, quite unlike anything that can be attributed to the Holy Mother Spirit.

"How can you think such things?!" Eleena broke into my train of thought again—I'd forgotten she was still listening. "The *Divine* Mother Spirit is stainless. She would never foment a rebellion! Why? Why would she do that? It would suggest an imperfection in Mother Spirit's character. No, no, no, that couldn't be!"

This was the point I'd reached before, the first and only time I'd broached the possible involvement of the Mother Spirit with this enigmatic voice. The sane objection. It couldn't have been her because she is perfect, incapable of such a devious act as covertly encouraging a bunch of revolutionary angels.

I was going to argue that I'd observed enough examples of cruelty and indifference in the natural processes on Earth—of strangler vines and wasps that lay eggs in the paralyzed bodies of small mammals so their hatchlings can eat their way out of living flesh. Didn't this speak to the degree of cruelty and violence being deeply imprinted into the evolutionary processes of a dog-eat-dog world such as Earth? And didn't the design of biological systems fall under the general aegis of the Mother Spirit?

Again, Eleena picked up on my thoughts. But before she could form a response I was relieved to see two figures stepping out of the darkness of the trees and crossing the lawn in our direction and to where we were sitting in the spacious Hall of Travelers. When they saw us through the glass panels they increased their speed a little, and I could see smiles of greeting settling over their faces.

I knew them, of course, when I could see them more clearly. It was from my last trip here, so I rose to greet them as a glass panel slid aside. It was Unava, Prince Zanda's chief of staff, who stepped forward first. (Prince Zanda, you may recall, was one of the two Planetary Princes of Zandana, the other being Prince Janda-chi.) Unava and I bowed our heads to one another. Then it was Sephira's turn. I remembered her as the council member who'd so callously dismissed the fate of the barbarians unwilling to be seduced into Zandan's more advanced culture. It wasn't simply her indifference that had disturbed me when I was leaving on that previous trip. No, it wasn't just that she seemed not to care but also that her tone was so sardonic that I couldn't entirely dismiss the sense she was protesting too much. As an original member of the Prince's staff, Sephira wore the most beautiful of bodies, and there must have been some lusty attraction to strong-minded barbarian warriors that she needed to suppress under a veil of scorn. Of course, I made sure not to focus on this observation at the time, yet I could sense we hadn't parted as the best of friends. So it surprised me when she bowed her head, inclining it in a manner signifying a certain respect.

I told them I admired the ease with which they had slipped so fluidly into our shared frequency domain in the fourth dimension and that I was grateful for their coming to meet me. I hadn't expected it—I really hadn't—since I still wasn't sure how all the details of my suggested strategy of love not war might have worked out. If anyone was going to blame me for something going wrong with the plan, I thought it would most likely be Sephira. And yet there wasn't a hint of mockery in her greeting.

As readers of the previous volume in my *Confessions* series might recall, my idea had arisen as a suggested approach to resolve the conflict that had long been brewing on the planet. The more backward tribes, the so-called barbarians, had finally gathered in force and were threatening to attack and overrun the capital city of Zandan. After much confusion at the highest levels, Prince Janda-chi had asked me, much to my (and all the others present at that meeting) surprise, if I'd an opinion as to how this might be best handled. This was an unheard-of request. Imagine Prince Caligastia ever asking me for my opinion on anything! Let alone something as crucial as a threatened invasion. At the time I felt it spoke to how desperate they must have been to involve me, a visiting Watcher from another world, in such a key discussion. In retrospect, I can but admire Prince Janda-chi's willingness to break with tradition. Watcher's watch—we are not asked for our advice.

There'd been no major hostilities in Zandana for at least two thousand of their years, so it was their Prince's particular brilliance to recognize that in coming from a planet with such a long history of belligerence,

I might have something of value to contribute. His question was so unexpected it caught me off guard, and I found myself blurting out what was on my mind while the council was wrestling with the issue. My suggestion that they experiment with making love and not war, much to my surprise, seemed to appeal to them as an ingenious solution that would be entirely unforeseen by the invading forces. The women of Zandana's largest and most advanced southern continent, known for their grace and beauty, were to be asked to greet the invaders with flowers and open arms and promises of the erotic pleasures to come. Such an unorthodox ploy could never have worked on my home world, so, despite being encouraged by the Prince's initial response, I didn't yet know if they'd really had the courage and foresight to put the plan into action.

When we had completed our formal greetings I turned to include Eleena, only to find she'd disappeared back into the inner recesses of the Transport Center—to pick up her next traveler I assumed.

When I turned back to my greeters they seemed to have barely noticed Eleena, or her absence. They felt anxious to me, their emotional bodies churning beneath their professionally placid exteriors. Once the diplomatic formalities were over, Unava made it clear they were on a mission and I should accompany them back to where Prince Janda-chi was wishing to see me.

That took me aback, I can tell you! I couldn't imagine this would end well. And try as I might, the pair were masking off any knowledge of why the Prince wanted to meet me, and I could get nothing out of them.

The three of us walked back through the woods in silence and caught one of the monorail cabins back into the city.

* * *

It was inevitable that the celibacy the community had voluntarily adopted ever since Xtul would have to be addressed at some point. Coming back to London in the throes of a sexual revolution was bound to bring a certain focus on second-chakra concerns. I'd no doubt that the community's aspirations to psychological and spiritual clarity were sure to come into conflict.

The core group who'd been through the Xtul experience together knew each other so well by this time that they could be brothers and sisters. I've heard some of them claim it was the closeness of this familial bonding rather than any acknowledged stricture forbidding sex that would have made sexual intimacy between them tantamount to incest.

There had been a few exceptions to this tacit agreement to abstain, but those relationships soon flickered out, or in one couple's case, caused them to leave the community.

I observed Mein Host during this celibate period, and for a healthy young male he appeared remarkably unaffected by the absence of any sexual activity. He'd had his fair share of sex prior to joining the community, so perhaps he didn't miss it as much as those of more modest experience. In fact, I heard him later claim how valuable refraining from sex was. Stepping back in this way allowed him to appreciate just how massively oversexualized the modern world was becoming. My ward was no prude, but I've heard him say he didn't feel that greater sexual freedom should be confused with licentious profligacy.

Behind the scenes, Mary Ann, with her senses more finely tuned to the sexual energies of the group (no doubt informed by her previous professional interests), must have been concerned that someone would strike up a relationship over which she'd be unable to exert her control.

Up to this point, I'd observed little that would really confirm Mary Ann's pathological need to control everything and everybody, largely because everyone in the community appeared willing to be controlled by her. My ward might have asserted that it was the very reason for being in the community. Yet Mary Ann's need to exert control became progressively more evident as the years passed. However, I can now say with some retrospective certainty that it was when the issue of sex raised its head in London that Mary Ann shifted her game into the next gear. The members of the community would have their sex, but it would be strictly on Mary Ann's terms.

Mary Ann's motives for doing this were more evident to me at the time than to Mein Host, whose devotion to the Oracle disallowed any thought that the reasons for her actions could be anything but what was required.

It was the late 1960s and the London Chapter of the Process was modestly thriving. After a challenging start after they'd returned from Xtul, their message was beginning to be heard and more and more young people were attending lectures and workshops, as well as coming in for sessions with one of the Process empaths.

These sessions require some explanation as they represented a deeper shift in the group's psychic abilities and its relationship with the "World of Men." It was also the time when, by discarding the use of the galvanic skin response meter (the E-meter), they cut the final thread of the umbilical cord still attaching them to Scientology.

Mary Ann and Robert had met at L. Ron Hubbard's Dianetics training center in Sussex and then left, believing Hubbard was misusing the E-meter. They thought highly of the E-meter, and the community used them in their sessions, but at the same time, they had wanted to distance themselves from Scientology. They considered Hubbard a fraud and a trickster who happened to have stumbled on to this valuable piece of technology, but who'd then set out to use the E-meter to "create a lot of little Hubbards," was how Mary Ann had put it. A year earlier Robert had overseen a repackaging of the mechanism—still the same simple Wheatstone bridge, but housed in a better-looking shell. The device measured and displayed that galvanic skin response by running a minute electrical current through the body. Think of it as a simple lie detector with the difference perhaps that they were using it to reveal what lurked in their subconscious minds. Robert had renamed it the P-scope. It was sleeker and more modern-looking than Hubbard's clumsy wood box, but on the inside the device was identical.

However, for a number of the senior members of the community, the years of these sessions, together with their meditation practices and the experiences they'd had with channeling other beings, was rendering them increasingly open and sensitive to subtle energies. Their focus on empathy and the intuition, and in developing their telepathic abilities, was now allowing them to conduct their sessions without the aid of a P-scope.

Mein Host was one of the half-dozen members who, after a period of intense training and practice with their colleagues, was authorized to conduct empath sessions with the general public. Because designing the magazine took priority, he didn't give as many of these sessions with outsiders as some of the others, yet he'd been continuingly astonished at how effortlessly effective these empath sessions could be.

"Almost too effective!" I heard him say to Juliette when they were comparing notes on the sessions they'd been conducting with members of the general public. My ward was telling Juliette about an hour spent working with a middle-aged English businessman. "It was all going fine," my ward was saying, "the guy was really getting it. Then, suddenly, it was like it was all too much for him. He kept getting hung up on how the hell I was doing it."

Juliette was nodding. "That's happened to me a few times too—especially with men. It's like they need a machine there . . ."

"They're holding on to the cans . . ." The cans, held in each hand, complete the electrical circuit and registers the subtle changes on skin resistance to specific probing questions.

"They're connected . . . they know something must be happening, right? Now, here we are, sitting in front of them, reading their minds . . ."

"Yeah! No strings attached." Mein Host was chuckling quietly.

"Seriously! Do you see the paradox?" Juliette was saying thoughtfully. "It's our accuracy that freaks them out . . . like 'How on Earth did you know that?!' If we were telling them stuff that wasn't true they wouldn't be freaking out."

"So? Well, we can't really censor what we get, just so they don't freak out? Perhaps we should have them hold the cans but not connect them to the P-scope? They wouldn't know the difference!" They were both laughing now.

"No, no, silly! That'd be wrong. I've thought about this, and I don't think there's much we *can* do. Go a bit slower, I suppose. But there's no gilding the lily; we can't not say what we get. That's what they're coming to our sessions for . . . to hear what we get from them . . ."

"Not to waste their money arguing with us, right?" Mein Host was shaking his head at the stupidity of going to an empath and then arguing about feedback received. Reject it, by all means, but *argue*? And how do you tell someone the very reason they're protesting so vigorously is because they are subconsciously resisting the truth?

"Weird, isn't it?!" he continued, no doubt forgetting his own two years of subconscious resistance. "They'd be quite content if we missed the mark. They just wouldn't come back. If we pick up something from them they don't want to hear . . . that pushes their buttons, they freak out and challenge us . . . it really is a bit crazy!"

"But have you noticed," Juliette asked after a moment's pause, "that they are often the ones who come back for more . . . after they've thought about it?"

"Well, the Process ain't for everybody," Mein Host parroted with a wry smile. It was a phrase that would come to be used with more regularity as the community became more widely regarded as infamous.

If the Process wasn't for everybody—and it certainly wasn't—it appeared to appeal to a surprising number of young people, some of whom were prepared to submit to the stern restrictions required of those who wished to actually join the community. This trial period, in which people were expected to show their dedication, could last from six months to two years and was deliberately devised to filter out the kind of freeloaders often drawn to community life. Not only were the novices expected to be out on the streets selling magazines alongside the Internal Processeans at the hours that they weren't at work, but they had to attend the community's activities and spend time working in the Cavern, attend numerous empath sessions, forego alcohol and drugs, and donate as much money as possible to the community. All of this had to be done in preparation for a total renunciation of all personal possessions when they finally, officially, became an IP.

It was a challenging filter, but it worked. Only a dozen or so young men and women actually made it into the community during this period. After devoting themselves so wholeheartedly for as long as it took to become an IP, they found themselves at the bottom of what was rapidly hardening into a rigid hierarchy. In my opinion it was always inevitable— with Mary Ann so firmly in control of the community—that a hierarchy would be bound to develop. The Oracle was not a woman to accept parity with grace. That's just the autocrat's way.

As people in any contained social system tend to reflect the characteristics of their leaders—if they're not consciously emulating them—it was quite natural for Mary Ann's inner circle of initiates, in turn, to believe themselves special and chosen. My ward was somewhat more fortunate than the others in coping with the group's collective ego inflation, as he'd already had the insight to tackle his own sense of specialness. This had sprung up in his child's mind when survivor guilt led him to believe he was being saved for some important purpose—which, of course, he was but he wasn't to know that for many years. I believe he felt he'd gotten through his own personal delusion of importance, and he showed no desire to repeat it.

Although Robert was more conciliatory by nature than his wife, he was never able to moderate Mary Ann's insistence on making it almost impossibly challenging to get into the community and become an IP. I've seen Robert attempting to soften his wife's autocratic ways from time to time, but he was no match for her manipulative skills. To be fair to Robert, he was of a far more democratic temperament, but he was not a natural leader. He had the intellectual brilliance to understand and sympathize with every side of a complex argument, but that also tended to be equally matched by his frequent inability to discern the moral and emotional difference between the opposing sides being presented. He had the dry intelligence of an academic, as much as Mary Ann had the instinctive cunning of a politician—and a dictatorial one at that!

There were already four distinct levels of hierarchy within the community. The Oracle (Mary Ann) and the Teacher (Robert) were at the top. Below them was their inner circle, which itself was divided into two camps at any given time, between those in Mary Ann's favor and those currently in disgrace. Beneath the inner circle were the remaining IPs who'd been at Xtul and yet who had never been favored sufficiently by the Omega to be invited to be close to them.

Thus, those who'd met the challenges of becoming an IP, who had given up everything to become one of the Elect, now found themselves on this bottom level of the pyramid, with a capstone that had disappeared from their sight. It was a jarring awakening for them, scarcely mitigated by the constant iteration of the maxim that it was only by learning how to follow that they would learn how to lead.

The influx of these new IPs into the community reopened the sexual conundrum. If the senior members were not sexually attracted to one another for all the reasons previously suggested, this didn't hold true for many of them regarding the new IPs. The new ones were an exceptionally fine-looking crew.

This raises a somewhat idiosyncratic issue that I've touched on before. Why was it, as a number of articles about the Process have pointed out, that Processeans appeared to be invariably good-looking? For no reason the writers could ever explain, the women were almost always beautiful, and the men—undeniably handsome. Was it the Process that was having this beautifying effect? Or, was it, as one wag suggested, a matter of only the beautiful people need apply?

And the new influx was no exception!

Before the sexual pressure swung out of Mary Ann's control she must have realized that she needed to step in. Celibacy can have its value, but when it becomes a state of constant sexual frustration, everything suffers. People become distracted; they don't sleep well; their work becomes lethargic; and, as Mary Ann would be the first to identify, they don't bring in as much money.

Another factor further complicated this already ambiguous situation. As frequently happens when people set off on a spiritual path, they may be liable to form a fixation on one person whom they feel has the answers they seek. In psychotherapy this can manifest as transference, and in spiritual communities as devotion to the guru. To the uninitiated this giving away of self has many of the same sensations as falling in love, and the two states can often become confused.

A responsible therapist or guru will understand this fixation as a normal and necessary early stage in a person's spiritual journey. They will either return the power to the person, or they will press to retain the power in order to create the challenge of "killing the Buddha on the road." This giving away of personal power becomes particularly pertinent when it applies to spiritual groups such as the Process. In most cases the new IPs had already become devoted to someone in the community during their long period of preparation. The commitment to celibacy hadn't deterred them. They would already have been mentored by their special person; they'd have opened their hearts and spilled their secrets; they'd have been comforted and loved and encouraged; the women would have felt safe for the first time, knowing their celibate mentor wasn't trying to seduce them; and they may well have believed themselves to be deeply in love with their special IP. Perhaps most painfully of all, they will most likely have deluded themselves into believing that their mentor was also in love with them.

They might, in some cases, have had good reason for this. Celibacy practiced by the person desired can act as a powerful aphrodisiac, especially for those accustomed to having their way. It presents an irresistible challenge to the sexual predator on the one hand, as celibacy can also create a safe space in which the person can express their needs and desires, thus allowing them to observe their compulsive sexuality and how it has been driving them in the course of their lives.

Catherine, one of the young women who'd just moved into the community as a new IP, had something of this provocative quality. She was a petite girl in her early twenties with a fiery nature and an impish laugh. She had a wide mouth and a freckled face and wore her auburn hair long enough to draw strands of it over her face when she was amused. Her body was slim and well formed with long, slim legs. If anything marred her appearance, it was the way she carried herself: her shoulders slightly rounded and pushed forward as if to protect her chest. She had something of the air of a naughty fifteen-year-old girl, which made her a bit dangerous—and intensely seductive at the same time.

Catherine's background was both unlikely and appalling, as Mein Host was to discover when he came to know her better. She was the daughter of an immensely wealthy Anglo-American family. Her mother, who hailed from an American banking dynasty, had the misfortune to marry into an equally ancient line of English gentlemen—only to find out that her husband was penniless and a con man to boot.

It was a familiar story, the stuff of Hollywood movies, and in this case it produced a drama as morally ambiguous as a scene in a Bette Davis film.

"I killed my own mother," Catherine had told my ward when she was trying clear the air. He clearly hadn't believed a word of it. He knew the girl enjoyed shocking people.

"So?" he said, humoring her and playing it cool.

"I poisoned her . . . one night, when I was fifteen . . . I just wanted to put her out of her misery . . ."

"Generous motives indeed, Catherine!" This was so outside Mein

Host's grasp that he hadn't been able to take her seriously. She'd already told him her mother was a hopeless alcoholic and that she'd died some years earlier under somewhat mysterious circumstances, so who knew whether Catherine was telling the truth?

"Were you caught? How did you get off?"

"The family lawyer . . . he covered it up somehow. Listen, I was only fifteen . . . it was easy to get me off."

Listening to her go on, I pondered what a lot of justice all that money could buy.

I was also aware I was taking Catherine's claim of matricide a great deal more seriously than my ward. Whether or not her horrifying story was true (and I'm not inclined to reveal that), the fact that she'd related such a story about herself, and without a hint of remorse, has to reveal some clue to her character.

There was certainly no irony in the flatness of her delivery. She appeared completely serious and, if anything, seemed eager to share her tale. But poisoned her mother? I really think not. Could she have deprived her miserable alcoholic mother of her lifesaving medication? My ward said he believed this to be more likely if there was any truth to it at all. The whole idea was so extreme and outlandish that I could see it was difficult for my ward to take the young woman's confession at face value. Besides, Mein Host really had no wish to believe it. He'd been celibate now for almost three years and was far too sexually drawn to Catherine to want to know for certain whether the girl, in an excess of sympathy for a woman already drinking herself to death, had resorted to a sort of mercy killing; or whether she was simply a cold-hearted killer who'd murdered her helpless old mum.

My ward will never know the answer to this question, but as events unfold over the ensuing twenty-three years, signs will manifest to suggest the answer.

8

A Meeting with Lucifer

The Time of Nigredo, Sexual Desire and Sacred Marriages, and the Failure of the Visitors' Mission

Prince Janda-chi of Zandana was in conference when I was ushered into his august presence. He looked up from a table covered with maps as Unava and Sephira quietly left the room. I saw the Prince adjust his perceptual apparatus before he could take me in—then he was smiling a greeting and beckoning me over to join him around the table.

Unlike Caligastia's ostentatious palace back on Earth, Janda-chi's dwelling was modest. Even his choice of setting it in such close proximity to where Zandan's administrators lived was a thoughtful gesture of openness to the council members, a gesture that would have been entirely alien to Caligastia. When the Princes' mission had first arrived on the planet of Zandana and they started building their city on the coastal plain, both Prince Janda-chi and Prince Zanda had, quite sensibly in my opinion, created their main dwellings high in the foothills that overlooked the city. Whereas, until recently, Caligastia had always insisted on micromanaging both his staff—when he still had them—and his midwayers, the Zandana Princes had opted for a more hands-off policy. They didn't appear to be driven by Caligastia's obsessive need to control their staff. Yet, by locating their dwellings among the rolling hills above the city, in the parkland reserved for the nation's administrators, the Princes had succeeded in separating themselves from the daily grind of governing while simultaneously making themselves more personally available to their staff of administrators on an individual level.

Once again I found myself wondering at the startling differences between the Planetary Princes of Zandana and those two on Earth and the choices they'd made in interpreting Lucifer's revolution on their home worlds. Both missions had arrived on their appointed planets at approximately the same time; both chose to align with the revolutionaries; both have had to manage their worlds despite the quarantine throughout the System—and yet how very different were these two worlds in the way they were turning out!

"That's exactly what I wish to speak to you about," I heard Janda-chi say in my mind. He'd joined me at the floor-to-ceiling windows, and we were standing in silence together, watching the lights blinking in the city below us. Monorail cabins, lit from within, curved through the darkening forests and meadows surrounding the city like glowworms on speed. The air was so clear I felt I could almost reach out and touch the first glimmering stars.

"No fossil fuels at all now," Janda-chi said proudly. At these words I recalled those massive hydroelectric plants I'd seen on my previous visit and remembered how I'd admired the advances made in applied electromagnetics by the scientists of Zandana that had led most obviously, I assumed, to the monorail cars snaking silently over the landscape on their filigree of silver tracks.

Together we gazed out of the window for a few more moments with Janda-chi pointing at some of Zandan's more recent developments that we could make out from this distance. I could see that the port had been enlarged, and there seemed to be more pinpoints of light from fishing vessels way out in the ocean than I'd previously remembered. I couldn't help but remark on the delightful illusion this created as the stars imperceptibly merged with the glowing lights of the boats so as to make the night sky appear to descend to the very coast itself.

I heard the Prince beside me chuckle. "I must be getting too familiar with the sight," he murmured. "I'd never noticed that before. Lovely, isn't it?"

We turned back into the room at the same time, and as we did so

I noticed a slight etheric disturbance in the darkness at the back of the chamber. Prince Janda-chi took a few steps forward before bowing deeply from the waist to a figure even taller than he, who was now projecting himself into our frequency domain.

"My Sovereign, greetings to you," I heard Prince Janda-chi say as the figure, now more fully formed and seeming to be his own source of light, moved farther into the room. He was extremely tall, far taller than the Prince, and Janda-chi was one of the most statuesque beings I'd ever encountered.

I could see a lean, strong face, an aquiline nose, and piercing blue eyes under a high, smooth brow. For such an ascetic face, his mouth and lips were surprisingly sensual. Yet as I looked more carefully I could see a profound sadness just under the shining, glamorous exterior. As the figure moved closer to us, the overhead points of light appeared to move with him. They glowed brighter as he approached, while dimming behind him, so for those moments he seemed to be gliding on a pool of light.

Once again, I was taken aback. It was Lord Lucifer, the deposed System Sovereign of Satania.

I hadn't seen Lucifer, the leader we'd so loyally followed into the revolution, since back on System Headquarters—before we'd all set out on our planetary mission. I'd seen Satan a number of times on Earth, mainly in conference with Caligastia, but I wasn't aware whether Lucifer had spent any time on Earth since the outbreak of the uprising.

"Be at ease, sister," I heard Lucifer intone after I'd paid my obeisance. I felt myself uncomfortably graceless in his presence. Even now, when it must have been evident to him that his revolution was largely failing in terms of how he'd originally proposed it, he appeared to radiate self-confidence.

I need to stress the rarity of the position in which I found myself that evening on Zandana. As a Watcher it's not my role to become involved in planetary affairs, and I'd managed to hold to this on Earth. However, in inadvertently contributing my unconventional strategy of how I thought to handle the barbarian invasion on my previous visit, I had to wonder whether I may have overstepped my mark. It's unusual enough for a Watcher to be required to attend a Planetary Prince of another world, but to find myself in the presence of Lord Lucifer was both astonishing and somewhat daunting.

Of course I was aware of MA's vicious propaganda against him; of how they'd portrayed Lucifer as driven insane by his arrogance and greed; as a monster with no redeeming features whatsoever; as a rogue agent, a deceiver, and a betrayer of everything MA holds sacred.

Yet here he was! Much as I remembered him in the days before he'd been deposed as System Sovereign, radiant with the same conviction that had drawn so many of us to his revolutionary ideas. Deposed and despised by the administration of the Local System, like it or not, Lucifer was still *my* System Sovereign. And he will doubtless remain so until there is a resolution to his revolution; a reconciliation between these two forces whose long enmity has created such chaos and confusion in this Local System.

"You appear surprised," I heard him say in my mind. His voice was soft and almost feminine in tone. Of course! He would have been listening to my thoughts. Had he heard my reservations too?

"Be at ease, sister," he said again, gesturing both Janda-chi and myself toward the comfortable seats on the far side of the conference room.

All three of us had adjusted our senses to match the dominant frequencies within the domain in which Janda-chi had created his dwelling. The dwelling's chairs, sofas, and its circular table cut from a single quartzite block; the ceiling carvings with their delicate, embedded points of light: a precise replication, I realized, of the night sky I'd just been observing; the polished basalt floor with its streaks and splashes of gold and copper glittering in the lamplight—all of this felt and appeared as solid and real to us as your material reality feels to you.

I have to admit it's a curious sensation at first. I'm used to the finer frequencies of the fifth dimension, so when I have to downstep to one of the denser third- or fourth-dimensional frequency domains, it's always initially somewhat uncomfortable. I imagine it felt even more confining for Lucifer, who would have had to downstep his sensorium even more than I had. It was likewise amusing to note that as we sat down the chairs readjusted themselves to conform to the different size of our bodies. I smiled my gratitude to Janda-chi when I realized the chairs were a device he'd deliberately contrived to put his interdimensional guests in a more relaxed mood.

The overhead lights brightened slightly as we made ourselves comfortable. An elegantly formed crystal decanter and three glasses filled with a dark violet liquid that I knew to be one of Zandana's finest wines had manifested on the table between us at Janda-chi's unspoken command.

As befitted his station, Lucifer opened the discussion, addressing me. "We have wanted to meet you since Prince Zanda informed us of your suggested tactic for defusing the invasion. Proposing the women of Zandan set out to seduce the invaders was an ingenious strategy indeed."

I replied in a rather feeble, self-deprecating tone, suggesting that surely another would have thought of it if I hadn't.

He cut across my mumbles. "We believe you were not originally posted here on Zandana. Are we correct?"

I'd no need to answer. He continued picking the replies out of my mind.

"Ah, yes. Prince Caligastia's mission. And within my Lord Satan's protectorate. A difficult world, if we recall correctly. With many setbacks . . ." and there he paused, while I felt the familiar tingling in my consciousness signaling the presence of one considerably more telepathically skilled than my function has ever required of me. As System Sovereign of up to a thousand worlds, Lucifer, as all System Sovereigns, was trained in the more arcane arts of telepathic espionage—although I'd heard they prefer to think of it as diplomacy—to be used sparingly, we're assured, and only when necessity demands it. To put it in the language of the digital age, beings such as Lucifer have the ability to make a complete scan of another's mind, transfer the raw data to their own minds, filter out all that is not immediately relevant, then bringing the core issues to the surface in times of confusion, conflict, and duplicity—all at the speed of thought. That he was using this technique on me suggested that he did not altogether trust me and used it to match my post-guarded thoughts with the answers I gave to the questions he asked. This entire telepathic transfer and analysis is completed with such rapidity that, done with skill (and Lucifer was skilled!), the subject will remain completely unaware of what occurred. This makes the technique an invaluable tool for System Sovereigns in their wide-ranging territories.

But I am a Watcher. My sensitivity spans a wider spectrum than, say, a Planetary Prince. I was aware of what Lucifer had just done, so I wasn't surprised how direct his first question was. Yet it slid into my mind so smoothly it could have been my own thought. He was focused entirely on Caligastia and what I'd observed of his strategies.

This was putting me in an awkward situation. I may have disliked many of Caligastia's actions, but I had no desire to be actively disloyal to either of the Planetary Princes of my home world. My concern must have been apparent to Lucifer, because I then heard his soft voice reassuring me that it was to my System Sovereign I owed my true and deepest fealty.

What's the worst that could happen? I thought. It was a big step.

Back on Earth both Prince Caligastia and Daligastia already distrusted me. They couldn't really make my existence any more challenging than it already was; and besides, I wouldn't be telling Lucifer anything he couldn't find out from other sources. This is what I told myself; how I justified my betrayal of the Princes of my home world.

Then, unexpectedly, another thought swept in, sending me sliding off in another direction, a direction I found shamefully self-concerned. It was consuming me. I could think of nothing else. Why was I here? Why have I been singled out? Have I been singled out, or have I chosen freely to betray my superiors? Or, am I being used in ways of which I'm unaware? Is this some near political game I'm being inducted into, one that supersedes my obligations to my masters on Earth? And where does this leave me in this shifting equation? There was more along these lines, swinging me between self-doubt and self-importance. I was horrified and embarrassed to reveal so much of my confusion and self-concern to Lucifer, but I simply couldn't hold back the thought from coalescing and spilling out of me. Oh! The shame of it. I could not stop the question from bursting free. I am still ashamed to repeat it here, but I pledged, when starting these *Confessions,* to relay as openly and honestly as I am able what I've observed and experienced, however personally uncomfortable the circumstance.

So here, patient reader, is what finally burst forth in all its ego-trivial banality.

"Why me, Lord? Why me?"

It wasn't a question that required a reply. Lucifer's soft laughter rippled through my mind, and I realized it was a question the Sovereign must have heard all too many times before. I felt I'd betrayed myself. I knew I was somewhat credulous by nature, and I'd probably already demonstrated that I was somewhat too trusting of others and too unsure of myself by following Lucifer's revolution in the first place.

The Sovereign was kind enough to overlook my self-doubts.

"It is Prince Caligastia who concerns us, not you, little sister."

I relaxed back into the formfitting chair and closed my eyes. I felt deeply relieved at Lucifer's forgiving response and this time held nothing back. Images from the moment our mission had first arrived on Earth began spooling through my mind: of building our beautiful city of Dalamatia and its destruction by tidal wave after the revolution began turning sour, of the constant struggle the Prince's staff had with recalcitrant natives, of the emotional stresses of a third-density world, of the horrible deaths of the staff who followed their Princes . . . I laid it all out, everything I'd observed and went through in the 496,060 years I've been connected to Prince Caligastia's mission on Earth.

Lucifer was clearly more interested in the events following the revolution. I felt his delicate touch reaching into my mind to guide the torrent of images and information streaming through it, as you might use a touchscreen on an advanced computer. I was required to do nothing but be the observer observing her observations.

The process was extraordinarily rapid. Images sped by faster than I could discern them; sometimes they would suddenly slow down and then speed up again. Every once in a while they'd reverse and then play forward once more. Lucifer's ability to scan, take in, sort value from noise, and then absorb the relevant information was utterly remarkable. I touched on this facility before but although this scan was slightly slower, it was done with my compliance, cut deeper, and was far more thorough. Even though Lucifer had been deposed as System Sovereign of Satania, he evidently still retained the finely tuned ability possessed by all System Sovereigns: to process massive amounts of information extremely rapidly.

And he was courtesy itself. I wasn't asked for my opinions or to betray any attitudes that could be held against me later. Although Lucifer never confirmed this, I received the impression that it was primarily Satan's relationship with Caligastia that was of the most interest. I had the sense that Lucifer felt Caligastia's actions and behavior on Earth were letting down the whole revolution and that somehow Satan was behind this, sabotaging and thwarting Lucifer's grand plan and his high ideals.

Before I could take this line of thinking any further, I heard Lucifer's soft voice in my mind again.

"We thank you, sister, for your invaluable service to us. Much of this need not concern you, and with your permission, at the end of this meeting I will mask out the event in your mind until it serves our purposes to have it revealed to you again."

I'd no need to think twice about it. This was all far above my pay grade. I recall I was more than happy to forget about the whole encounter until the right time—which, I can only assume, is occurring now as I write these words.

It comes back to me . . . It must have been from Prince Janda-chi that I'd heard that Caligastia's world was considered among the System Sovereigns as being one of the three most troubled of the thirty-seven worlds aligned with the revolution. That had hit me hard, I can tell you! I knew conditions were difficult on Earth—but right at the bottom of the list?! That horrified me. And I didn't want to imagine how dreadful the conditions must be in those other two worlds.

"Be at rest now, little sister." It was the soft, cajoling, seductive voice again, stroking my mind. "There's much you don't know. But we will meet again. There is time yet for the Great Work to more fully evolve and manifest."

Lucifer rose to his full height as the encounter drew to a close. Prince Janda-chi, to my surprise, remained seated.

"Know this one thing, sister. There is more to our revolution than you know. Take courage. What you see on Earth are the first tears of the freedom we promised."

I must have seemed like a novice to him, this High Son of the Lanonandek Order, and I have to admit to being puzzled by his enigmatic statement.

"There have been many before us," he continued to reassure me, "who have called for the new freedoms. We have been accused of heresy. Let me quote from the records, 'The tendency to fall into error though fallacies of personal liberty and fictions of self-determination.' You see, it's nothing new. We are always misunderstood and vilified for wanting to mold our own destinies. I fear it has always been thus."

For the first time I could hear pain underneath the confident, knowing voice. It pitched me straight back into my fears and doubts. Had it all been a massive misunderstanding? The revolution, all the turbulence and suffering, everything we held so dear . . . a *misunderstanding*? Is that what Lucifer was telling me?

Before I could dwell on the possible truth of this, I heard his voice again, his confidence returned.

"You may call this first stage Nigredo," he was showing me. "Or, you may prefer to call it the Time of the Black Sun, when Caligastia cultivates the soil of corruption and blackens that which is to be transformed . . ."

Lucifer paused, concerned, I now believe, that he might be revealing too much.

I saw Prince Janda-chi—I'd quite forgotten he was there—now leaning forward, his eyes alive with interest. I had the impression the Prince hadn't heard Lucifer speak in this way before. But, then again, the Princes of Zandana evidently weren't cultivating the soil of corruption on their world with the dedicated and overt malevolence that Caligastia was enjoying on Earth.

For a moment I believed I saw the whole wonderful pattern fall into place. And it was perfect. The Multiverse . . . the revolution . . . all the horror and misery . . . just the cracking open of the chrysalis that the butterfly might fly free. Is that how it will be? Could it all truly be working for the best despite everything I've witnessed?

How I wished that were true.

"Be patient, my sister," Lucifer's tone soothed me. My desire to drink in his words almost overwhelmed me. "Have courage and faith in your vision of unification with the Supreme. It is a Great Work we have embarked upon and we will not cease until the transmutation is complete. It remains for us to reiterate our gratitude for your service to us. More will be revealed in time."

With that I believe he must have masked the encounter in my mind, because the last thing I remembered until recently was Janda-chi bidding me good-bye after a short meeting with him and someone else—was it a member of his staff? I'd never been able to remember.

Then I was alone again, out in the darkness, with the last of the city lights in Zandan below flickering out for the night.

There was nothing left for me to do on Zandana. I felt an urge to return home, even if "home" was one of the third worst of all the inhabited planets in this System. In retrospect I realize that this longing for home must have been derived from Lucifer telling me that my part in this Great Work of his lay back on Earth. And although I couldn't recall the words of our conversation, something of our meeting had apparently soaked up into my emotional awareness after all.

The smaller of Zandana's two suns was just being swallowed by the horizon, and it was suddenly darker than I'd ever remembered that planet to be. I felt confused. Then I recalled my sensorium was still tuned in to the finer vibrations of Prince Janda-chi's frequency domain. Before I readjusted my senses, I felt moved to make a pledge. Not to Lucifer, not to Satan, certainly not to Caligastia, but to the ultimate transformation of all beings.

So I vowed silently to myself in the language of planetary alchemy: "If this is the time of Nigredo, I will wait on Earth with courage and patience for Albedo, for the slow burning out of the impurities. I will do this having faith it will lead us all to Citrinitas—to spiritual enlightenment and to our ultimate unification with the Supreme."

* * *

I wasn't present when Mary Ann (and it can only have been Mary Ann) came up with her solution for coping with the sudden buildup of sexual energy that occurred when the new IPs joined the community at Balfour Place. I say that it could only have been the Oracle who devised the system because she made sure that all aspects of it remained firmly under her control. This system also served to reinforce the hierarchical structure in ways it's hard to imagine she hadn't carefully considered.

Mary Ann and Robert presented the idea at one of the late-evening meetings wherein the community typically gathered to share their stories from the day, drink tea or hot chocolate, or coffee in Mein Host's case, and smoke a last cigarette before their final meditation and sleep. After returning from Xtul, the Omega had stopped attending these evening meetings, so their presence suggested that something new and important was about to be introduced. The new IPs hadn't yet met Mary Ann or Robert, so there was even more of an atmosphere of nervous excitement than usual.

One of Mary Ann's admirable qualities was her ability to open up difficult and often confrontational issues. Her technique appeared to involve making some surprising or outrageous statement. Then she would ask probing questions, without settling for superficial answers, before directing the ensuing discussion in such a manner so as to achieve the results she'd originally intended.

On this occasion, the Omega presented the new idea in their usual convoluted way.

There were approximately thirty-five people in the room, some on chairs, most sitting on the carpeted floor, their backs against the wall. Mary Ann and Robert were seated in two comfortable armchairs, which stood against a wall that featured a fireplace long blocked off from use.

Mary Ann began by drawing the group's attention to the sexual energy that hung in the air. That brought everybody up with a start!

"It was as if," Mein Host commented later, "being celibate had made sex taboo to talk about."

"Or even noticed," Juliette had added.

"Or admitted to . . ." Mein Host said thoughtfully. The evening had forced him to admit to himself what he'd been holding at bay for weeks: his unacknowledged desire for Catherine's sexy little body and his admiration for her feisty ways. But mostly, if I'm to quote him, "It was lust for that sexy little body."

He believed he'd successfully repressed this desire—he was a celibate, wasn't he?—and that nobody, including Catherine, would have noticed. As it turned out, he wasn't alone in this. The influx of new IPs had apparently stirred up more libidos than merely my ward's, and, as was revealed by Mary Ann's aggressive questioning, almost every one of them had been repressing and denying their feelings. After all, they were all trying to be good little celibates.

"And thus the heavy sexual atmosphere," Mary Ann remarked with a certain measure of scorn in her voice. The scorn was no doubt due to their denial of the obvious; or because no one had the courage to act on their feelings; or because they hadn't yet mastered their sexual desires, and it was up to her once again to sort it all out.

I could see that the ambiguity of Mary Ann's attitude—openly stated or merely implied—was a device she employed to maintain a certain amount of tension. She was a mistress of manipulation of shame and guilt, so no one knew—when admitting to their lusts—whether she'd give them a tongue-lashing for their weakness of character or a wink and a nod of approval for remaining celibate in the face of their passions.

Mein Host found himself sitting next to Catherine at this particular gathering. He'd so effectively tried to ignore the girl over the previous months, repressing his desire and deliberately avoiding sitting near her at meetings, that he was seemingly quite unaware that Catherine had also been secretly lusting for him—despite her being somewhat less repressed about showing it. Thus, unknown to my ward, it was her decision, when she came in a few minutes late to the meeting, to lower her slim body into the gap next to him.

Mary Ann had set the scene the way she liked it.

Now came the revelation. The group hung on her every word.

The Omega had been shown, so she said, that one of the key dynamics to be examined in the community was the "spiritual parent/child relationships" that were emerging between the Elect.

"Parent/child relationships?" That was something new. What could she mean? People were looking at each other in puzzlement. Where was this going?

She spoke then of all the cultural baggage associated with father/daughter and mother/son relationships; of how so many peoples' sexual hang-ups can be found in the distortion of feelings, experienced in childhood, toward parents of the opposite sex.

So far, so good. Dr. Freud would have no disagreement with this generalization. What came next, however, might well have surprised even the good doctor himself.

Before I embark on this next bit of narrative, I feel it may be necessary to remind the younger reader how much that times have changed in the sexual arena over the past fifty to sixty years.

The young men and women of the Process in 1968 had been raised and educated in the 1940s and '50s—a very different time. In a society that was still class-ridden, most of them were of middle- or upper-middle-class backgrounds and were particularly subject to the strictures imposed by centuries of repressive traditions. They might well have been in the midst of a sexual revolution happening around them—and they'd all had to rebel against something: their parents, their education, their religion, just to have summoned the nerve to join the Process—but, in truth, they were creatures of another era, subject to the sexual guilt and shame that had been bred into them.

Mein Host, having had more sexual experience prior to joining the community and being more acquainted with celibacy than many of the others, was less susceptible to Mary Ann's emotional manipulation. This was not wholly to his credit, because he was so blindly devoted to her by this time that she really didn't need to manipulate him. However, he was no longer struggling in her web, which paradoxically left him freer to express his emotions over a sustained period, perhaps for the first time in his life.

So when Mary Ann explained that these mother/son and father/daughter relationships that seemed to be developing would have, among their other features, a sexual element, Mein Host greeted her words with some excitement. He must have felt the warmth of Catherine's body pressed softly against his side and smelled her scent when she shook her hair.

However, he was to have little choice of a partner, for this is where the hierarchy came in—in the subtlest of ways. The sons were asked to name their mothers, and the daughters were required to choose their fathers. And it should come as no surprise that the children in these spiritual/sexual relationships were the new IPs, and the parents were the senior members.

There were some tense moments as the sons and daughters staked claim to their spiritual parents. Mein Host appeared to have no idea he would be chosen by Catherine (although I'm sure he had his hopes). He became increasingly nervous as Mary Ann worked her way through the new IPs, many of whom must have been astonished to hear all this talk of sex when they'd thought they were joining a celibate community. But then again, if they could see what lay in their future, they would realize that this was only the first of many such radical changes of direction and beliefs that would characterize the group's erratic course over the years—with the Oracle at the helm. This is the reason I consider the community more aptly a Mystery School than a religion.

Mary Ann wasn't finished yet. She didn't want everyone jumping into bed. It wasn't going to be like that, she said. These were to be sacred relationships, and they were only to be consummated during a one-week period in which the happy couple would be given a room to themselves and wouldn't have to work alongside the others. Thus they could devote themselves completely to one another for an entire week.

Interestingly, Mary Ann said nothing about birth control, although it was generally acknowledged among the inner circle who knew her better, that she was uninterested in children and could be witheringly disdainful of childbearing and rearing. In fact, in checking Mein Host's memories alongside my own observations, neither of us have witnessed even one occasion that we'd seen Mary Ann with children.

As my ward came to know the Oracle better over the years and learn more of her appalling childhood in the slums of Glasgow—unloved and passed from reluctant hand to reluctant hand until she could escape the horror—he was able to better identify with her. Not because *he* was unloved but because of the horrific conditions of the Second World War into which he'd projected himself. He too had never wanted children of his own, and I know he has pondered whether his war-torn childhood was responsible for his disinterest in having a family. I can't be certain of this, but a statement I've heard him say from time to time—"This is no world to bring a child into!"—does support this position.

Yet there is always sadness in his voice when he says this.

The Oracle would have doubtless agreed with the sentiment. Yet sadly, I believe she was far too proud to think of her disparagement of children and childbearing as anything other than her own consciously chosen attitude. As well, she was too deluded by her own self-importance to realize that her vanity contributed to her disdain for the pregnant state.

Mary Ann said that she would be deciding when and who would be having these sacred marriages—or "Absorptions," as they came to be called. In giving these week-long affairs a sacred gloss, she was able to keep firm tabs on who was having sex with whom, while at the same time implying it was a sacred duty for the various pairs not to have sex with one another at any other time. She finished by emphasizing that these Absorptions were never to be talked about to outsiders and that for all intents and purposes the community would, with these one-week exceptions, remain essentially celibate. Those who knew Mary Ann better had heard her justification for this sort of hypocrisy before: to wit, all spiritual paths, all Mystery Schools and religions, have their esoteric and exoteric elements. She spoke of how outsiders wouldn't understand the parent/child relationships; of how cruelly they would ridicule them and use the ensuing scandal to discredit the Process. She said it was a secret the Elect would have to keep to themselves.

Of course, she was right in saying this. No one wanted to contemplate what a delirious massacre the Sunday newspapers would make of week-long sacred marriages in an organization claiming to be celibate. The press had already told enough lies about the group. They would have no compunction about making hay of the truth.

Mary Ann's instruction to keep this relatively harmless hypocrisy in place unfortunately reinforced a pattern of secrecy that became progressively more troubling as the Elect came to have more and more secrets to keep. This preference for secrecy also had an unforeseen consequence that wouldn't surface for a while. Then they would discover it was their very secrecy and the cloak of mystery with which they surrounded themselves that allowed the most ridiculous lies and distortions to be written about them—just to fill the vacuum created by the mystery.

However, all of this trouble lay a few years in the future. At the time, I could tell from Mein Host's emotional body that his excitement at the prospect of a week of making love with Catherine was matched by the feeling I've observed in humans when they possess secrets others do not.

Catherine and Mein Host were not the first pair to be chosen for their Absorption, so the delay just added to the delectable anticipation of the sensual pleasures awaiting them.

After three years of celibacy, my ward was now living in a constant state of erotic excitement.

"Soon the time will come," he whispered to Catherine as the meeting broke up.

"And so shall we!" she'd murmured back with a sly grin.

* * *

When I arrived at dawn my friendly Transport Seraphim Eleena wasn't at the transport station on the other side of the bay from the city of Zandan. I hoped she wasn't avoiding me after our previous conversation, given that I had the sense she may have felt she'd been indiscreet, or had overstepped her position.

Zandana, like Earth, is the third planet of its primary star; however, its orbit, due to the minimal gravitational influence of its distant secondary star, can draw the planet slightly closer to its sun. Zandana's solar system consists of twelve planets, four of which are gas giants. Although I was told by another Watcher that the fourth planet in the system has been prepared for the physical evolutionary processes, it is still in the early stages.

Dawn has a magnificence all its own on Zandana. As the world turned and its sun broke the horizon, the shining orb grew so large that it seemed to be extruding itself from the planet—to be sucked up into the sky. The clarity of the air and the lack of clouds on this particular morning only seemed to emphasize the size of the sun.

I finally managed to drag myself away and turn in to the station to go through the tiresome business of arranging my trip back to Earth and lo, there was a Transport Seraphim right there. But it wasn't Eleena. Yet it seemed that someone had been waiting for me. Once again I had the odd sensation that someone or something was easing my way, much as I now feel someone or something is organizing this narrative and guiding my attention.

My new Transport Seraphim was courteous but largely uncommunicative. I wondered if she'd heard about me and wasn't sure how to relate to my presence. As I've previously mentioned, there appeared to be a taboo throughout the System that prevented loyalist angels from communicating with those of us they've labeled rebels. I'm aware that in my case this may have become more complicated for loyalists, because they would likely be picking up on my growing ambivalence about the revolution. I'm sure that my conversation with Eleena had gone around the seraphic circuits with viral speed, which would only have further confused the many angels who had not heard the mysterious female voice that I'd heard.

I was folded in the seraph's embrace, and we were well into subspace when I realized the music generated by this seraph's magnetic envelope as we sped through the ether was remarkably different from the music that had issued from Eleena's heat shield. I was thinking about this, and wondering whether the quality of the music was in some way codependent on the personality of the Transport Seraphim modulating the sound, when I must have fallen asleep.

I awoke as she was slowing down and docking herself in the Transport Center on Earth. When I emerged and orientated myself, I was surprised to find that I'd been delivered to the almost defunct Salem Transport Center. This had never occurred before. Previously I'd always been returned to the center from which I'd embarked.

Yet here I was, dumped down in the middle of Prince Caligastia's kingdom! I pondered briefly whether the same invisible hand that had eased my way through the travel bureaucracy had also been the one to deposit me here in this unwelcoming place.

It is against a Watcher's nature to ignore such an obvious sign. Whoever may have been guiding my way became less immediately relevant as I realized that my services must be required, either by the Prince or by those I felt were tacitly encouraging me to observe and monitor the Prince's actions.

A quality all angels possess—being primarily creatures of function—is the ability to allow ourselves to be drawn to where necessity requires us to be. As a human being this might be difficult to immediately grasp, because mortals are thought of in Multiverse terms as "will-creatures." You constantly choose or decide what action you're about to take. Even tasks that might seem automatic to you carry the choice of not doing them. As angels, we don't possess anything like the same freedom of choice. I know I've gone on about this issue before, because it was so central to Lucifer's revolution—certainly as concerned us angels.

You see, choosing to follow Lucifer, deciding for ourselves on a course of action in direct opposition to MA's injunctions, was the first time any of us had made such a serious decision for ourselves—as an act of will. Prior to Lucifer's revolution, for example, my life was a simple one. As if guided by an invisible force I would simply find myself in the right place at the right time. As you'll have seen from my narrative, the revolution changed all that. As a Watcher I now have the ability to choose where I wish to be and what I want to observe, and yet I still find myself liable to be blown by the strongest wind to where I can only imagine I am *meant* to be.

It was in this way that the strongest wind had blown, and I found myself once again overlooking the peninsula on which the off-world visitors had made their home.

Much had changed since I'd last been here.

And not all for the better!

The parkland had a rundown look to it; trees had been left where they'd fallen; and the mass of flowering bushes had withered and died from lack of water and loving attention. I even saw a pride of sleeping lions who'd managed to take over a wide swath of the grasslands at the tip of the peninsula.

The two visitors, the Material Son and Daughter, sent from Jerusem to upgrade and refine the human genome, were in no better condition. They no longer glowed as brightly as when they'd arrived. When they walked, they stooped as though the weight of the world now lay on their shoulders, which I was to discover much later was how MA understood the situation too.

If their mission was to biologically uplift the natives by creating many tens of thousands of offspring who would then interbreed with the native stock and thus gradually raise the overall quality of human genetics—if this had been the task MA had sent them here to accomplish—then the few children I saw wandering around did not augur well for the mission.

There was a particularly dispirited atmosphere around the visitors' dwellings. The fountains were dry and their basins were full of leaves and muck; a roof had partially fallen in at one end of the main house and nothing had been done to fix it; the grassy meadows outside had turned into dusty, sunbaked dirt; and the fenced-off pastures, in which the visitors' animal husbandry and domestication programs had once taken place, had reverted to desert. I could see none of the cattle they'd been so carefully and selectively breeding, nor the goats of which they'd been so proud . . . then I remembered those fat, contented, sleeping lions.

This wasn't at all what I'd expected!

As I moved farther east toward the great wall that Vanu's workers had built across the neck of the peninsula, I found dwellings burned to the ground and cultivated fields reduced to bare and stony ground. Rocky outcrops had been blackened, and there wasn't a tree in sight. It seemed as if a terrible fire had swept across the land, cursing it into an inhospitable, scorched desert.

When I came to the wall, it was obvious how the lions had entered the interior, protected area, because one end of it had completely crumbled and there were smaller breaches up and down its length. Well outside the wall I could see the camp of a Nodite raiding party, the smoke from their fires rising in the still air like pillars supporting the sky.

It was a terrible and depressing sight, made even worse when I recalled the excitement the visitors had brought with them when they'd first arrived. Another Watcher who'd been assigned by Prince Dalagastia to specifically observe the visitors, told me something of what had been happening while I was away. She said the problems had started with the natives who lived on the peninsula alongside the visitors. Many of these people were the descendants of those who Vanu and Amadon had gathered to prepare the garden and build the wall and dwellings.

Although Vanu had told the people of the imminent arrival of the visitors, the garden had taken so long to prepare that a growing number of them had become disenchanted with Vanu's promises. Thus, when the two off-world visitors had finally shown up, the exhilaration created— after such a long time of almost giving up hope—started building to unrealistic proportions.

Apart from Vanu and Amadon, who'd always done their uttermost to disguise their true identities from the masses, the people of Earth thirty-eight thousand years ago had comparatively little awareness (although perhaps more than nowadays) of the Multiverse and its personnel. Had this System not been quarantined and had Earth been a normal inhabited planet, its mortals would have been familiar with different Multiverse personnel—both extraterrestrial and celestial—functioning on their world alongside them. Such people would not have needed to deify the visitors. They would have known the visitors for who they were.

The problems had started, so the Watcher told me, soon after the couple had arrived. Knowledge of this had spread like wildfire around the region, bringing thousands to pay their respects. Vanu had discouraged this adulation before leaving for Lemuria, but his protests had made no difference. The people were convinced that the gods themselves had finally descended to Earth, and there was little Vanu could do to quell the crowd's mounting religious hysteria.

Beneath this level of emotionalism, however, was a deeper concern.

While the visitors had appeared to be somewhat overconfident at the meeting I'd observed, my informative Watcher assured me they proved to be more modest and democratic in action. They apparently were too unassuming, however, for the excited crowds who demanded they behave more like the gods they believed them to be. Lest this compulsion to deify sound absurd to the modern ear, at the time of the visitors' garden, and for long after, there were some rebel midwayers controlling their worshippers by *pretending* to be gods and goddesses. Unlike these midwayer pretenders who weren't generally overtly discernible, the visitors at least appeared real. And wasn't that what they'd always demanded? A real god they could see and touch?

The Watcher told me that matters had progressed uneasily for a while, with the visitors introducing a number of significant developments. The most civilizing of these had been in the arena of law and education. Unlike Vanu's Lemurian culture in which the simple admonition to "Be Kind" covered most social contingencies, the visitors reintroduced many of the same laws and codes of behavior by which the citizens had lived in the days of the city of Dalamatia. Both in the laws and in the education of their young, the visitors stressed fairness and adherence to the Golden Rule, which is really the essence of any truly democratic society.

These new conditions allowed for the rapid growth of a trading culture among the clans on the peninsula, which soon reached out to the tribes beyond the wall. This progressed well for a time, and some of the Nodite tribes even became trading partners. The problems invariably arose when the visitors attempted to expand their influence too far beyond the wall.

Whereas Caligastia was powerless within the confines of the visitors' domain, those outside the wall remained far more vulnerable to the Prince's connivances. In fact, the Prince had numerous meetings with both visitors, trying to persuade them of the rightness of Lucifer's cause and the brilliance of his own actions in carrying his orders out in the world of mortals—all to no avail. The visitors had apparently been repeatedly warned about Prince Caligastia's deceptions prior to their arrival and, I sensed, came to regard themselves as beyond temptation.

It's not my purpose here to dwell on the many positive developments that the visitors introduced before their mission collapsed into tragic failure. These are described very well by the seraph who transmitted the relevant papers in *The Urantia Book*.

What I needed to know was: What had gone so terribly awry?

Was it simply the nature of life on Earth that led to such chaos and confused thinking?

What were the true dangers that might lead the visitors to betray their sacred trust when they'd been so vigorously warned against just such a thing?

Was there some potential weakness in the character of the off-world visitors that made them particularly vulnerable to Caligastia's machinations?

As the visitors were due to make their home on the planet for many thousands of years, how was it that their mission could be failing so spectacularly after a mere 117?

If Caligastia was behind the collapse of the visitors' mission, however could he have managed it so quickly and effectively?

As I moved slowly around the peninsula, I could see all the signs of the imminent disintegration of the visitors' mission. Despite my formal affiliation with Caligastia, I knew I was witnessing a terrible setback for the people of the world, at the same time that I was observing the unfolding of one of the Prince's most heinous crimes.

Could I allow myself to accept and enter into Lucifer's planetary alchemy—Caligastia's Nigredo? And just how bad did conditions on Earth have to become before the critical transformation could occur?

9

A Violent Absorption

The Unleashing of Sexual Energies, Subtle Seductions, Pleiadean Evacuation, and Sacred Orgasms

Back in Balfour Place the sexual energy was humming along. It touched everybody in the community, brightening their days with erotic promises and making them appear even more attractive.

It seems that if there is anyone, male or female, who is more attractive to the opposite sex than a celibate, it has to be a celibate who is having unashamedly secret sex on the side.

Although only one pair of IPs consummated their Absorptions each week, the effects of this intense sexual activity pervaded the community. Selling the magazines on the street—the source of the group's main financial revenue—picked up noticeably, and the Cavern was increasingly overcrowded with London's bright young things, there for an ogle and an Ogmar. The Telepathy Development Course was proving to be a great draw for adventurous souls; the weekly lectures were featuring intellectually provocative speakers; the movies the Process showed were attracting a regular crowd; and more people than ever were signing up for the empath sessions.

Now forgiven his incessant daily grind of magazine selling, Mein Host was spending all his time in the art department working on the Sex issue of the magazine, with brief breaks to wait tables in the Cavern when the crowds became overwhelming. I was amused to see how much he enjoyed working in the Cavern. Much the same energy he'd learned to draw on while selling magazines in the street seemed to carry over to when he was waiting tables in a crowded café.

But I was starting to notice a subtle difference in my ward, in the way he was presenting himself.

This wasn't quite the same Gabriel Stern who'd been the initial driving energy behind my ward's magazine selling, but a gentler and more humorous version. He was just as quick-witted as he was on the street, and he moved with the same fluidity through a crowded Cavern as he did through the river of pedestrians pouring along a Kings Road sidewalk on a busy Saturday afternoon. Yet it was a softer, kinder energy, less acerbic than I'd seen before in Gabriel Stern.

I soon realized, on seeing this different energy coming through quite regularly whenever he worked in the Cavern, that Mein Host's primary personality was starting to assimilate the Gabriel Stern subpersonality back into himself. I imagined it was only the beginning of a long process. This turned out to be true, because it would take another thirteen years before there was no further need for Gabriel Stern's intervention. By 1983 the subpersonality had become fully absorbed.

Yet, it was not going to be an easy ride for either of them to get there.

The week that Catherine and Mein Host were due to have their Absorption finally came around.

Waiting for it had evidently been an awkward time for them both. Not having yet kissed or embraced each other with affection, and all the while knowing this week of intense intimacy was facing them, their personal contact hadn't been particularly simple. They certainly couldn't claim to be in love. The situation was more similar, perhaps, to that of an arranged marriage (which, in fact, it was) or a Victorian engagement in which a forced courtesy descends on the couple and their repressed sexual desire renders them clumsy and inarticulate as awkward children.

Yet, for all that, it must have become increasingly obvious to my ward how emotionally out of balance Catherine was and how few interests they actually shared. In fact, during this interim period, and as Mein Host came to know his "spiritual daughter" somewhat better, while his lust remained as strong as ever, her erratic and volatile personality made her someone with whom it was quite impossible to reason.

The Absorption started with a ceremony held in front of the whole community—although the Omega wasn't present for this—before the couple was shown to their suite. All very formal. It was a small room on the fourth floor at the back of the house, with the rare luxury of having an attached bathroom. Its furnishings included a double bed, a couple of upright chairs, and a desk. A bookshelf contained some popular novels and a record player with a handful of vinyl LPs, including—to my ward's pleasure—the Beatles' recent album *Revolver,* had been kindly provided.

Mein Host also moved a drawing board in for the week so that he could continue to work on designs for the magazine. He was still too inexperienced with women to know what a mistake this was, although he'd had enough prior clues to understand it if he'd been paying more attention. Half a dozen times over the course of his seven-year architectural training, when he'd been sitting working at his drawing board, his mind on his designs but with a girlfriend talking to him, he'd said something without thinking that had deeply upset the woman. This had occurred with several different girlfriends over the years, so he'd had every chance to have spotted the pattern by now.

What he couldn't have known at the time, however, was that this was another manifestation of the ease with which he could dissociate. With his conscious attention elsewhere, a more direct and somewhat acerbic subpersonality would pop though and make some painfully truthful comment to whichever young women it was. And then the sub would disappear again, leaving Mein Host to pick up the pieces. I don't say this to excuse Mein Host in any way, because a person needs to be responsible for their subpersonalities, but to clear up a mystery for my ward that continued for many years after the event that I'm about to narrate.

As I've already stated, companion angels and Watchers avert our gaze when our mortal wards make physical love, not because we are prudes, but to allow a veil of privacy to descend over the lovers. I am an observer, not a voyeur. Yet it was impossible not to note that my ward and Catherine's coupling must have been extremely vigorous, because whenever they emerged they would both be covered with sweat and exhausted, with deep scratches etched into my ward's back.

It seemed to me that such a passion is inherently unstable, and, when added to Catherine's emotional unpredictability, this mix quickly became dangerously volatile. It came to a head one evening when, predictably enough, Mein Host was working at his drawing board while Catherine was standing on the other side of the room trying to talk to him. Their conversation was desultory and unimportant. Mein Host's attention was on his design, and his replies to Catherine's questions were getting progressively mindless. He was clearly getting fed up with her demand for attention.

Whatever it was that ignited Catherine's fury isn't relevant. She was so temperamentally high-strung that it could have been anything. She picked up a wooden T-square that was leaning against the wall, stepped quietly up behind Mein Host, and brought the edge of it down in a swinging arc on the back of his head. Luckily it was a glancing blow or the T-square would have buried itself in his skull—but it must have been extremely painful.

I saw Mein Host pull himself upright and turn slowly toward Catherine. His hands went to his head, and blood seeped through his fingers. There was a shocked silence. A look of baffled surprise crossed his face as it twisted with pain while a bitter smile of triumph seemed fixed on Catherine's catlike features.

The T-square rose again and started arcing down toward my ward's head. Since I had no access to his interior experience at the time, this is how he later described it in his words: "The pain and the surprise were intense. Then I saw that T-square coming down at me again . . . that's the last thing I really remember. From the bruise on my shoulder afterward, I think it hit me there, but I didn't even feel it. It's like I wasn't fully there, because the next thing I was aware of my eyes were covered with a red film, which was blinding me. Worse than that, my fists were thrashing out at Catherine.

"When I came to and discovered what I was doing, I was appalled. I stopped immediately. I'd never hit a woman in my life in spite of the occasional provocation. On the two previous situations in which violence had exploded in my relationships, I had been the one who was hit. And in neither case was I at all angry. In fact, although I can't remember for sure, it was most likely my cold and hyper-rational behavior that must have set them off!

"But this thing with Catherine wasn't like that. I'd never experienced anything even vaguely similar. I'd never "seen red" or lost control before. I was horrified at how my fists were wildly and uncontrollably striking out at the girl. At the time I'd never come across this 'seeing red' effect; I'd never even heard about it. If it was out there, no one was really talking about it, except the mentions of 'bloodlust' or 'going berserk' I'd come across. But reading about this state and experiencing it are two entirely different matters; Catherine ended up with a few bruises, but she wasn't hurt. In fact, she might even have enjoyed it. Of course, when I came to understand her better, she became less of a mystery to me.

"I was left with a deep need to discover what it was inside me that seemed to autonomously take over, and with such a horrible result. I could never allow this to happen to me again. God knows what damage I might have done if I hadn't caught myself before it got too bad."

The attentive reader will have doubtless noticed that the previous explosions of interpersonal violence so far in Mein Host's life have all put him on the receiving end of it. Granted he could be irritatingly detached and probably appreciated a lively argument more than most, but this shouldn't have been enough to have produced such a physically abusive response from very different people.

Yet, a catharsis of sorts was taking place.

Catherine's attack, coming out of the blue in my ward's terms, served to wake him up to the fact that something else less obvious was going on under the surface. I knew he'd never considered himself a victim—in spite of having been victimized through no fault of his own as a child of the Second World War, and again at school by the resentment and fury of a senior boy. Yet he had never responded as a victim would have. Instead, he wanted to know why these assaults were happening.

The Process community's belief in taking total responsibility for themselves also helped, in that it directed his attention back to himself. He couldn't blame the other people; no doubt each of his attackers had their own issues to work out. What was inescapable was whatever the immediate justification for the person's action, the result was invariably the same—someone else was beating on him. So why was he attracting these violent outbursts? What was he exuding that was inciting these out-

of-control episodes? Was he subconsciously punishing himself for something he was unaware of doing? These were the kind of questions I knew
he must have been asking himself.

Unfortunately, his knowledge of general psychology at this time
didn't extend to understanding the dynamics of projection. He wasn't yet
consciously aware how much anger had been beaten into him, so successful had he been at repressing it. But with the Catherine incident he at
least woke up to how much damage he had sustained over time, and the
need to do something about it.

What he wasn't to know was that it would take the next thirty years
to fully exorcise that demon. It was critically entangled with a previous
incarnation and the fear-impacted thoughtforms he'd received when he
was a small child living through the war.

* * *

The longer I stayed on the peninsula, the more I came to recognize Prince
Caligastia's hand behind the impending final collapse of the visitors'
mission.

Of course he hadn't been able to act directly on the visitors. They were
too intelligent and forewarned for that. In the Prince's frequent meetings
with the pair all he could do was try to persuade them to continue his
policy of accelerated evolution. He tried doing this from every viewpoint
he could think of, but to no avail. The visitors stood firm. They hadn't
aligned themselves with Lucifer at the outbreak of the revolution, now
more than 150,000 years ago, and they weren't going to start now. That
was their stand, and they were quite resolute.

The years passed in a stalemate. The visitors were faced with an
almost hopeless task. The situation was far worse than they could have
imagined. All their efforts needed to be devoted to attempts to bring the
native population back up to the point of cultural advancement—where
it should have been were it not for Caligastia's destructive policies. This
proved to be desperately difficult for the pair.

Under normal conditions, if we hadn't followed Prince Caligastia into
the uprising—or, more particularly, if the Prince hadn't taken over and subverted Lucifer's revolution—the visitors would have found a rather different

world waiting for them. For a start, people would likely all be speaking the same language. It would not have been a population fractured into a thousand different tongues by millennia of warfare, invasions, and the movement of refugees. A Planetary Prince and his staff, had they remained loyal to MA's mission, would have had some 462,000 years to prepare the people for the arrival of this, the second of MA's primary interventions. The illustrious visitors would have then heralded in what should have become a golden age of progress on the planet—but a progress that balanced material advancement with spiritual values. This is what normally occurs on inhabited third-density planets, or so I was taught.

As we've seen, on this world, this just wasn't to be.

There appeared to be a permanent feud, for example, between the Nodites—descendants of Nodu and the rebel staff—and a tribe that called itself the Amadonites, which counted the many descendants of Amadon and Vanu as their forebears. Both these tribes had reached about the same point of advancement, although what inspired them and drove them was very different and bound to keep them at odds.

It was generally through priest/kings that Caligastia indirectly controlled the northern Nodites, as well as most of the other tribes on the mainland. It hadn't been difficult for him to goad the already belligerent Nodites into constantly harrying those inside the garden who were loyal to the visitors. With the main group of Amadonites forming the spiritual aristocracy in Lemuria, the much smaller tribe in the area around the peninsula had been no match for the aggressive Nodites.

The visitors tried to draw all the tribes together under a representative government to replace the monarchs and tyrants who were always at each other's throats. But they found no one capable of governing in a fairer way. The visitors established a number of new trading centers on the mainland, yet much of the knowledge they tried to disseminate was rejected out of hand. Their much-needed attempts to breed out defective genetic traits in the natives, while welcomed among the garden dwellers, was considered tantamount to murder by the mainland tribes. Caligastia had seen to that! The visitors' perfectly sensible emphasis on eugenics was roundly mocked by the Prince as another example of MA's overreach. Where human beings were concerned, Caligastia evidently favored numbers over quality.

Lest I get across that the visitors were somehow foolish or incapable, they most certainly were not. They were fine and noble characters, as brilliant and able as any of their order. Even I could see that. They tried everything they knew, everything they'd been taught back at System Headquarters, to put the planet back on course.

But was it truly was an unachievable goal? Perhaps the visitors might have achieved it had they remained on the planet for many millennia, but after what occurred their mission fizzled out within a fear hundred years and Caligastia reasserted his primacy. The Prince, as self-proclaimed God of this World, had far too powerful a grip on the tribal imagination. With his priests and the kings who were under his control, the Prince was able to nullify most of the advancements the visitors introduced, so after the first hundred years the visitors could see almost no progress for all of their tireless efforts.

Because the visitors were pacifists and insisted no one was to be killed on the peninsula, the hostile Nodite tribes understood they needed to refrain from an outright slaughter to avoid alienating their less sanguinary allies. More subtle methods would have to be employed.

I'd watched Caligastia probing the visitors for their weak points during his meetings with them in the garden, and I wondered then if they knew the Prince was playing them. Although Caligastia had been formally denounced by MA after the revolution, neither he nor his deputy, Daligastia, had been replaced and both had been permitted to stay on the planet. I believe MA must have allowed this in the hope that the Princes would see the errors of their ways, but obviously this hadn't yet happened. Caligastia was still dedicating all his efforts to subverting the visitors' mission, even though he pretended to support them.

The visitors were no fools. They'd have been quite aware of Caligastia's hypocrisy from the warnings they'd received. Yet the constant obstacles and the depressing conditions, along with relentless pressure from the Nodite aristocracy to interbreed with them, had been steadily wearing the visitors down. The more frustrated they became with their lack of progress, the more vulnerable they became to Caligastia's unctuous sympathy for their plight. For more than a hundred years the visitors had rejected the Prince's persuasive arguments urging them to ignore MA's directives.

"Look around you," Caligastia would tell them. "What do you see?

Everything is falling apart, right? You know you never had a chance down here. You were set up!"

The visitors had heard most of Caligastia's arguments, but this appeared to be a new one.

"Listen to me. MA's put you in a completely untenable situation. You never had a chance—there's no point in blaming yourselves. None of your order could have done any better. Don't you understand? You were sent here to fail. You weren't expected to bring in a golden age."

Now the visitors were looking puzzled, for what he said was true. They *hadn't* received any real support from MA.

"How did they expect you to manage?" Caligastia asked, seeing he'd hit a nerve. "How long is it since you've been able to consult a Melchizedek, for example? Don't you get it? They're not that interested in us. They don't know what it's like down here on Earth. They don't know how thick-witted and intransigent the people are. They didn't appreciate everything we tried to do *before* we'd had enough of MA's harangues."

The female interrupted him. "Set up, Prince? What did you mean, set up?" Even if her face looked tired and drawn, and her startlingly blue eyes were duller than when I'd first seen her, she was still an extraordinary beauty. She was pregnant, as she invariably was, yet for all her exhaustion she radiated a still-glorious femininity.

"You think it was any easier for us back then?" Caligastia's tone was rising in complaint. "Why do you think we were demanding more freedom?" He was starting to go into one of his self-pitying moans. The visitors caught one another's eye. Was it simple courtesy that demanded they hear the Prince out?

"We could have made this place a paradise if we'd been given a free hand. But, no! MA tied our hands—and now look where we are! And they sent you two to clear up their own mess! Hah!"

"*Your* mess, Prince Caligastia. Not their mess. Yours!"

I'd noticed previously the male visitor's tendency toward defensiveness.

"Doesn't matter whose mess it is," Caligastia said impatiently. "The point is it's you who are expected to turn it around. Just you two. If it was so important don't you think they'd have sent more of you?"

I don't think this had yet occurred to the visitors. The Prince hurried on.

"You've seen what happens when you've tried taking your ideas out to the mainland tribes . . . you can't impose your way of life on these people—you must understand that by now. And if we have to wait around until you've had all those children before we act, it'll be too late."

"MA's not going to stand for that, Prince Caligastia," the female replied. Her mate looked at her sharply, and it came to me that her choice of words might have suggested she was softening in her views.

"You will come to see the truth of what I'm telling you," the Prince's tone was softer now, almost seductive, and he was addressing himself to the female. "There are times," I heard him intone, "when each of us must make decisions for ourselves. We have to take responsibility for our own actions. Each of us has to grasp the moment and respond accordingly. Do you understand? You can't look to MA anymore—they've deserted you. You're on your own. You can do what you think best. That's what freedom means. That's what we're fighting for."

Caligastia must have felt his inspiring words carried the day, because he phased back into his dimension, leaving the two visitors sitting silently at the polished basalt table in their rundown garden. After a few moments, the female broke her mate's gaze, placed her arms and elbows flat on the slab, and buried her head in her hands. Her flowing blond hair hung disheveled over her shoulders, and her long swollen body was shaking with sobs.

"I promise you . . . we'll give it serious thought," the male said helplessly.

"You know he's right," she said between sobs. "We've got to do something. We can't wait."

The male chose not to reply to this. It was obvious he deeply loved and trusted his mate. After all, she knew MA's instructions regarding their breeding program as well as he did. And the Prince did have a point—it would be centuries before the next step of the uplift could be initiated. As we were taught, at a certain point in every inhabited world's development a pair of these off-planet visitors (beings of the Order of Material Sons and Daughters) arrive with the instructions to bring a new genetic boost to the indigenous mortals of that planet. This "violet blood" genetic uplift had to be administered with great care and caution. That was why MA made it an absolute rule that a full complement of up to a million pureblood offspring of the visitors had to be produced before violet blood could be introduced by interbreeding with the indigenous races simultaneously all over the world and with the finest examples of human beings from all tribes and races. Any failure to achieve this large number, warned MA's tutors, would result in a premature expression of the genetic boost. They told us that in a few cases this upset had occurred, and the consequences were "unfortunate"—a word MA's agents reserve for the very worst of eventualities.

This is how it had always been done, and Earth, in MA's judgment, was no exception. I recall thinking at the time how even the minimal infusion of violet blood into a small, select group or tribe would favor them unfairly over other peoples. Not only would they be blessed with the higher intelligence of violet blood, but they would be cursed with the arrogance of regarding themselves as special and superior—as a master race, perhaps.

The male visitor sat, silently thoughtful, while his mate on the other side of the table wept on uncontrollably.

I feared even more for the future of this unfortunate world.

* * *

Mein Host and the art department were now toiling around the clock on the magazine's Sex issue in order to meet their printer's tight schedule. Creating the pages was extraordinarily laborious in an era before computer graphic-design programs made such tools as pencils, Letraset, X-Acto scalpels, and drawing boards irrelevant. The focus necessary to cut and precisely register the four acetate overlays needed for handmade color separations was so intense that on a couple of occasions I observed my ward's head, after countless hours of concentrated effort, slowly dropping to his board. He was fast asleep, an X-Acto knife still twitching in his cold, dead hand.

Whether or not it was a coincidence, Absorptions were occurring at the same time that the team was preparing the Sex issue. After the long years of voluntary celibacy, a less-repressed sexual energy was now permeating the London Chapter. Mary Ann was keeping a close eye on the forces she had unleashed by opening up this Pandora's Box of sexuality, but it wouldn't be long before she would need to reach deeper into her sexual grab-bag of tricks.

The Process cosmology had been becoming progressively more formalized since the group had returned from Xtul. The four gods—Jehovah, Lucifer, Satan, and Christ—had first emerged out of the community's psychological explorations into patterns of human behavior. However, it was their experiences in Xtul that had crystallized these god-patterns into "The Four Great Gods of the Universe."

On this topic the Omega had produced three slim volumes with provocative titles; they were being printed on the Heidelberg Press in a room at the back of the basement of Balfour Place. Mary Ann was thought to have channeled *I, Jehovah* and *I, Satan,* while Robert appears to have written *I, Lucifer.* (I thought it fortunate there was never an *I, Christ.* That might have been one conceit too many.)

There is no point in trying to explain the intricacies of the Process cosmology or how these Great Gods relate to one another, as it bears little relevance as to how the Multiverse Administration is actually structured. Yet the god-patterns themselves did have some limited value in allowing the community to become aware of how deep-seated these patterns of behavior really were.

To oversimplify, a Jehovian personality might have the characteristics of a powerful leader, self-confident and inspiring to others, but also capable of becoming autocratic and ideologically rigid. A Luciferian might be intellectually brilliant and socially nimble, but with a tendency toward self-adulation and unrealistic expectations. A Satanic personality might be adventurous or filled with artistic passion, yet can be cruel and destructive if opposed. A Christ personality will lean toward balance and unification and yet might also lapse into indecision and self-pity.

In this way, each Processean identified themselves with one pattern or another. In some cases Mary Ann would be the one to make the identification. Later on, as the belief system became more intricate, these god-patterns doubled up. Thus Mary Ann thought of herself a J/S (a combination of Jehovah and Satan); Robert was cast as a J/C (Jehovah/Christ); and Mein Host and Juliette each came out as an L/S (Lucifer/Satan).

No doubt there were those in the community who felt a genuine connection to these four gods, but I never saw any sign of this in Mein Host. He's written that he found Robert's religious writings unreadable, and that he never thought to worship any of these four gods. He said that he'd never even had an experience of them. Nothing like the Godhead that absorbed him behind five hundred micrograms of the purest LSD.

"Indeed not," I remind him, as we write together. "You were far too focused on Mary Ann as your Goddess to include anyone else, God or otherwise."

"So one delusion saved me from falling into another delusion, is that what you're implying, Georgia?"

"All belief systems are delusionary to one extent or another. They're delusions to the extent that they're incomplete. Your conviction of Mary Ann's divinity was delusionary, but even so, it provided you with the potential for far deeper spiritual insights than if you'd believed in those silly gods."

Although Mein Host did not accept the basic tenet of this Four Great Gods belief system, there were curious aspects to this system that were ultimately extremely helpful to him, and I can only think his companion angels must have foreseen this. All the talk of Lucifer and Satan by the Process community allowed my ward an ease and a familiarity with names he'd later encounter in *The Urantia Book* in a somewhat more authentic context. Still more important was the Process belief in the reciprocal interdependence of the gods and human beings. Mary Ann liked to say that "The gods need us as much as we need the gods."

The implications of this grandiose, but not ungenerous belief, was probably the clue that Mary Ann needed to make her next move.

* * *

I must have been getting more sensitive, because I found I had no wish to observe how the tragedy on Earth that Vanu had warned Amadon about was going to play out. The prophecies of the Star People—that fire would come from the sky and that the waters would rise over Lemuria—seemed to be too unbelievable to be true. Besides, I'd last been on the Islands of Mu at an equally key moment in Lemuria's development, and I was keen to know how the Pleiadeans' warning of the coming calamities had been received by the people. And that thought was enough to take me back to the large southern island that was Vanu's administrative center.

After linking up with one of the local Watchers, she told me that word of the extraterrestrials' predictions were apparently spreading rapidly through the islands. No one had known quite what to make of the warnings of fire from the sky. The people were living on volcanically active islands so they were familiar enough with eruptions and earthquakes, but—*fire from the sky?* That hadn't rung true for many of them.

On the other hand, Vanu and Amadon evidently believed the predictions—however diligently they were trying to avoid a panic—so, surely there had to be some truth to them. Each person was thrown back on their own spiritual resources to sort out their intuitive feelings. Yet, with time, the stresses of trying to make such life-or-death decisions dissipated as the demands of everyday life reasserted themselves.

Thus, when the first of the Pleiadean evacuation ships had arrived to transfer the inhabitants as promised, the massive arc had departed, according to the record the Watcher had heard, almost half empty. She told me some Lemurian families had actually arrived at the Pleiadean ark only to change their minds at the last moment. People were that unsure of themselves!

The Lemurian civilization at this point represented nearly thirty thousand years of continuous existence. In their enormous Hall of Records there were even a few treasured written records, carved onto flat jade plates, from a time before the great emigration to Lemuria had taken place. Lemurians were intensely proud of their motherland, and it seemed inconceivable to many of them that their beloved islands could be wiped out. Mu was the mother who took them in and offered them refuge, as Father Sun had warmed them and Mother Earth supported them for a hundred generations.

The more religious among the citizens simply couldn't believe Father Sun and Mother Earth would ever betray them—the gods never had and surely they never would! Amadon, however, wasn't so confident. It had been Amadon, after all, who'd persuaded a reluctant Vanu to replace the Invisible Father God that no one could see with Father Sun and Mother Earth.

Given the present state of affairs, Amadon was nervous and Vanu was vexed. I knew Vanu blamed himself for ever listening to Amadon and compromising his most scared dogma. And for what? Now his people didn't know what to believe or who to trust. And worse still—and I could tell Vanu didn't want to address this—might it have been their actions,

Vanu's weakness and Amadon's thoughtless pressure, that was bringing the catastrophe down on them all? True or not that their spiritual betrayal played a causative role in precipitating the disasters, I could see from his emotional body that Vanu certainly felt it to be so. I could appreciate why he wouldn't want to let the thought into his conscious mind. I think it would have crippled him. He knew he was soon to leave the planet; that the Islands of Mu, his brainchild, were going to be vanishing forever. This was "somehow tolerable" was what I heard him muttering to himself when he couldn't push his self-blame away any longer. But to think he might be responsible through his own cowardly irresolution? No, no, it was intolerable . . .

"Oh well," I could hear him say, as I did more than once in moments of weakness. "There's really nothing much anyone can do about that now . . ." and he'd drift off into silence. But never for long. It was one of Vanu's great strengths.

Because, of course, there was much to do!

Amadon was doing his best to make up for his error before it was too late. He must have known it would be hard-to-impossible to redirect the peoples' spiritual attention after so many generations of the worship of Sun and Earth. However, after he'd consulted with Vanu, a decision was reached to repeat a pattern that had worked so well for them in the early times of the Prince's mission. It was when the staff had reached out telepathically to call in the brightest from the surrounding indigenous tribes to be educated in the city. In this case it was Amadon who set up a major university on one of the main southern islands that would be devoted to teaching the teachers. Following that original pattern, Amadon sent out his envoys to the farthest reaches of Lemuria to gather together the brightest and bring them to the new university. There, Amadon could explain the reasons for the decisions he'd made so long ago, telling them how their distant forebears had needed something more solid in which to place their faith. It was by reassuring the Lemurians that they were now more spiritually endowed with the truth and would benefit from returning to the faith-driven belief in the Creator God, assuring them that in the experience of the Indwelling Spirit, they would find the strength to return to their people and restore the old ways.

Framing the change in this way was evidently designed to flatter his teachers and make the redirection of their religious enthusiasm more palatable, thus making it more likely they'd be able to communicate the urgency of this restoration when they returned to their islands with the good news.

It was a desperate time for the people of Lemuria. Disaster was hanging over them. The Earth itself was shifting under them. An entire island and all its inhabitants could disappear overnight, sucked back down to the depths from which it was once thrust up. In the light of this imminent threat of extinction, it appeared that Amadon took it upon himself to give his audience of teachers a crash course on planetary history, starting from the time the Prince's staff first arrived on Earth. I knew the situation must be serious, because I'd not heard so much revealed that had been previously withheld from general knowledge. I was a little shocked, I have to admit, but not nearly as shocked as those who would go out to spread news of the "New Revelation," as Amadon was calling it.

When the savants had absorbed as much as they could, Amadon offered them three choices. They could either return to their islands and relay the teachings to those who chose to remain on their motherland; or, they could accompany the Pleiadean evacuation arks and continue teaching at their new planetary home; or, they could join the boats that were taking Lemurian emigrants to their settlements in Central and South America, mainland China, northern India, and Tibet.

Before the teachers left to return to their islands, Amadon reminded them that Vanu's plans for the future and the continuation of the Lemurian culture depended on their responsible choices. Until the time came for action, so he'd told them, the teachers were to remain silent about what they'd learned in order to allow all citizens to make their decisions free of coercion. These decisions, he emphasized, needed to emerge from the deepest intuition of each individual. Clans might well be split up and families separated by people making different choices, but Vanu had decreed it a necessary corrective, a redirection toward listening to and heeding the guidance of the Indwelling Spirit.

If this seems irresponsible to the modern mind—that a leader such as Vanu wouldn't take stronger action given the threatening conditions—it's my understanding that Vanu was taking the larger picture into account. In terms of the mortal lifetime, it was of lesser concern to Vanu as to which decision a particular mortal might make than encouraging each to listen to the truth of their hearts. Some would live longer than others; some would die on Lemuria; others would die in India; while still others would die on another planet.

But they would all die. Sooner or later, they would die. Did it really matter that much where and how it happened?

And because Vanu had once been a mortal on another world—long before he ever volunteered for this post on Earth—he knew from his own experience that mortals will awaken from the sleep of death to find themselves in the loving care of angels. He understood, because he'd been there, that the souls of mortals ascend through the many levels and dimensions of the Multiverse, because that was the other choice offered before he volunteered and was chosen to join Prince Caligastia's staff. Yet Vanu had grown to love his people and to think of them so dispassionately I knew must have been difficult for him. He was kindness itself.

I'm not privy to Vanu's thoughts, but I've no doubt they were such as these that kept him awake and tortured his dreams. Yet he said nothing of any of this to Amadon, who, having been born fully human, from human parents, and due to his extraordinary longevity, has never had the opportunity of dying to the mortal flesh.

So knowing this and accepting that even the worst catastrophe can work for the ultimate benefit of all beings concerned, Vanu was able to make peace with the knowledge of the disasters to come, for he and Amadon had done everything required of them to prepare the way.

As more years passed, life on the islands tried to settle back into its normal, easygoing rhythms, and talk of fire from the sky no longer dominated peoples' conversation, although the thought and the threat of it always lurked just below their collective awareness.

Meanwhile, in the darkness of space, a massive piece of ice and space debris some miles in diameter, drawn out of its own orbit by Jupiter's gravity, was speeding on a nearly elliptical path that curved out beyond the sun. Implacable and unstoppable, trailing a glowing tail of ice particles, the comet was now hurtling toward the sun for the first of its three passes through the inner solar system before it would be slung out into open space to follow a new and less catastrophic trajectory.

* * *

Mary Ann's announcement that masturbation was to become a holy duty had the predictable effect. So, I thought, is that how she's going to resolve the sexual pressure?!

The sexually charged atmosphere had been building steadily in the chapter as the various couples had their Absorptions. It hadn't diminished, as Mary Ann might have hoped. Did she really believe it would? Having followed a celibate life for the previous three years, and then to have a single week of voluptuous sexual pleasure, made all the more intense by the limited time allowed, was scarcely liable to reduce the sexually charged atmosphere.

The erotic energies floating around the chapter were most confusing for the public attending activities or eating in the Cavern. Indeed, one celebrity—the Australian satirist Barry Humphries, Mein Host tells me—was heard to have asked, "When's the barefoot job going to begin?" making clear what he thought was going on!

Mary Ann had stressed that the general public was to know nothing of any of the sexual activity going on inside. Outsiders were to continue to believe that all Processeans were celibate, for if they ever learned the truth of what was really happening they'd be sure to misinterpret it and make it a subject of ridicule. However, if Mary Ann had known to frame it this way, she might have added that esoteric sexual pursuits were also the very stuff of Mystery Schools. At least, this was how I observed Mein Host interpreting the information.

Robert, always an expert with a pen in such situations, wrote a short ceremony to be intoned before the sacred act of masturbation, which wasn't intended to be an act of worship as much as a gift of energy to the god of choice. The act of masturbation was to be undertaken by the sacred couple and was presented as a way of sacrificing back to the gods the most intimate and personal offering a human being can make.

A room was set aside at the front of the mansion on the second floor for the devotionals. The floor was carpeted, the paneled walls were painted white, and the ceiling was lofty in the manner of Mayfair mansions. A low altar stood in the middle of the room; on it were two silver bowls, one for water and the other for fire. Smoke from copal incense drifted up from a holder. They called this room their temple.

It was not my manner to observe the IPs at their devotionals in the temple but merely to note that most of them took up their sacred duty with unbridled enthusiasm. While individual IPs could reserve the room, it also gave those who'd already undergone their Absorptions an opportunity to continue the intimacy by simultaneously masturbating and dedicating their orgasms to their respective gods. There was to be no physical contact between the couple, who were positioned as the ceremony required on either side of the altar. I've heard Mein Host claim the most profound orgasms occurred when he and Catherine were maintaining eye contact as they ceremonially carried out their devotionals in the Temple together.

There were also a few times when I saw that small groups were gathering to make their offerings as one.

"Odd how entirely lacking they are in real eroticism," I overheard Juliette saying to my ward as they were filing out of the temple after a group devotional.

"Not exactly orgies," he'd grinned back. "But quite good fun anyway."

While it was unlikely the Great Gods of the Process cosmology could have been affected in any way by all this devotional sexual energy, I observed that it allowed for a far more relaxed atmosphere in the chapter. By making the orgasm a sacred gift and providing a formal situation in which to offer it up, Mary Ann had accomplished her ends. She'd managed to release much of the pent-up sexual repression hanging in the air; she'd combined sex and religion (her religion!); she'd maintained her control over the IPs' sexual impulses; and she'd helped to dissipate the shame and guilt associated with masturbation during that era.

It was a masterful move, I have to admit that, and I gave Mary Ann full credit for loosening the group's typically English sexual rigidity. However, her next move was more questionable and carried consequences far beyond the event itself.

10

Impending Doom

A Parisian Challenge, America Beckons, Caligastia's Cunning, Planetary Differences, and the Complexities of Lucifer's Revolution

My recent time on the Islands of Mu was a tense one. It seemed to me as though the people were all living under their own collective Sword of Damocles. Even those who hadn't quite believed the Pleiadean's warning were affected by the subtle shift that had taken place in a populace that was quietly contemplating the possibility of its own demise. With the exception of the few remaining worshippers of the sun god, fewer and fewer people were attending their four great solar ceremonies. I overheard a number of mumbled conversations about the pointlessness of life and even some comments suggesting the people would rather never be warned about an impending disaster. It seemed to me as I moved around that the joy had drained out of their lives.

Granted, a couple of Pleiadean arks had docked, taken on their passengers, and quietly slipped off again into the galactic night. Boats had been crossing the Pacific, delivering teachers to Lemurian outposts in mountainous regions throughout the world. Yet, taking the island nation as a whole, not much really seemed to have changed. People went about their daily lives much as they had before the warning but with an uncharacteristic indifference. More tellingly, the birthrate had been dropping steadily.

Although the imminent catastrophe was spoken about less and less, I could see how a subconscious awareness of the disaster heading their way was wearing down the spirit of the people.

I observed, for example, that there was virtually no recent building taking place anywhere on the islands. Some of the massive temple structures had even been left half completed, and their superbly constructed and terraform pyramids and plazas were being reclaimed by the jungle, unloved and uncared for. Two large and once important Temples of the Sun lay completely deserted, many of their gargantuan stone blocks defaced with the angry graffiti of those who felt betrayed by their solar deity.

Yet, despite the sadness I'd found in my travels around the islands, the problems their people faced—devastating though they threatened to be—had all the purity of a natural event. While this isn't the forum to discuss the intentionality behind an erratic elliptical path that brings a comet so close to Earth, you may take it on faith that no such significant natural event occurs without the knowledge and sanction of the living Multiverse. Once again, this might sound improbably callous to some people, or simply downright improbable. Yet, whether a natural disaster is thought simply to be the consequence of unavoidable physical processes, or whether it is the result of an intentionality beyond current understanding, the effects of the disaster will be precisely the same.

And when I say the oncoming disaster that will force so many fine Lemurian minds into a global diaspora has "the purity of a natural event," I'm contrasting it to the disaster of a very different kind that was concurrently unfolding on the other side of the world. It focused, not surprisingly, on those two worthy off-world visitors on their peninsula at the eastern limit of the Mediterranean. This was a drama that has turned out, over the longer term, to have a much more deleterious effect on human life than the disappearance of the Islands of Mu under the waters of the Pacific.

The visitors' sad little drama was far more personal and humiliating than what would befall the Lemurians. Yet, in many ways, it also shows a poignancy and tenderness that is quite absent from the simplistic and twisted version of this story that has filtered down to the modern era. It's the reason I haven't yet named the visitors although I'm sure the astute reader is aware by now that our visitors are the Adam and Eve found in the Holy Bible and to whom is attributed the creation of the human race.

Plate 1. *A Relaxing Moment.* Enjoying the luxury of
such a rare abundance of clean fresh water.

Plate 2. *Shifting Realities.* Momentary shifts
in consciousness can reveal deeper
layers of intentionality.

Plate 3. The *Panentheistic Journey.*
In reincarnational time, all belief systems
will yield to the deeper truths
of the open heart.

Plate 4. *Emergence Moving Forward.* Dragging oneself out of an ancient quagmire can be a messy business.

Plate 5. *Pax Natura*. The overlooked power of Nature to take care of her own.

Plate 6. *A Moment of Truth.* Such life-changing events can occur when least expected.

Plate 7. *An Alien Presence.* Imaginative invocation of a small android
seen to accompany an Arcturian agent.

Plate 8. *End of the Day*. Mission accomplished, tired of cloaking,
a last chance to buzz the canyon before it's back to the mothership.

It should be obvious that this creation story couldn't be so. Humanity long preceded the visitors' arrival. Yet the biblical story does capture some element of the truth. While not the first humans, that they are remembered for having a hand in procreation is remarkable and speaks to the importance of the visitors' mission and its consequences, especially that anything should remain that occurred almost forty thousand years ago.

I will describe as best as I can what actually happened, and you will be able to see the distortions that have crept in over the millennia as religious revisionists through the ages have spun the event to suit their purposes. In doing this, to give one example, by casting the female of the pair in such a negative light the reverberations of her actions, sorely misunderstood and distorted, have been used to demean women to this day. While the biblical story hasn't been the original cause of discrimination against women, it has certainly reinforced and legitimized it through the centuries.

It has been my observation, based on comparing sexes on Earth and Zandana, that the more difficult the planetary conditions are, the more those difficulties can bring out both the aggression of men as well as the natural compassion of women. This is a generalization, of course, but one that, by and large, holds true. The women of Zandana, for example, would never have been able to adopt such a shameless military strategy of seducing incoming armies bent on conquering had they not been emotionally secure enough to handle the consequences of their actions.

So I've asked myself whether it was inevitable that it would be the female visitor upon whom Caligastia would set his sights, although as far as I could make out at the time, she was no more vulnerable than her mate. Or was it merely that she was more compassionate than her mate? Was it, then, her legitimate concern for their mission's slow progress that made her the most tempting target for the Prince?

Was she, therefore, merely a dupe of Caligastia? Was it really "the devil who made her do it"?

Or was it her impatience and ambition that rendered her susceptible to the Prince's manipulation?

Was she so overcome with frustration that she turned with full knowledge to the dark side to accomplish their mission's ends? Or did her action spring from the depths of her compassion?

Perhaps, when understood in the larger context of Local Universe politics we may find what she did accomplish was part of a far deeper and more occulted strategy to prepare this world for the events that lay ahead.

* * *

If Mein Host had had more of his wits about him he might have been curious as to why he and Andrew, the magazine's production manager, were so unexpectedly instructed to go to Paris. The final and most punishing deadline for the magazine—when they had to actually deliver the flats to the printer—was merely weeks away, and the art department was only just keeping up. But an instruction from the Omega, however unreasonable, was not to be ignored or refused—and certainly not to be argued with! Leaving Balfour Place was a hurried affair. They were told on a Tuesday and left for France that Thursday morning. The only reason given was that they were to encourage and support the recently founded Paris Chapter.

Arriving in the city on a wet Parisian afternoon, they were picked up and driven to the chapter, some forty miles outside the city suburbs. The chapter was housed in a pleasant French country house, large enough to fit the eight IPs and the two visitors from London with rooms to spare.

The sprawling one-story house was set in an unkempt garden with half a dozen ancient fruit trees whose barren, blackened branches were now dripping with rain. And because the house was so far from the city and wasn't set up to admit members of the public, it was deemed to be a closed chapter, with no outsiders to be invited in.

Yet the moment the pair arrived they couldn't help but notice the thick feeling of depression hanging like a veil over the house. Back in London they'd been told that morale in the Paris Chapter was at a low point, but I could tell from my ward's emotional response that he had no idea the atmosphere would be quite this grim. Much store was always set by sales of PROCESS magazine and the money this brought in, but clearly this hadn't been going particularly well. Just how poorly he was yet to find out. The IPs living there knew nothing of the parent/child Absorptions or the recent sexual explorations in London. Even if it might have encouraged them, neither Andrew nor my ward were about to enlighten them.

Dinner that first evening was an awkward, stilted affair, with the

Parisian chapter IPs straggling back in from the streets of the city as the night wore on. Stories had to be repeated and re-repeated for the late-comers, as all of the residents were expecting and probing for news of the Omega—while Andrew and Mein Host were doing everything they could to avoid talking about what had really been going on back in London.

This evasion was made even trickier because all Processeans were trained specifically to be empathic and tended to be highly sensitive as to whether information was being withheld. Having been sent there to inspire the Paris Chapter IPs to greater efforts, and yet being prevented from telling them the very news that may well have uplifted their spirits, I watched as Andrew and my ward had to tamp down their own enthusiasm and weave their way through the many pointed questions asked of them that night. Thus their arrival at the Paris Chapter did very little to immediately lift the depressive atmosphere that, as Mein Host would soon discover, was far more deeply embedded than either of them had expected.

Finally the meal and the questions were over. Everyone had returned, and, as in London, they'd put on their long, black robes for the evening meeting and their final meditation for the night. Exhausted and clearly relieved to have survived the evening without betraying any sacred trusts, Mein Host took to his mattress and fell asleep with the rain still hissing down outside the window.

The next day they all set out in the downpour to catch a train and two buses to reach the Left Bank and what were reputed to be the primo streets for selling magazines.

If they could sell magazines.

At the best of times, urbane Parisians aren't known for their civility as they hurry about their business. They especially don't enjoy hearing their language mangled by schoolboy French. They also don't relish a magazine written in a language they don't understand, about a subject that offended their secular souls, sold to them by someone with unfashionably long hair and dressed in the robes of a priest. For Parisians it must have been a choice combination of aversions, because they felt free to let their invectives fly with a complete lack of inhibition.

A word about Process clothing and symbols because—as has been pointed out by others—the group's use of dress and symbols has been recognized as a remarkably savvy marketing technique.

Processean men and women dressed alike in black shirts and trousers, worn with black shoes. Their violet capes had been replaced by longer, black, hooded cloaks falling to their ankles. Triangular patches sewn onto each shirt collar featured a Goat of Mendes embroidered in scarlet thread on a black background. To further confuse the uninitiated, around each of their necks hung a silver cross with a serpentine dragon engraved in red and black coiling up the vertical axis and stretching sinuously out onto the horizontal one. On their fingers flashed heavy silver rings adorned with Process symbols emblematic of their different ranks within the community.

Frankly, looking like this, I was surprised they could get *anyone* to stop and buy their magazines.

Mein Host, who was accustomed to selling more than a hundred magazines a day in London, now counted himself lucky to return to the chapter late at night having sold more than a dozen. Day after day their endeavor became an exercise in dealing with almost constant rejection. Rejection was nothing new to anyone selling magazines on the street, yet somehow this was made even more unpleasant, as my ward observed to Andrew when they were making their way back after another frustrating day, by not understanding what their potential clientele was saying. In fact, with minimal exceptions, the only people who ever bought their magazines were American and English tourists—and during a cold, wet November, there were few enough of them around.

When orders came through some days later for my ward and Andrew to return to London, the only task they'd accomplished was to reassure the Paris IPs they'd tell the Omega about the almost impossible conditions they faced daily on the streets. The IPs evidently believed that this message—coming from Mein Host, who was accepted as a top seller among the men in London—would finally convince the Omega of the very real difficulties they encountered.

Arriving back in London, the art director and production manager needed to get straight back to working on the magazine and do their best to catch up on the time lost in France.

When they were both cross-examined by Mary Ann a couple of days later about the problems in Paris, they felt bound to lay out the frustrating and depressing conditions they'd met over there. They told her about the exhausting two-hour trip to get in and out of the city, and in so doing it became clear that Mary Ann hadn't understood the distance the IPs had to travel each and every day to do their work. It turned out that the senior IPs in the Paris Chapter hadn't wanted to admit to themselves, or to the Omega, just how far from the city was the only house they'd been able to find and rent.

Mein Host talked about how hard it had been trying to sell a magazine to an unwilling Frenchman, and he acted out the man's reactions for the benefit of Mary Ann. This dramatic display was much to her amusement, given that she had never shown much affection for the French.

Andrew then added the idea that he and my ward had previously discussed, as to what they believed to be one of the root causes of the French IP's depression. "If the house was in the city," he said, "say somewhere on the Left Bank, if it was an open chapter with a coffeehouse, then even those people who'd had a rotten day on the street would have somewhere to invite people back to if they were interested. That way they still feel they're doing some good. They're not just selling magazines, they're helping people."

"And then they'll feel good about themselves even if they didn't sell much," Mein Host agreed.

This was true; I'd seen it happen again and again in the Cavern. Processeans were highly trained to listen to someone speak and display no attitude or judgment. They did it without interrupting and waited for the other person to finish saying their piece before speaking themselves. This was a Processean at his or her best. True listening such as this was a rare talent and frequently drew out intimacies and guilty secrets from people—secrets that they'd never before spoken aloud.

Mein Host has written previously about such an occasion one afternoon in the Cavern with the unfortunate Brian Epstein. Ashamed and terrified of his homosexuality, locked in his closet but terribly teased by those lads from Liverpool, he was finally able to blurt this all out to my ward, who heard out the anguished confessions of the Beatles' manager with an open heart. Although Brian Epstein would commit suicide some months later, he left the Cavern that afternoon having spoken his truth for the first time and in considerably better spirits than when he'd arrived.

Mein Host finished by telling Mary Ann how it was really only English or American tourists who ever stopped to buy the magazine. "Forget the French," my ward said, playing on Mary Ann's prejudices, "they're hopeless. I don't think the chapter will make it with their current setup."

He clearly had to be careful in his analysis, because by this time he understood Mary Ann well enough to know how quickly she'd dismissed any rationale given as mere excuses and lame justifications for failing to rise to the challenge. She had every reason to believe in the power of the will, having dragged herself up from the slums of Glasgow, and she seldom had any time for complaints about difficulties.

Yet it was that reference to America, to Americans being the ones buying the magazines, that seemed to grab her attention. Mary Ann, as it turned out, was the only one of them who'd been to America. She'd spoken of it fondly and had hinted to her inner circle of her relationship with the American boxer Sugar Ray Robinson.

So it was that within a couple of weeks my ward's friend Chris—another L/S—together with a couple of other IPs, were on their way to the United States to start the Chicago Chapter of the Process. (There had been a long-standing injunction from the Omega that a Processean must always be accompanied by another Processean whenever they left the chapter.)

While a cynic might suppose this was one of Mary Ann's control mechanisms, allowing her to keep tabs on everybody, the IPs were generally grateful to have another Processean covering their backs when they went out. There were other times, however, when having to drag along a second person was downright inconvenient, and in Mein Host's case when visiting his mother it proved to be intrusive and annoying for both mother and son.

His mother, Diana, especially, felt deprived of the normal closeness she typically shared with her son on my ward's infrequent visits. She disliked having to make polite conversation and feel obligated to include the other Processean when there were so many more interesting matters to talk about with her son. He'd always been included in her important business decisions, and his invention of the Viewpack System for photographic slide storage remained the core moneymaker of her educational filmstrip production company. When a stranger was present, she found it impossible to discuss her business openly in the way she preferred.

Always an ingenious woman, Diana soon came up with a solution that only modestly bent the rules.

"Why not bring along Little Daniel?" she'd suggested, leaning back in her chair with a bark of triumph, clearly amused at the thought of outwitting Mary Ann's rules for the group. Diana had not taken to Mary Ann the one time they'd met. "Little Daniel's a Processean, isn't he? He could be your pair."

Little Daniel was the three-year-old son of a young American woman who had joined the community in London after splitting up with her husband. Daniel was the only child in the group at the time and needed the constant attention required by any child of that age. As all junior IPs were required to spend most of their time out on the streets, Daniel's mother was seldom available to care for her child. This caused a certain amount of resentment in those who were switched from tasks they enjoyed to having to look after a highly energetic and rebellious little boy.

Some months earlier Mary Ann had instructed my ward to be the caretaker for Little Daniel on a daily basis. Hard though it is to believe, she conceived this as a punishment for one of my ward's long forgotten, minor transgressions of the rules. Mein Host, in turn, seemed pleasantly surprised to find himself enjoying looking after the boy. His energy appeared to chill out the rambunctious three-year-old. They'd chatter away happily to one another, entertaining each other endlessly with scary science-fiction stories while Mein Host was on his hands and knees scrubbing the staircase carpet (another punishment).

Mein host was as surprised as his mother was grateful that Mary Ann had acquiesced. Little Daniel (the "Little" denotes his rank in the hierarchy) could accompany my ward when visiting Diana.

Thursday afternoon and evenings were the only times in the week that the IPs were given time to themselves. Many of those whose parents or friends weren't living in London spent their free time relaxing in the chapter. Diana, however, was living in an apartment above her office at the top of Baker Street—"Two doors up from Sherlock Holmes," she liked to tell credulous Americans—and Balfour Place was only a short bus ride away. It would have been inexcusable for Mein Host not to visit his mum—considering how seldom he was in the country. But neither mother nor son was to know yet just how seldom this was going to be as the years passed.

The afternoons my ward spent with Diana were happy afternoons, welcome breaks from the intense pressure of life in the Process. During these times they could speak openly to one another, with Little Daniel happily drawing with crayons at their feet. These afternoons also had a less obvious value for all three of them: for Diana, it was the pleasure derived from having a surrogate grandson; for Daniel, they were afternoons—unlike those in the Process—spent in a stable family setting; and for Mein Host, it was an opportunity to get to know a young child.

There was something about his and the child's rebellious natures that allowed them a sense of mutual recognition, which obviously surprised my ward, who'd never shown much affinity for small children. It was a regrettable aspect of the Process that, due to all the traveling around they did and the number of chapters they set up in different cities, Mein Host would never again be able to share such unparalleled quality time with Daniel.

To Mein Host's surprise, the strength of this early bonding showed itself many years later, after he'd left the community behind and was one day sitting quietly in his New York studio. He'd not thought of Daniel for years, although he'd heard the boy had had a rocky time in the community and had finally left the group when he was in his teens to be with his father. Apart from that, my ward knew nothing more of the boy.

"And then, suddenly!" to quote Mein Host, "there Daniel was! Standing on the other side of my desk. He'd come to show me how he'd died."

Daniel had just been killed. He'd been at a party in Los Angeles, given by his best friend in the family's house while the parents were away. When the party broke up Daniel half-jokingly refused to leave. His friend went upstairs and got his father's gun. When he threatened Daniel to leave or else, Daniel had ended up daring his friend to shoot him. That's what he had demonstrated to Mein Host.

"It was when his friend actually shot him—that's what he wanted me to see!" Mein Host has said. "Daniel couldn't believe his friend had just shot him. He told me he was almost immediately overcome with a terrible, terrible sadness. He said he just stood there, unable to believe that he really was dead."

When Daniel came to Mein Host in this way, he hadn't stayed for long, and it appeared that he only wanted Mein Host to know what had happened to him. There was nothing Daniel wished done about it, and, after he phased out, he was not seen again. Mein Host was more familiar with the spirits of the dead by this point, and he was able to handle the encounter with considerably more equanimity than he could have mustered earlier in his life. His near-death experience a few years later in 1973 would change all that!

* * *

Caligastia's influence has been so pervasive on this world that I frequently find myself thinking of him as a physical and material presence. But, of course, he was never a creature of your dimension and was only able to influence human affairs through his midwayers and their willing mortal collaborators. If there was ever a candidate for the devil's role, far from it being Lucifer or Satan—who rarely graced us with their presence here—it would have to have been Caligastia. Although not exactly the horned goat of religious fantasy, Caligastia has certainly used every trick possible to attempt to pull down or poison anything that threatened his hegemony.

The Prince was bound to attempt to subvert the off-world visitors' mission. By now it was his nature to do so. The visitors' presence on the peninsula was abhorrent to him. It represented an insult to his proclaimed divinity and presented a constant prospect of losing control over those he'd co-opted. Setting himself up as God of the World meant he would have to oppose any of MA's attempts to intervene in planetary life.

The visitors were eventually able to adjust their senses sufficiently to see Caligastia as a physical being, but normal humans were unable to perceive his presence. As I've previously stated, your mortal minds are inviolate; you are protected—as your forebears were—from the direct mental intrusion of any of the rebel angels unless you specifically request it.

This had made Caligastia's plan to subvert the visitors' mission all the more complicated. Although he'd tried many times to persuade the visitors to follow his example and accelerate the lethargic progress of human development, they hadn't been deceived by him. But neither had they reckoned on the subtlety of Caligastia's intrigues.

The Prince knew he couldn't directly intervene, so he'd been cultivating and working through a couple of Nodite priest-kings—Nodu having once been his greatest supporter. I have come to believe the Prince must have long been cooking up a plan with the Nodite priests to trick the visitors and do this by working through highborn members of the Nodite aristocracy.

Caligastia had all the time in the world to develop his strategy and his plot will turn out to be one that features multiple betrayals, a Machiavellian deception, underpinned by profound sexual shame and guilt. It would be a tragedy of world-changing importance, and yet it will also reveal a level of true tenderness and a touching depth of love that continues to reverberate in the best of humanity.

However, the most unfortunate result of Prince Caligastia's conspiracy was that it would effectively seal the fate of this planet and the human race for the next thirty-four thousand years. Planetary life was going to get a great deal worse before there would be any light. It was with a nagging sense of the visitors' inevitable downfall that I once again took what I've come to think of as my coward's way out. I just couldn't watch another fiasco. So I decided on a quick trip to Zandana to clear my mind.

I felt sure that life would be a lot more balanced on that world.

After a smooth and uneventful trip to the planet with a Transport Seraphim I hadn't encountered before, I found myself once again on the other side of the bay from the city of Zandan. I settled into meditation beneath one of the massive old-growth trees overlooking the ocean and allowed myself to be drawn to where my presence would be of most benefit.

You might imagine my befuddlement when I next found myself in a beautiful garden setting—every bit as glorious as Vanu's peninsula park back on Earth. It was a place I'd never seen before. I could tell from the position of the shadows on the mountains that it couldn't be far from the city.

Fine, I thought. What now?

I moved closer to the dwellings that I saw through the trees. As I watched, two tall beings, a male and a female, emanating and surrounded by a glow of the lightest violet, strolled out of the main entrance, arm in arm.

Off-world visitors? They looked so similar to the visitors on Earth whose fate I'd come to Zandana to avoid watching.

And yet here I was, observing what appeared to be another Material Son and Daughter! Here. On Zandana.

As they drew closer I could see they looked almost identical to the unfortunate pair on Earth with the important exception that these were smiling and laughing. Both of them were quite obviously radiantly happy.

I moved slightly to my left so I could see where they were heading. Although they couldn't perceive me without adjusting their senses, I found myself following them as discreetly as possible while they walked toward the monorail terminal that I could now see in one of the forest glades ahead. A silver cabin was silently drawing to a halt, and in the next moment Prince Zanda stepped smoothly out of it, accompanied by a small retinue.

I have to admit to a moment of fear. Caligastia and Zanda are of somewhat the same appearance from a distance, and I must have flashed back to my preoccupation with the imminent catastrophe I'd just eased myself out of back on Earth.

Yet, when *this* Prince caught sight of the visitors, I watched his face light up with genuine delight. He started moving faster, his retinue struggling to keep up, until he reached them. And here again, I couldn't quite believe what I was seeing. The noble Prince Zanda was bowing his head and going down on one knee in front of the softly glowing pair.

I had never once observed Caligastia greet the visitors back on Earth in this deeply respectful way. Rather the opposite! Although I hadn't seen him ever be openly discourteous to the visitors, he always seemed to have a slightly patronizing tone when he addressed them. Here I was watching an entirely different display from Prince Zanda.

Rising to his full height again, Prince Zanda and the visitors looked at each other for a long time in silence, and then the three of them burst into simultaneous laughter and fell into a joyful embrace.

A bell rang from somewhere in the building behind me. I turned to see a mass of children of all different ages pouring out into the gardens, squealing with joy, running and skipping off in different directions to go about their separate tasks for the afternoon.

Prince Zanda and the visitors walked slowly back through the woods, stopping every once in a while to admire different flowering bushes and revel in their scents. Their laughter rippled through the trees, the sounds bouncing off branches so as to reach me as a rich micro-tonal chord of mutual pleasure.

It was an idyllic scene; more beautiful than anything I'd yet observed in the material realm.

And it made me suddenly feel terribly sad!

In those moments I had the shocking realization that I was watching everything the visitors' mission back on Earth could have been. It was then that something of the complexity of Lucifer's revolution dawned on me. Might what I was witnessing here on Zandana be exactly what Lucifer had hoped for when he was considering what might grow from his revolution?

How could these two worlds—both of whose Planetary Princes aligned themselves with Lucifer—be working out so utterly differently from one another? Was this contrast simply due to the difference in personalities between the two Planetary Princes, Zanda and Caligastia? Or, was it some specific quality in the two planetary populations that had fostered such different outcomes?

Not having had access to the other thirty-five worlds supportive of the revolution, I'd no way of knowing how the scenario on Zandana rated in terms of the other worlds. Was Zandana, despite its troubles, a fine example of the revolution working out for the benefit of all? Or was Earth the example of the worst consequences of Lucifer's revolution?

It was worth bearing in mind that Lucifer and Satan, in spite of being from the same order, were quite different personalities. When the Planetary Princes for the thirty-seven apostate worlds first gathered, they were informed that Lucifer had already divided up the oversight responsibilities between himself and Satan, claiming nineteen worlds for himself. The remaining seventeen fell to Satan, Earth being one of these.

Would this, I wondered, have made a difference? Would the quality of life on Earth be so radically different had it been Lucifer and not Satan who maintained overall responsibility for the world? If Prince Caligastia had been operating on Earth all this time with the knowledge and sanction of Satan, that would not be much to Satan's credit.

I'd had the one brief meeting with Lucifer when he'd made his case for cosmic alchemy, which is all I recalled at the time. It seemed to me of some significance that it was here on Zandana, and not on Earth, that I'd been personally addressed by Lucifer. And yet, for all my time on Earth, I'd seen Satan so rarely and had yet to be called to his presence.

It was not an encounter for which I yearned.

* * *

The Sex issue of the magazine was finally put to bed on time.

Andrew and my ward spent hours every day at the printers, overseeing and learning the intricate processes of photolithography.

I enjoyed watching this too—the professionalism of it. All down the line, everyone was looking for perfection, from the absolute precision demanded of the photographer shooting four acetate layers, to the swift and sure movements of technicians patiently removing the blemishes from the negatives, to the meticulous registration required to burn the four plates accurately. It was fun to then watch the massive, clanking machine, as large as a locomotive, with its many different-size rollers whirling and laying down each color one after another, and the printed sheets popping out at the other end, each sheet large enough for eight individual magazine pages.

Printer-technicians clambered lovingly around the huge shuddering contraption, stretching down to give this pot some ink or that one a stir to prevent the liquid from pooling in its tray. I admired the foreman, moving fluidly from one roller to another, checking each color as it was laid down and confidently calling for minute modifications of chromatic value. Then, as if punctuating the end of the affair, came a little puff of air and talcum powder—as the final, cut sheets floated out the other end of the machine, each powdered sheet dropping smoothly on top of the previous one.

It excited me to see this, and I found I shared my ward's and the team's enthusiasm when the printed and bound copies were finally in their hands. I could see it was a time of intense excitement for them as they hadn't had the privilege of seeing the multicolored illustrations before. They had originally worked on acetate sheets, blocking out the shapes representing each color on the respective four sheets with Rubylith masking film. So they never knew how a page was going to come out until it was in their hands, making the entire process largely an act of faith.

This time, just as the Sex issue was finally in their hands, down came the Omega's instruction for Mein Host to prepare to leave for America. This edict was as surprising as his sudden orders to go to Paris had been a month earlier; however, he greeted this plan with far more enthusiasm. Like any adventurous young Englishman of the time, he'd always had his eyes on America. Many of his closest friends were expatriate Americans, and his favorite musicians and artists and writers were almost always in the United States.

America represented everything that England did not. Obviously he couldn't wait to leave.

There was, however, the matter of Diana, Mein Host's long-suffering mother.

Diana had treasured the few Thursday afternoons she and her son had managed to spend together, with Little Daniel in tow. She had evidently taken heart at her son's return from Xtul—after his threat never to come back to England—and received the news of his upcoming journey to America with what I took to be renewed stoicism. She was a courageous woman, well practiced in covering up her feelings and equally intent on supporting her son's choices (whatever she might have thought of them). So she bid him off with an open hand. Neither mother nor son could have anticipated the conditions under which they would next meet any more than they could have guessed the disturbing reasons as to why various Processeans were being moved around like pieces on a chessboard.

Unlike my ward's previous major trip, which had taken him to Nassau and then on to Mexico, and for which he'd sold his last possessions of any value to purchase a ticket, this time he had no possessions, and a ticket was provided for him out of Process funds.

A month later, with an American visa stamped into his passport and his small suitcase packed with black clothes, he was winging his way to join Chris and the others in Chicago. They'd already found a place to live and now only needed to find somewhere in the city where the action was to start a coffeehouse and begin to take meetings. Given that this new chapter in Chicago was to be located in the city itself, it would appear that Mary Ann had taken heed of the recommendations that my ward and Andrew had made regarding the Parisian problem. This made Mein Host appreciate the Oracle all the more.

The residence of the Chicago Chapter turned out to be a small, two-story house on the South Side of the city, within a block of Lake Michigan. Walking down to the lake in the bitter cold on the morning after he arrived, Mein Host had a chance to witness the first of many curious sights America would present to him over the course of the next forty years.

The lake had frozen over to such an extreme extent that as it lapped the shoreline the water had frozen so as to form a series of perfect waves. Frozen waves. England might have been cold and damp, but these improbable ice waves in Chicago were demonstrating a cold of quite a different order. Mein Host perched himself on a tree stump overlooking the frozen waves. His gaze met the endless white expanse of lake stretching to the horizon, a barely etched line against the gray smudge of sky. Considering the closeness to the water, the area was surprisingly impoverished; some of the houses in the street behind him were boarded up and deserted.

I could only imagine what he must have been thinking. He'd finally made it to America (albeit under somewhat curious circumstances). He'd given up everything: his career, his books, his Martin guitar, his other possessions, any personal money, and now his country, his mother, and his friends back in England—all to follow a dream of a more perfect way of living.

He'd shown no interest in the group's developing theology and yet loved the excitement of being part of a community, every member of which was pursuing the same goals. He'd never been happier than when the art department was going full bore, or when he was having a good day selling magazines on the street. He firmly believed Mary Ann was the incarnate

Goddess and that the Process was an authentic Mystery School. He was equally sure he was giving his life in service to a higher cause and obviously enjoyed the freedom such a monastic life allowed him.

Now, here he was in America, perched on the edge of a whole new phase of his life.

* * *

As I look back over that time—when I was flitting back and forth between Earth and Zandana and trying to sort out my feelings and reactions—I can see more clearly how the comparison I was trying to make between the two worlds was only confusing me. How could they be so different?

And if Lucifer's claim that Earth was part of an alchemical experiment was authentic, didn't this suppose a high degree of intentionality behind Caligastia's stirring up his planetary Nigredo? Or was I once again falling under Lucifer's spell? Was I believing the Great Lie all over again?

And so it went . . . back and forth . . . forth and back . . . so much so that I felt I was going through my own Nigredo! What I was coming to know about Zandana was only making me feel more discomforted by what was happening on Earth.

I had to let go.

The tension was more than I could stand.

We Watchers are observers first and are simply not equipped to handle so many conflicting ideologies.

I knew then I would have to examine the dynamics of the visitors' tragic actions back on Earth. I couldn't avoid it. The fact that I've been promising to narrate the events but have managed to avoid doing it for so many pages is an apt comment on my resistance to facing the issue. And yet, as I write, I feel I will soon be able to relate the incident and its consequences with more confidence than I could muster at the time.

11

Arriving in America

The Spiritual Challenges that Mortals Face, the Fate of the Visitors, and the Differences between Mortals and Angels

It had been an overcast winter's day in 1969 when Mein Host first arrived in America. He'd described his previous trip a few weeks earlier to a cold, wet Paris as "spectacularly unpleasant," yet I could see that estimation must have paled in the face of the bleak, windy cityscape of downtown Chicago. He was later to joke ruefully about the moment he was turning a corner on Michigan Avenue and was blown off his feet by a ferocious gust of wind. His armful of magazines went flying across the busy street, and his long, black cloak ballooned him off the ground, depositing him inelegantly onto the icy sidewalk before he slid on his bottom to a final thudding halt against a road sign.

His instructions were to join his friend Chris and the three other Processeans who'd been sent to America previously to start the Chicago Chapter. They'd already rented a house on the city's South Side for the community to live in (and commute *from*), but at the time of Mein Host's arrival they hadn't located an appropriate place in the city for a coffeehouse and assembly rooms. So the search was on for the ideal location somewhere in the most exciting part of Chicago: a place where they could create a London-style Cavern as well as a large, comfortable space to hold their regular meetings, with some additional, smaller rooms for offices and the empath sessions they were now offering.

As with much of what the Process had taken on in its heyday, the plans for such a large place in the midst of prime Chicago real estate were somewhat ambitious, and made even more unrealistic by their complete lack of funds. The Process back in London may have paid my ward's ticket to America, but that is where the generosity ceased.

The Chicago Chapter was on its own.

There were no free lunches! Each chapter was expected to make its own money with, as we know, a substantial percentage going "up the line," directly to Mary Ann and Robert's "Central Fund." The remaining funds were to be used to pay rent and other expenses. This practice of passing money up the line wasn't generally known by the rank and file members of the group and only became contentious later when it appeared the Omega was taking advantage of the financial arrangement.

These were the early days, however, and the four IPs in the Chicago Chapter were fired up with righteous enthusiasm. Convinced of the rightness of their cause, these members of the Chicago Chapter resolutely set out to sell their books and magazines on the crowded downtown streets of the Windy City.

Here came the first surprise. Compared to the cynical English and the uncomprehending French, the Americans were an utter delight. They were simple to stop and appeared fascinated by the magazine, which they invariably could be induced to purchase by the silver-tongued Englishmen. I could see my ward was almost disbelieving the ease with which magazines left his hands. The first few days on the street were evidently a revelation. It had been an eye-opener for the others too when they'd first arrived, but curiously they'd said nothing about it to Mein Host. He was amazed to find himself selling three or four times as many magazines as he had in London. I watched him take the art of selling to a whole new level. He'd been accustomed to people back in London reluctantly buying a magazine more to get away from him than from any particular interest in the periodical. He had no illusions about that. Yet here in America the people seemed genuinely interested. Their faces lit up with enthusiasm, and as often as not they would start reading their magazine as they walked happily away.

This was fertile turf indeed. Processeans had the streets to themselves, interrupted only by the infrequent passage of half a dozen Hari

Krishna devotees, chanting and dancing their way down the icy sidewalk. The citizens hadn't yet been pestered by Moonies or panhandled by the Children of God. They hadn't been cajoled into buying *Avatar,* the newspaper produced by followers of the self-proclaimed deity Mel Lyman. No Scientologists had yet lured them in for a session, and the idea of systematically setting out to sell magazines directly to people on the streets of the cities hadn't yet occurred to other potential rivals.

This was virgin territory, and the money rolled in.

But it was still, clearly, ruinously hard work. As in Paris, they had to commute in and out of the city every day, returning exhausted and freezing to their small house on the South Side. And lest you, my devoted reader, find yourself likening the South Shore region to Chicago's Lakeshore Drive, with its tree-lined boulevards, elegantly designed high-rises, and a sandy beach stretching its length, allow me to quickly disabuse you.

The house the IPs had managed to rent before Mein Host arrived, in spite of being within a stone's throw of the lake, was as dilapidated as the area around it. Not quite a slum, it was an area in which the workers in the old meat-processing plants must have lived, and regarded themselves as fortunate in so doing. But as the years passed and the meatpackers moved on, other immigrants came and went, and in the way of all transients, they invested little care in the places they lived. More recently, a new influx of middle-class African American families were recolonizing the few surrounding blocks, and the place was just starting to straighten itself up.

However, this did not apply to their house, a small two-floor, wood-frame shack, clad in paint-chipped aluminum siding and set in a patch of dirt that only a realtor would call a garden. It had obviously never been a well-built house in the first place, and age, and presumably its many previous occupants, had not been kind to it. An arctic wind blowing off the frozen lake whistled and roared through the structure while the four Processeans piled on sweater after sweater under their black uniforms. The rooms of the house were tiny and poorly lit, with mean little windows, their metal frames rusted and the wind hissing through cracks in the plaster.

"They're small all right," I heard my ward saying to Chris the morning after he arrived, "but at least each of us gets a room to ourselves!"

When I heard him say that I realized that having to share a room with three or four others, as he'd had to do back in Balfour Place, must have been more trying than he'd let on at the time. Having spent his life from the age of seven to sixteen and a half at English boarding schools, he was no stranger to sharing space. Yet his early childhood—with no father, no siblings, and a frequently absent mother—had allowed him the opportunity to appreciate his own company. His early love of reading stemmed originally from those endless, early times in London, when, on holiday from school, alone and parked out for an afternoon by himself in a garden that was more of a bomb crater than garden, books became his closest friends.

This was not a unique story by any means; many writers have similar backgrounds. Yet what is somewhat unusual is that it took Mein Host so long to discover his love of writing.

It was when I heard him talking about a room of his own that I found myself relieved to know he hadn't altogether forgotten the pleasure of being alone. And here I have to briefly break my own rule of avoiding retrospective pondering, merely to point out how easily my ward could have been swept away at this stage by his devotional nature. From my observation at the time of his emotional and spiritual bodies, I could see he remained devoutly loyal to Mary Ann. He didn't doubt that she was his incarnate Goddess, and that seemed enough for him to commit himself unreservedly to serving her with no thought of his own personal future.

As with so many young people who grew up under the threat of nuclear annihilation, I never heard him give any real credence to the future. His fascination with architecture, for example, was always more involved with the problem-solving aspect of the design process than with any ambition he might have shown for actually making a career as an architect. Even the dreams of the utopian community were more concerned with life in the moment. Convinced of the inevitability of global war, the Process teachings gave little serious thought to a future they didn't believe would really exist.

Regardless of this dire prognosis, it was with all the enthusiasm in the world and focused only on the immediate demands of money and the search for a downtown locale in which to establish the chapter that Mein Host threw himself into his new life in America with no idea that in five years he'd be dead.

So much for the future.

* * *

Arriving back on Earth from my recent trip to Zandana, I found myself being pulled in two directions at once, neither of which I found particularly appealing. I've been finding this business of having to choose between two difficult options occurring more frequently, and, although I was still unaware of this at the time, it must have been part of my long preparation for mortal incarnation. As I've previously mentioned, normally we angels simply find ourselves in the right place at the right time—there's very little personal volition involved. Our function draws us to where we are needed.

However, as a Watcher—a rebel angel who remained on my planet subsequent to the revolution—I've found that I'm not subject to quite the same functional strictures as many of my sisters, and I'm allowed a somewhat wider field of choices. I still had no option but to observe; my *function* hadn't changed. But now I had far more choice in *what* to observe.

And I admit it, I'd made some poor choices.

I'd chosen to act like a coward, for example, by slinking off to Zandana when Caligastia's brutal indifference to humanity's well-being became too painful to observe. But at least it had been *my* choice. I learned something about myself—even if it didn't make me proud to know I was capable of behaving in such a shameful manner. And yet the discovery that I could act in this way also excited me. Not the cowardly act itself—no beings likes to think of themselves as a weaklings. No, it wasn't that. It was that I could have experienced a sensation such as cowardice. I'd never felt quite such a personal emotion before, and certainly not one that had been generated by me. I knew what cowardice was, of course—I'd both seen it in action and picked it up empathically in a very mild fashion from humans I was observing. I'd never really understood why men and women acted in such fearful ways, or why some would be so ready to betray their principles when their physical security was threatened.

This is a profound difference between our two species and an issue we are constantly warned about in our training sessions back on Jerusem. I've been writing here more about the differences between angels and mortals, and of course there are profound differences. Yet I fancy you would be quite surprised at our similarities. Were I to wear a human body, I could walk down any street on Earth with no one being any the wiser. The Multiverse is, after all, one vast family. We are all sons or daughters of the Divine. And I'm sure you must have noticed by now how similar the range of my interests are to a mortal who might find herself or himself in my position.

But it's the differences that we study in the Jerusem; our similarities can take care of themselves. And if it is my destiny to enter the mortal ascension program as a human being, even though all that I know will be forgotten at birth, I'm sure I'll be thankful to have some instinctive understanding of human nature.

"You will never fully understand a mortal's fear of death," we'd been informed by our instructors. "You will observe it again and again, and you will invariably be puzzled by it. You will see feats of unaccountable courage by some in the face of death; others you will observe denying the fact of it, even unto the moment of mortal death itself; while still more will give themselves over to their terror."

"Surely," we students would argue, "this will not be so hard to understand. Death cannot hold that much terror if mortals believe they're eternal souls . . ."

"Perhaps some do!" the instructor would wearily interrupt at this point. They'd all heard this sort of comment a thousand times before. "But you will find for mortals that the act of believing is profoundly different from knowing. For them, believing is an act of will; knowing is the result of experience."

Now that really confused us novices. What could she have meant by that?

"To confuse you further," she was evidently practiced at this, "you will find many humans who believe they know the truth of eternal life and who will kill their fellows in the name of their belief." She paused at this, looking around at our horrified responses.

"But you will never find a human being who really knows the truth of their own eternal beingness, who would then go out and willingly harm another being who thought differently."

Well, of course they wouldn't! I recall thinking at the time, with the simple innocence of one not yet aware of the revolution seething in

Lucifer's mind. Why would any mortal who knows the truth of their eternal soul ever wish to kill or harm another person?

"Let me put this as simply as possible," she'd continued, "because this quandary will present itself many times as you go about your tasks among mortals."

I could just imagine the lecture coming. I was starting to get mildly irritated with all this talk of mortals.

She must have heard the boredom in my thought, because I got a pointed look from her before she went on with her transmission. I wasn't the most attentive of students.

"Mortals have many beliefs, some of which resonate more closely with the truth than others; yet the truth itself transcends all belief. The truth simply is. You know this; you wonder how could it be otherwise?"

She let that hang in our minds, allowing us to assimilate what is an essential difference between mortals and angels. Angels have no need for belief: we either know a truth, or we don't. We have faith, of course, but that is quite different from belief. Faith emerges with a developing spiritual intelligence, while belief can be thought of as an epiphenomenon of the emotional/mental intelligence. Humans have to believe in something. Even an atheist has to believe in his or her lack of belief.

"This will be self-evident to you," her dry, papery voice continued in our minds, "as you are created to be aware of your eternal life. But you will find that for mortals who have no direct experience of their immortality, this is one of the spiritual challenges they wrestle with as they grow in spirit. It's inevitable. There is nothing you can, or should, do about it. You are there to observe only. It will be the business of the individual mortal's companion angels to know what action is appropriate."

There'd been a small ripple of resistance in the telepathic web from some of the more senior observer angels. These were the ones who'd returned for a refresher course after serving on their different worlds and seemed to many of us to be exuding a smug sense of their own superiority. I admit I enjoyed seeing the telepathic ripple spun back at those self-satisfied seniors with such practiced and consummate skill. I'll warrant the tendril she hit them with slapped them wide awake. It sent a shudder through the rest of us, I can tell you. And we didn't hear any more of their arrogant whispers for the rest of the course!

"To return to the quandary I mentioned earlier," our instructor continued after she'd withdrawn the tendril—and I could feel the seniors somewhere behind me, their minds slowly relaxing back into her words—"you will be sure to face this quandary in your dealings with mortals, so hear me well."

She had our full attention now. No one wanted to feel her lash.

"You will never be able to predict why one mortal will choose to be courageous when threatened, while others in a similar situation will give in to their animal fears. So, simply accept this. It is part of the mystery of the mortal nature. It is also why you should avoid placing any expectations on how a human being will act when they're fearful. Even if you are sure you can anticipate their response from their previous actions, we advise against any such predictive indulgence. You will be almost certain to be wrong."

The thrust of her lecture seemed to be that we angels could never experience an extreme emotion like terror or cowardice. But, of course, that was long before the revolution broke out, and the instructors clearly never anticipated such an event occurring on their watch.

So I can say with some certainty that it was as a result of Lucifer's revolution that I was experiencing the effects of the sort of extreme fear-for-self that I'm told only a mortal can feel. I thought then (foolishly, as I realize now) when I recalled her lecture, that if this is the sort of ambient fear that humans live under on a daily basis, I never want to be mortal. This type of fear was a horrible sensation, which I found extremely emotionally painful; it depleted my spirit and confused my mind. Yet underneath all that self-concern was an unexpected feeling of exhilaration rising up from within me.

I was free to choose! To *choose*!

Even my bad choices would be mine to make.

I was now faced with having to make a decision as to which scenario unfolding on Earth I should follow most closely: there was Vanu's Lemuria, warned by the Pleiadeans that it would soon disappear in the worst natural disaster the world had seen for many thousands of years, or there was Prince Caligastia in the Middle East, whom I'd last observed concocting his mean-spirited campaign to corrupt the two visitors.

Some choices! Is this what it's like to be mortal? Constant, impossible choices?

But—no more cowardice! If I have to make a choice, I decided I would choose the most challenging of my options.

There was no evading the fact that Prince Caligastia was still my immediate superior, although he had no real power over me at that stage. Well, he'd never actually had power over me because I serve at my System Sovereign's behest, but because Caligastia had followed Lucifer into the revolution, this left me in an uncomfortable position. As you may have gathered, I was never a particularly enthusiastic admirer of Caligastia, even before the revolution. And if you've been following my narrative you'll know of my increasing disenchantment with him and the unfortunate level of chaos and suffering he and his midwayers were bringing to this world.

My interview with Lucifer, whom I'd encountered recently on Zandana, had mitigated my concerns somewhat by his assurances that all was well. He told me that I was observing an experiment of cosmic alchemy: it was Caligastia's function to prepare the initial stage of the alchemical process. He told me that one such as myself couldn't be expected to understand the intricacies of the Great Work—and that I was simply there to observe and report.

But it still pained me to watch the Prince's callous indifference to human beings as he cooked up his brew of putrefaction and despair. I'd been able to avoid him recently by sneaking off to Zandana, but having aligned myself with Lucifer's cause, and having originally been willing to serve Caligastia in his revolutionary plans, I knew I owed it to myself to see what noxious brew the Prince had been fermenting for the visitors while I'd been away.

And so it was: the Prince was my choice.

On arriving back at the visitors' peninsula, I was, quite frankly, horrified by what I was seeing. There was no sign of the visitors, and their elegant dwellings now appeared to house the clan leaders of just those northern Nodite tribes about whom Vanu had tried so hard to warn them. To say "it only felt like yesterday" that I'd been observing the august encounter would be a cliché, if it wasn't for the fact that to an angel, when a memory is evoked, all past events can feel as if they happened only yesterday!

What I observed was a farce. The Nodite leaders were trying to emulate the visitors on the one hand, while on the other they were trashing their garden and dwellings and fighting among one another for dominance.

The beautiful garden courtyard had been ruined completely, and the trees were now just burned stumps sticking up above layers of discarded rubbish. Leather tents had been thrown up in the once-clean white minimalist inner chambers of the houses; the tents were now crammed with grubby children. The elegant ancillary buildings Vanu had built for the vast gathering of followers he'd anticipated coming and living alongside the visitors—all of these had burned down. The tilled fields and animal compounds were long gone, and the irrigation channels and ditches that threaded through the meadows and orchards had dried out, their banks collapsed and overgrown with weeds.

I had no idea what was happening. From what I'd seen of the visitors I wasn't holding out much hope they would have been able to resist Caligastia's corrupting influence, but it was hard to believe matters had fallen this far out of control quite so fast.

I was less than half-a-mile from where the visitors had held their gatherings. The nearby temple had been reduced to a pile of rubble. The sacred tree was picked clean of its fruit and leaves and was clearly dying—if it wasn't already dead.

It was then that I perceived her, and it must have been my appalled disbelief and the intensity of my need to know what happened that drew her to me. It was Astar, a Watcher I'd come to know and with whom I had a casual arrangement to fill each other in on what we'd observed. She was standing to my left and a little behind me, yet I hadn't noticed her until she spoke quietly in my mind.

"They left three years ago," I heard.

"The visitors?"

"With whomever was left after the troubles."

Well, I knew there must have been troubles. I could see the results of the troubles all around me.

I heard her again. "They headed eastward in one long caravan, but everything was falling apart before they left. I've become used to it now."

But how, I thought, how could this have happened? This was MA's second intervention, intended to maintain its presence on Earth for the unforeseeable future. And it appeared they'd already folded their tents and left the garden. Vanu and Amadon would have been heartbroken to see what had become of all the preparatory work they'd done to welcome the visitors. Well, I certainly wasn't going to enlighten them, and I hoped they'd been taken off the planet before they had a chance to witness the devastation.

"I don't know if they ever arrived where they were going," she was saying, and I could hear the puzzlement in her tone.

But so fast?

"Perhaps you should know what occurred if you are to understand the nuances of the Prince's maneuvering."

Hearing these words, I knew I needed to be careful with this Watcher, so I quickly veiled my growing disenchantment with Caligastia, behind an enthusiastic agreement to hear what had occurred.

We retired to a grove of sacred trees that grew tall and straight in the center of a meadow that was within a frequency domain in our fifth-dimensional reality. We were comfortable lounging in the long grass. The sweet scent of crushed stems filled our senses, and we felt all the pleasure and relief of being able to enjoy the thoroughly bearable lightness of being we were both experiencing back in a higher vibrational frequency domain.

Sitting with our backs against a couple of standing stones, we conjured up two long-stemmed flutes and a jug of potent apple cider, and I listened to the story my Watcher colleague unfolded for me.

* * *

Mein Host had been in Chicago no more than a couple of weeks before he and the other IPs in the chapter found a building on Wells Street that fulfilled most of their requirements. More importantly, Wells Street was turning out to be the Kings Road of the Windy City. It was ideally placed to pick up the sort of street trade that even the London Chapter, stuck away as it was on a Mayfair side street, would have been unlikely to draw in.

This was still a year and a half before the Rolling Stones' free concert at Altamonte in December of 1969, and the young of America were on the move. Wells Street, like Greenwich Village in New York, or Haight-Ashbury in San Francisco, had turned into one of those hubs that became the focus of the growing number of young women and men streaming up from the suburbs. They were disenchanted with their lives; TV and travel had opened their eyes to the wider world; and many of them resented their parents' attempts to control them. They were inherently suspicious of all authority—the admonition to distrust anyone over thirty originated in that era—and they were intensely distrustful of a government that was sending them to war for reasons that made no sense.

Many of the young, like Mein Host, had rejected the religions of their birth and were searching for spiritual paths they could relate to with their whole beings. Again, like Mein Host, some of the more adventurous among them were exploring entheogens, while at the same time there was a great deal of irresponsible use of mind-altering drugs.

This isn't the place to discuss the use or misuse of drugs, except to point out that the generation of people coming of age in the 1960s were the first to use mind-altering substances so widely and in such large numbers. There were many immediate reasons for this—from the increasing availability of the substances to the freedom to travel to countries in which such substances were used without restrictions—but it will be no surprise to my reader to know this generation also contained the second major wave of fallen rebel angels entering human incarnation in the twentieth century.

Whereas previously the rebel angels had been incarnating in small groups, or as a rare individual amid purely human cultures, the social transformation occurring in the West over the latter part of the twentieth century provided considerably more fertile turf in which to integrate themselves.

Perhaps I should elaborate on this a little more, because it's been one of the best-kept secrets since it first started occurring and has been hidden, in most cases, from the incarnate angels themselves. There was good reason for this, or so I've been told, for both the incarnate angels and for the mortals who live alongside them. While incarnate angels might have flashes of their previous lives, the real value of their mortal lifetime is just that: their humanness.

Incarnate angels invariably feel different from mortals, often to an extreme extent in childhood, and they have no way of explaining this to themselves. The truth of their angelic heritage would be meaningless unless they had a context within which to place themselves. The handful of people throughout history who appear to have stumbled on their angelic background (as did, for example, a few of the English eighteenth-century romantic poets), found this knowledge of little value to them. As happened to the Cathars before them, they will have discovered that any such knowledge that included reincarnation would have set them in direct opposition to the prevailing religious beliefs of the time. And humans, religiously driven or not, have invariably treated those too unlike themselves with suspicion and disdain, or with undue adulation—which are very human reactions that have most often ended in tragedy.

However, times have changed so dramatically over the past half-century: conditions on Earth have made it simpler for an angel to come into mortal incarnation. Because of this, waves of rebel angels have been choosing lifetimes among virtually all cultures across the face of the planet. Many have chosen lives foreshortened by famine, war, or disease in order to pay their dues by briefly taking the brunt of human violence before dying and being accepted as an ascending mortal. Others have thrown themselves into attempting to resolve the problems of the world, unknowingly trying to dig their way out of the chaos and confusion that resulted from the decision to follow Lucifer at the time of the revolution. Still others will find themselves placed where a rebellious consciousness is required in the world of humanity, as has recently manifested in the spring of 2011 among many of the young Arabs in the repressive countries of the Middle East.

This is not to belittle the courage of human beings who are facing up to the weapons of their despotic rulers, but merely to say that some of the leading spirits behind any revolution will be incarnate rebel angels. Additionally, the impulse to rebel against an unjust authority will frequently be generated initially by an individual incarnate rebel angel, or a small group of them, all of whom are likely to be completely unaware of the ancient pattern they are acting out.

I've overheard a Melchizedek Brother in an offhand moment, riffing, I assumed, on the famous Tibetan yogi and poet Milarepa, referring to this strategy as "getting the demons to *destroy* the monastery for you." The Melchizedek aren't known for their humor, and as a joke it wasn't a particularly good one, yet as simple a statement as it may appear to be on the surface, it conceals a deeper truth that is far less evident.

You see, as mortals you have the chance to undergo a review of your human lifetime after you have shed your material body. You have the opportunity to examine your life with the help of your spiritual counselors and to understand the nature of the decisions you've made over the course of your lifetime. You may be surprised to discover that what you considered so important when you were alive fades into irrelevance when viewed within the larger context of your Multiverse career.

It may be unnecessary to emphasize that this life-review process is a privilege extended to mortals of all the various inhabited worlds. It is not, for example, anything that I as a Watcher have yet undergone, because I have not yet embodied myself as a mortal. And I believe this will apply to all Watchers who await mortal incarnation.

It is also true that in all but the rarest cases a sincere appraisal of a mortal lifetime, when reexamined and placed within a spiritual context, permits the mortal in question an opportunity to become aware of the deeper implications of their actions during their lifetime. They can observe with dispassion both their good and bad actions and understand and then forgive themselves (and others) for their ignorance. This should not be confused with the punitive "Judgment Day," which priests of a variety of belief systems have used to terrify their flocks. It is instead a profound life review conducted by your angels, who have great kindness and an authentic desire to see you grow in spirit and move on to higher worlds.

I believe this digression has been necessary, because this particular aspect of the mortal after-death experience has been so misunderstood, and thus has been open to the manipulation of those using their threats of hell and their equally fallacious promises of heaven as a primitive control mechanism. Although this unfortunate distortion has been rejected, together with other long-held religious dogma, and dismissed by most sensibly minded people, it has not yet been replaced by a more authentic and accurate account of the first overtly spiritual encounter all humans face after they have shed their mortal bodies.

If it seems odd that a mortal, whether or not an incarnate angel, should receive such compassionate and respectful treatment during her or his life review, remember that every mortal of sound mind is indwelt by the Creator in a way that no celestial is. This has remained one of those divine mysteries that none of us angels claim to understand. Just how an aspect of the Creator of All resides in the heart of the lowest of evolutionary creatures capable of sentient intelligence is something we just have to take on faith.

When you have completed your life review and you are continuing on your Multiverse career, you will retain everything of spiritual value that you've learned from your mortal lifetime, and you will be accompanied by your Indwelling Spirit.

Bringing this digression back to my original contention that rebel angels have been incarnating in waves over the past half-century, it shouldn't be thought a coincidence that this has been happening while the biosphere is rapidly deteriorating and as the global population has been increasing. The timing of this blossoming of the more wide-ranging implications of the angelic conspiracy provides insight, I believe, into a deeper intentionality at work.

So little is known about the three previous revolutions in this Local Universe that I'm not able to discern whether there is a pattern to the timing of these waves of incarnated rebel angels, or even whether MA would have employed the same strategy in response to the previous uprisings. I have already suggested that the veto placed on the archived reports, with all the details of those other rebellions, must have been withheld from us for a good reason.

However, it's not for me to second-guess MA's responses to the previous uprisings but only to suggest that one rebellion, or even two, might be considered anomalous. But four rebellions? Against the same administrative system? Surely this points to some deeper and less obvious theme, which brings into question the true source of this intentionality.

Of course, there is MA's basic stance: rebellions become a risk whenever angels relate closely with mortals—although I've noticed they never tell us why this is. Then there is the question I've previously raised: if MA is as benign and well organized as her celestial administrators maintain, might rebellions be the way change, or novelty, is introduced into a stable, balanced system? Revolutions can be unpleasant for those caught up in them, and yet they serve a valuable purpose overall. While this doesn't signal any real level of intentionality on behalf of MA's senior administrators, it couldn't have been that much of a surprise when Lucifer fomented his revolution, given that it had happened three times before.

If angelic revolutions are considered radical agents of change, then it would make tactical sense to allow rebellions to play themselves out for as long as possible. In that way, everything of value can continue to be plucked from the debris. It turns out that like most mortals, some celestials learn more thoroughly by understanding our errors and making amends than from performing our functions faultlessly. The Melchizedek Brothers are known to have claimed that the positive consequences of the Lucifer Rebellion already outweigh the negative.

And then there is the far more radical possibility: that fusing angelic and human consciousness has always been the plan on the highest levels of Local Universe administration, and angelic revolutions are merely one of the primary mechanism by which this can be accomplished.

I trust by the time I've completed this narrative I will know the answer to all of this. And if I'm wrong and perceived as besmirching MA's integrity, then I shall simply hold Mein Host responsible for putting such revolutionary ideas into my simple head.

So it was that my ward was unknowingly meeting a number of incarnate angels among the hundreds of people he was confronting daily on the streets of Chicago. He'd encountered such beings before, back in London, and he'd always felt a natural kinship with them. And although he'd never have known the reason at the time, a number of his friends and his occasional mentors had been incarnate rebel angels—as unaware of their angelic heritage as Mein Host was of his own.

The hours that he and his fellow IPs spent on the streets were long. When they weren't selling magazines, they were in their new chapter house on Wells Street renovating its two floors. To enter the place they had to climb an unstable timber staircase that ran up the outside of the building to the front door, which was above the shop below. Inside, the place was not in a good state, with nicotine-bruised walls and a worn red carpet, badly stained and frayed around the exits. Half a dozen theatrical lighting cans clung from the ceiling like sleeping bats and were arranged to focus on a small stage at one end of the room. A kitchen, its sinks and cookers encrusted with brown grease, were tucked into the dark end of the space. It had most recently been one of those jazz clubs that flourished briefly on Wells Street, before the proprietors had put too much cocaine up their noses and their accountants were last seen gambling at a casino in Monaco.

It was a battered old place that would eventually burn down some years later, but the four of them worked wonders—by dint of hard work and with the help of numerous volunteers—to create a tolerable coffee-house. Replicating the one in London, it was another Process Cavern, which they hoped would draw in like-minded people who'd be interested in what the Process had to offer.

They spruced up and repainted another large room on the next floor up, this one accessed by an inside staircase, and turned it into a space for their meetings and meditations. They used the smaller rooms at the back for offices and a place to conduct their empath sessions.

Within a few weeks, the Wells Street Chapter was open to the public and, much to the surprise of Mein Host and the others, it was an immediate, if modest, success. I say they were surprised because the London Chapter had taken a slog to get going, and Paris, of course, was a nonstarter.

They were simply not used to the immediacy of success, or to the intensity of the interest they'd aroused. But this was America, after all, the land of the free—as I'd hear them reminding each other after a busy evening in the Cavern. However, as surprised as Mein Host may have been at the success of the Wells Street Chapter, a far more serious and long-lasting surprise was waiting for him in the wings.

12

The Watcher's Tale

Conspiracy in a Garden, the Dynamics of Envy, a Bun in the Oven, and a Dream of the Plumed Serpent

The sun warmed the Watcher and me as we sat together on the grassy knoll, content to be temporarily free of the stresses of third-density reality. "How long has it been since we've seen each other?" the Watcher was asking me as we sat with our backs against the sun-warmed dolmen.

"Oh," I replied cautiously, "no more than 120, or maybe 150 years . . . hard to pin down, you know how it is."

"Eternity can be a bitch," she said (or some telepathic equivalent of that). I joined her in laughing at our common complaint. It's not unknown for one of us Watchers to become lost in time for a while.

As we shared the same frequency domain we were surrounded by the beauty of the parkland that was flourishing in our dimension. But I knew that for all the easy familiarity of our surroundings, I was that much more liable to relax my guard. I didn't want this Watcher, who in my opinion had already shown her hand, reporting my doubts to the Prince behind my back. Besides, I wasn't sure I wanted the Watcher to know about my encounter with Lucifer, not that I recalled anything much of value to report. Were I to blurt it out, it would only be an attempt to impress her. And from what I knew of Astar, she wasn't easily impressed.

"I'm sure you observed the Prince in meetings with the visitors," she was saying. "It was before you left for Zandana." She evidently knew about my trip! Did she also know about my cowardice? I needed to mask off that from her probing intelligence! However, I needn't have been concerned, because I was soon the recipient of a torrent of images and words. Telepathic communication is so hard to reproduce in linear form that you'll have to forgive me if I haven't caught every nuance.

"It started soon after you left," she began. "The Prince obviously must have convinced himself that he couldn't get through to the visitors, not even after all those endless meetings he'd had with them."

I grinned to myself at the memory. Poor old Caligastia—he'd acted so sincere and persuasive with his talk about the desperate need to accelerate progress on the planet . . .

"How far behind schedule we'd drifted," she'd picked up my thought again. "Remember? MA had no idea what it was like to actually be down here on the face of the planet. Caligastia used to tell them that MA had just shoved the two visitors down here among all these fearful and primitive savages willy-nilly, dropped into a totally untenable situation, remember?"

"He just couldn't persuade the visitors and he couldn't charm them either, that's what I observed," I told her, recalling it well. "I reckoned I probably knew the Prince a whole lot better than the visitors did. I was pretty sure he'd find another way of getting to them."

She let that hang in the air before asking me: "Did you ever have the chance to observe what was happening in the Nodite kingdoms to the north?"

It wasn't a question; she could read me easily enough now. I hadn't known the details of the Nodites, because the prospect of watching Caligastia ruining yet more lives—of humans who had trusted him—was what had prompted me to take my leave for Zandana.

The Watcher was hurrying on. "Really, you should have seen it. It was like watching a master at work. The Prince made it look so simple. It was a lesson for us all."

"And it *wasn't* so simple?" I wondered. Nothing is simple on this world. I knew that.

"Easy, perhaps, but not so simple," she replied with a knowing snort. "You were aware that the Prince had been working through the northern Nodite priests, right?"

"It was at that point I had to leave . . ." I tried to make it sound more like a business trip, but of course she wasn't fooled for a moment. I could hear slight scorn in her tone when she continued.

"About that time, this is what you'd have seen: The Prince instructed a select number of his midwayers to make themselves personally available to members of the Nodite nobility, as well as to various clan leaders and the main trading families. He told them to manifest themselves in some cases as household gods; in others as the gods and goddesses of fertility; and as the gods of war, or fire, or death, or whatever, among the most belligerent clans."

This I hadn't known.

"But you must have noticed how envious the Nodite leadership was of the visitors, yes? Always, ever since they'd first arrived. For a start, they didn't know what the fuss was about, with Vanu and his volunteers sweating for all that time. It was more than seventy years, wasn't it?"

"No wonder! The Nodites always thought they were top of the pile," I said. "It must have really angered them to see all that attention being given to these visitors . . ."

"They never believed Vanu's prediction anyway," she broke in. "They thought the whole business was just another one of Vanu's tricks."

"I can see why they'd be open to Caligastia's tender ministrations."

She ignored my attempt to be clever.

"It was the visitors' immortality that tipped the balance," she told me. "It was the one thing the tribes were always denied . . . the Nodites who knew about it. They hated it. Why were they being prevented from being immortal too? Weren't they just as important? Weren't they the direct descendants of their most revered ancestor, Nodu?"

"And *that* was what the Prince was able to play on?" I was incredulous.

"For the clan leaders, yes, working through his loyal midwayers. He was able to stir up their desire for immortal life to an almost obsessional degree, while simultaneously pressing each one on the need for absolute secrecy. See what he did by this?"

I was starting to get mildly irritated by her patronizing tone. "'Did I understand what he did by this?' No! I wasn't there, was I? That's why you're telling me this, right? However, she was well into her story by now, so if she picked up on my annoyance she didn't show it.

"In one fell swoop he created a situation," she answered her own question. "A situation in which all the important Nodite aristocrats were immediately put on the defensive. They became even more suspicious of each other than they had been before."

"Preparing the groundwork?" I suggested.

"But the Prince's cleverest move was to work through one of his mid-wayers, one of those who can pop in and out of human ken. This mid-wayer made it his mission to appeal to the small circle of grandmothers who advised one of the leading Nodite kings.

"It turned out that the grandmothers had been watching the gradual decline of genetic purity in the royal Nodite bloodlines over the generations. In spite of everything they'd done to arrange appropriate matings, there had been this inevitable deterioration over the centuries.

"Then those beautiful visitors arrived with their plans to bear all those thousands and thousands of children, who would mate with each other to produce an entire race of new humans. If you remember your lectures back on Jerusem, you'll recall this can only happen when there are about a million of the visitors' pure violet-blood offspring. It's only then that they're permitted to mate with the indigenous natives. It's standard operating procedure, right? You do remember that, don't you?"

Yes, I thought impatiently, starting to get irritated again by her tacit assumption of my ignorance. So what if I hadn't immediately recalled that?! Get on with the story!

I think it amused her to taunt me.

"Well, guess what? Guess what happened?"

I sensibly didn't respond.

"When the grandmothers grasped it would take about a thousand years before they'd be able to regenerate their noble bloodlines by inter-breeding with the visitor's bloodline, well, they were seething with anger and jealousy. You should have seen their emotional bodies! They immediately started planning to find some way of getting around MA's rule that the visitors' offspring remain strictly out of reach until their numbers reached that million number."

"The grandmothers must have thought that downright unfair," I said, to show her I was getting her point. "And to have all those beautiful, blond, blue-eyed girls and boys romping around just on the other side of the wall must have been too tempting to resist. So what happened then?"

"There was quite a plot developing." It would have been a whisper had she been speaking. "There were three groups with similarly aligned motives: the nobles who craved the visitors' immortality and were prepared to fight and kill to get the secret; a smaller group led by the Council of Grandmothers, who were equally intent on grabbing some of that violet blood for the Nodite bloodlines before it was too late; and the rank and file of the tribesmen who simply wanted to overrun the garden and kill everyone there because it was in their nature to invade other people. It's what they did."

"A perfect storm," I agreed.

"Here's how the Prince finally outwitted the poor visitors," she was sailing on, ignoring my attempt at a summary.

"Do you recall Serapatatia?" The name came through with a sibilance that tickled my mind. "Was he around when you were last here?"

"Serapatatia? The Nodite leader? Don't think I ever saw him, but as I told you I never had much to do with the Nodites. But wasn't he the one I heard spent so much time in discussion with the visitors? Yes, of course, now I do remember seeing him once fleetingly, leaving the garden . . ." and, as I thought more about it, I *did* remember Serapatatia! It was because he seemed such a rarity. It could have been only in those few moments of watching him walking toward the wall. I could feel his kindness and intelligence. That's what stuck out for me. A genuinely kind and intelligent human living among a far more rough-and-ready crowd.

"It came about he was key to the Prince's plans. But here's how clever it was—poor Serap! I liked him too, but for all his kindness and intelligence, he had no idea he was being manipulated. Imagine that. Right to the end."

"But Serap was one of the good ones. I admired him."

"So did the visitors," Astar laughed, knowing what was to come. "The visitors loved their Serap and he loved them too. It was perfectly wonderful, especially when Serap brought in hundreds of his own clan to work alongside them."

"I missed all that. So then what happened?" I asked.

If you can imagine a Watcher sniggering, then Astar sniggered.

"This is what happened, and I was there for it," she told me with pride. "I was observing that first evening when Serap suggested his grand plan. He'd been having dinner with the visitors. I remember that because I could see he disliked having to eat all those fruits and vegetables. He wanted his meat, but he knew better than to reveal that in front of his hosts. It was hilarious watching him trying to swallow food he hated. One time he tried to palm some particularly unpleasant vegetable mess under his robe when he thought the visitors weren't looking . . ."

Now I was sniggering too. The visitors were telepathic—of course they must have known he disliked the food!

"They never gave it away, though," she flowed on, "and I never saw Serap do it again. Anyway, after dinner the male was called away, leaving Serap alone with the female visitor . . ."

"They didn't . . ." I blurted out.

"No, no, no, not *that*! Although you're right, in a way. There always was an intense attraction there, I could feel that. They were both beautiful creatures. How could they not have been drawn to each other?"

"But it's forbidden, isn't it? She'd never have counseled it."

"Just so," the Watcher agreed. "And I don't think Serap would've wanted to betray the friendship . . . anyway, that's not the point. He was after bigger game."

I must have appeared puzzled.

"Listen, you have to put yourself in the visitors' position. Progress hadn't gone well. The Prince made sure of slowing them down and sabotaging their efforts. He and his midwayers played those Nodites and the surrounding tribes like a fiddle. They just kept gnawing away at the visitors' project . . . and neither of them ever wanted to believe the Prince was behind all the trouble they'd been having."

The pride came back in her tone.

"Both of the visitors were getting more and more frustrated, yet they clearly believed they couldn't express it because so much was expected of them. And year by year it only got worse, more difficult to hold together, more defectors, and more skirmishes with hostile tribes who'd busted down part of the wall. Remember the wall?"

"Yes, of course I remember the wall! Now it's just overgrown ruins, most of it. Hard to believe!" I saw the wall in my mind again, just after Vanu's workers had completed it. How proud they had been of it—how proud because they'd finally be able to keep the wild animals out of the garden. And look at it now! It really was such a lovely wall."

My Watcher paused, surprised, I think, at my drift into nostalgia. And it's true, I *had* been excited by the visitors' arrival. I'd hoped the visitors would curb some of Caligastia's worst excesses—that they'd find some way of collaborating together.

When the Watcher continued, it was in a slightly different tone. I imagined she was trying to puzzle out whose side I was on, which was not anything I relished getting back to the Prince.

"So, what was the deal?" I asked quickly. "What was Serap's idea?"

"He told the female what the grandmothers had come up with; how it would be valuable to cooperate so as to speed up the visitors' mission. If the Nodites could produce a leader with some violet blood, then, as the most progressive tribe around, they could really help out the visitors."

"Naturally she rejected it," I said with enough sarcasm to show her where my sympathies lay. "Surely Serap must have known about the prohibition?"

"She did reject it to begin with, of course. She told Serap how it was in direct contradiction to their instructions. But Serap kept at her for years. Wearing her down . . . in the nicest way, naturally. Telling her how depressed her mate was by the pathetically slow progress. That it would improve everything for everybody and how it just made common sense to get the violet blood into Nodite veins as quickly as possible.

"As the mission hit obstacle after obstacle I could see she was softening to the idea. The visitors had been observing MA's rules for the past hundred years and look where it had got them! I could see she must have been thinking that."

"What did her mate think about all this?"

"Oh, they kept it from him. They knew he'd have turned down any thought of breaking MA's rules. And it didn't happen overnight—the decision to go ahead with the plan. It took more than five years of plotting and planning, choosing the right person, making sure the female visitor was prepared to fully cooperate . . ."

"So this was Serap's doing?" I asked.

"He was perfectly sincere, if that's what you mean. He really believed it was the best approach. After all, to him MA must have been a rather abstract concept. He also had the pressure from the grandmothers to contend with. They really wanted this to happen.

"The truth is, the female visitor wasn't *that* hard to persuade. Here's what I think finally convinced her. Serap was always supportive of the visitors' instructions to hold off on mating until there were a million of them. He could understand the reason for it."

"Which is . . . ?" I hadn't understood this either at the time.

"Listen, violet blood is a powerful boost, you must know that." There was that petulant tone again. "Weren't you listening to your lectures on this? It has to be widely distributed all over the world simultaneously, right? And if it isn't, and it gets out in dribs and drabs, or it gets too localized, remember what they said would happen?"

She didn't stop for my excuses.

"It'd produce a cultural anomaly, that's what they told us." Her voice took on a singsong rhythm. "'A severe imbalance in the distribution of violet blood will invariably result in cultural disharmony. If this genetic complement becomes overly concentrated in any one indigenous race or tribe before it can be widely distributed, the resulting phenotype will be unpredictable and will become a potential danger to global progress, as well as a danger to itself.' Isn't that how the lecturer spoke of it? C'mon! You must have been there!"

Enough! I thought. So she can rattle off the lecture word for word. Big deal! Lording it over me like that. But, hey! This story's too good to miss.

"You've not talked like this to anyone for a long time, have you?" Her tone was kind again. "Take a break. Get some rest. Let's meet back here again at the full of the moon."

She was right, of course. It was getting complicated, and I'm not really cut out for assimilating information secondhand in this way. I settled down against my rock and relaxed. The sun was setting and the scents of the night-blooming flowers were starting to waft over me with the evening breeze. I felt the Watcher slip away. That was fine by me . . . I'd see her again soon enough.

* * *

All groups or organizations with a centralized command structure face similar challenges as the organization expands over a broader geographical area. That is axiomatic. Empires have fallen as a consequence of their frayed borders.

Orders will come down from the center, in this case from the Omega in London to the Chicago Chapter, and of necessity those orders will be molded to fit local conditions. Depending on the degree of control demanded by the center, there will always be some level of tension that develops between the original instructions and the manner in which they are carried out on the ground. Compounding this tension, of course, are the varied psychological dynamics of the personalities involved.

Mary Ann, as you will have gathered by now, had the characteristics of a dictator. Like many of such an autocratic nature, she held personal loyalty as the highest value. She quite evidently believed she was complete unto herself. Her word was final within the community, and although Robert may have argued with her behind closed doors, she stood for no opposition from any other Processean.

Mein Host still appeared convinced that Mary Ann had revealed her divinity to him in Nassau, which had remained, to that date, the most profound spiritual experience of his life. He clearly felt deeply privileged to be serving his Goddess, and apart from the transgressions already described, I could see he was gradually mastering his overtly rebellious aspects. He'd chosen a harsh way of doing it, however. His was turning out to be a path of total renunciation, and I'm sure he was still telling himself that this was the path of a Mystery School.

Yet, if I was to put a date to when my ward first had an inkling that all might not be quite straight in his relationship with Mary Ann, it would have to be when Catherine unexpectedly arrived in Chicago, fresh from London, and very obviously pregnant. She came with instructions from Mary Ann to inform my ward that the baby was his and that he and Catherine were to get married at once.

Of course, Catherine's arrival wasn't completely unexpected. Chris—the titular head of the chapter—had received a call from Mary Ann a few days earlier, but either he'd been instructed not to tell Mein Host the news or he'd had his own reasons for not passing it along.

Although Chris and Mein Host had been longtime friends, given that they'd been at the same architectural college and had traveled widely together before either of them joined the community, their friendship had never been an altogether easy one. Mein Host will be surprised to hear this, but his friend Chris (now many years deceased) had long envied him. This manifested in Chris's small acts of covert aggression and the obstructions he'd put in Mein Host's path, unbeknown to my ward. Their relationship had brought out a competitive element between the two men. Nonetheless, they had enjoyed each other's company enough to take two long summer vacations together, one to India and one to Morocco. Yet I don't think my ward considered that his friend would ever want to have anything to do with a group. Like many others who were to join the Process, Chris thought of himself as independent and individualistic. However, he must have been intensely curious as to what Mein Host was doing during the time he was acting as Robert and Mary Ann's guinea pig when they were fine-tuning the psychotherapy technique they would offer, first under the rubric of Compulsions Analysis and later as the Process. It was only when Robert and Mary Ann formally set themselves up as psychotherapists at their apartment in London's Wigmore Street that Chris joined the group.

My ward wasn't to know this about his friend, because by that time he'd left the budding group and his friends, as I've previously related, only to return two years later to find the group much larger and more formalized. At this point Mein Host's friends Chris, Wendy, and Paul were all firmly embedded in the organization. In a group that was always prone to a hierarchical structure due to Mary Ann's autocratic nature and approach, this meant that my ward, on rejoining the group, found himself in a considerably junior position to his old friend. Chris, to put it baldly, was now my ward's immediate boss.

Chris was an unusual young man. He and his younger brother—who also subsequently joined the group—were the scions of a well-known Swiss/European musical family. Both boys had already disappointed their parents by not showing any interest in making music their career. The pressure for the boys to continue the family's rich musical reputation was further complicated by the decision of their father, a musician of international renown, to forsake his career and become instead a teacher of the Alexander technique, a physical therapy technique that was gaining some traction at the time.

Chris had the high intelligence that was expected of the offspring of an urbane European family, and the emotional coldness that might be expected from having such a high-pressure background. He was a tall, slim man, with the erect posture befitting the son of a practitioner of the Alexander technique. Sadly, the very stiffness of his bearing, capped by a long, thin, aquiline face with light-blue eyes and a shock of blond hair, reinforced a natural arrogance that he was never fully able to dispel. At some point in his young life he may well have stopped trying to not appear haughty, since he seemed to have come to terms with his aristocratic bearing and may have decided it was easier to actually *be* arrogant if that's what was expected of him.

For all his failings, Mein Host—and I know he's embarrassed to have me write this—is one of those natural aristocrats who appear every once in a while in families of various classes and backgrounds. And like natural aristocrats everywhere, he was completely unaware that this was a quality he possessed.

Chris, who was all too aware of his illustrious lineage and having horrified his parents by his decision to join the Process community, must have felt he had a great deal to prove to himself. Feeling deeply inadequate and yet never accepting this deficiency in himself, Chris saw in my ward what he wanted to possess for himself. Unfortunately, however, the desire to emulate another person's characteristics is inevitably bound to fail, because at best an emulation remains a mere copy of the original. At worst, the desire descends into envy, and, as in Chris's case, this turned into an ambient sense of resentment, which was then turned against the subject of that envy.

This issue of envy will raise its head at a number of key points in Mein Host's life in the Process community. The constant physical closeness of chapter life and the pressure-cooker atmosphere of so many vigorous young men and women living and working together twenty-four hours a day naturally brought out both the best and the worst in everyone. Of the negative qualities, envy invariably proved to be the most difficult one to spot and acknowledge, so much so it was only many years after my ward left the community during the bitter-cold month of December in 1977 that he first came to realize that his being envied had been the source of a number of previous, perplexing events.

In this narrative, Mein Host has encouraged me to be open and direct about his faults, since he claims to be learning what he hasn't hitherto grasped from my review of his life. As is true for many people who attract the envy of others, his lack of awareness of this was due to the lack of envy in his own makeup. I have never observed him envying another person, and I don't believe he actually knows what the sensation feels like. And when I've heard him talk of it recently, it has only been to say that if someone was to envy him, then that person was simply ignoring his (my ward's) many faults.

I've concluded over the course of observing how people have related to my ward that envy is the hardest of the social dynamics to recognize. Because it appears to be one of the more shameful (and unnecessary) emotions and is invariably sourced in a low sense of self, envy can manifest in a wide variety of covert ways. In some it can provoke anger or hostility— the "tall-poppy syndrome" of cutting the envied one down to size. Others will be ingratiating or clinging, hoping that the envied characteristic will somehow rub off on them. Envy can also manifest as teasing, or more aggressively as bullying, while other people might purposefully ignore or ridicule the one who is envied.

In the public arena I've noted how, by encouraging the concept of role models for the young, and national "heroes" (who have often done nothing more heroic than survive a disaster) for everybody else, a culture of envy has been sanctioned and applauded in much of the West. This strategy, which starts to bite for most people as children, is then, in turn, exploited by the marketing and consumer culture (there'll always be someone with a cooler gadget, a slimmer figure, or a better-looking spouse); by the celebrity industry (the worship of false idols); by religions (guilt in the face of illusory perfection); and by the sports and entertainment industries (encouraging voyeurism above participation). And although envy has always been a character weakness to which humans are prone, there doesn't seem to have been another culture in history that has manipulated it so thoroughly and for such crass and greedy reasons.

On a more personal level, envy appears to have become such an accepted shortcoming that I've frequently heard people quite openly state that they envy this or that quality in another person or situation.

In this case, on the surface, Chris maintained an affable front toward Mein Host, but as he was in charge of the Chicago Chapter he was able to exert his influence behind the scenes. While this did little to trouble Mein Host at the time, Chris's small acts of obstruction came to foreshadow a far more serious betrayal of friendship that occurred some months later.

Catherine's arrival in Chicago, with instructions from the Oracle that Mein Host marry the girl, threw him for a loop. The subject of children was not something Mein Host had ever discussed with Catherine, nor do I believe my ward had ever given a moment of thought to marrying the girl. He might have initially been sexually drawn to her, but the week spent together for their Absorption back in London had put to rest any real affection they had felt for one another.

And now here she was, with a baby in her belly, and orders to marry him.

What was the lad to do?

He'd made it clear enough he didn't love Catherine, and I could see he wasn't even sure he liked her much after she'd attacked and battered him with that T-square. But there was something more deeply troubling going on, which would result in many years of unnecessary complications and duplicity. It was also the first of Mary Ann's deliberate deceptions that she imposed on Mein Host, which he might have seen through had he more confidence in himself at the time.

You see, from the moment that Catherine's pregnancy was credited to him, Mein Host was intuitively sure the child was *not* his. Yet as far as he knew he was the only person with whom she'd had sex in the past six months. Catherine also appeared convinced the child was his, and it was only many years later Mein Host discovered that she had been instructed by Mary Ann to tell him he was the father, while knowing perfectly well that he wasn't.

Mary Ann had calculated well . . . very well.

Again.

* * *

I was well rested by the time my Watcher returned.

The moon, gloriously whole and silver, softly illuminated the meadow as it sloped down to the edge of the cliff. Beyond that I could see the waves, rolling silver-white stripes against an indigo sea, materializing from the distant darkness to break on the beach far below me.

When I woke up I found that the dolmen against which I was resting had retained its warmth, so I stayed there and weighed the dream I'd received while I was awaiting the next installment from my communicative Watcher.

My first impression was that the dream somehow connected back to an earlier one I'd had when I first came to the peninsula at the time of the visitors' arrival. And from the odd sense of familiarity that washed over me, I suspect I may have had other similar dreams that I've overlooked or forgotten. They seemed to be building to a climax, because the dream I'd just had was the most complete one yet.

I'm aware that other peoples' dreams can be tedious to hear, yet there was a lucidity about the theme that was being developed over the course of these dreams, which suggested I may have been receiving yet another level of Multiverse activity of which I'd been previously unaware.

This was my dream: I was hovering some four hundred feet above the peninsula. Below me I could see the two visitors relaxing together in a grassy glade. They looked perfectly splendid—much as they had when they'd first arrived. Both were tall, somewhat over nine feet, and they were holding themselves erect and proud, just as I'd recalled them. Their bodies were lithe and tanned, and they wore their fair hair in long braids.

Most noticeable to me were their light-violet auras, which seemed to join and entwine, creating a glowing globe of lavender light that surrounded them like a translucent bubble as they sat in the shade of the trees.

It was such a pleasing sight that it took me awhile to break my gaze. When I did, to my surprise I saw a flash of color beneath me. It was scintillating like oil on water—gliding stealthily through the forest canopy toward where the visitors sat. They appeared unaware of the creature's approach.

Next, I was poised lower over the treetops, where I had a better view of the creature. It was then that I realized I'd seen it before in my dreams. There it was gliding smoothly through the ocean. The creature seemed smaller than before. Its body was more compact, and its sleek head was capped by a plume of multicolored quills that ran down its backbone. The expression it wore was somehow one of a gentle intelligence. As it moved sinuously through the canopy, whenever it slid out of the shadows I could see its iridescent scales glittering against the dark greens and browns of the trees.

The visitors heard the music at the same time I did, although I had the impression it had been going on for some time. From where I hovered I could hear the sounds emanating from the creature, although the visitors seemed not to know where the music was coming from. They were both peering around into the forest with looks of charmed wonderment on their upturned faces.

Now I could hear that it was much more than music—it was the entire history of this creature's race, rendered in sounds and images that curled and coiled around the two visitors.

There seemed to be a break in the Dreamtime, because in the next moment (that I was aware of, anyway) I was among the trees at the edge of the glade, watching an astonishing spectacle. The two visitors and the creature were standing quite still and triangulated in the center of the clearing. They appeared to be entranced as the music swept around them.

I watched their three bodies, each exquisitely beautiful in its own way, starting to sway as they gradually moved closer together. The music—and I call it that for want of an appropriate word to describe this torrential flood of sounds and images—this music grew wilder as their swaying turned in to a dance that then became a sinuous ballet. Their bodies were soon twisting and winding around one another so as to appear to me as a single, entwined being in constant sensuous motion.

I knew this was a dream, yet watching this strange vision I wondered if I might have been as hypnotized as the three participants appeared to be. Soon the music was reaching a climax, and it seemed that great waves of pleasure rippled over the surface of this tangled jumble of ecstatic bodies.

As the music died away, the visitors gracefully disentangled their limbs, while the creature, its head turned up toward the sun, rose to its full height, its magnificent plume sparkling with mineral iridescence. It then enclosed the pair in a soft embrace of its magnificent wings.

I believe it was then that I turned away, because the next thing I knew I was awake—with the music still resonating in my mind.

I was thinking through the dream when I felt the presence of the Watcher approaching and slipping up to my side. I didn't try to mask the dream away before she picked up on it. Watchers have always found it hardest to mask thoughts from our peers—probably for good reason.

"Ah, yes, I understand, of course," I heard her voice again in my mind. "You've met the Helianx, haven't you?"

It must have been obvious to her that I was still looking startled by what I'd seen in my dream.

"And the conjoining? You saw that too?" she intoned.

I'd no need to reply. She'd read the whole dream out of my mind as quickly and easily as you might take in a single image on a screen. Watchers are good at that. But, then again, might Astar too have had the dream? How could that be if it was only a dream?

"Other Watchers as well have had such visions," she confirmed. "I too have dreamed up the Helianx several times while I've been here."

"You know its name. You called it the Helianx, didn't you?"

"Like you, I've received dream glimpses of that creature before. I've learned a little about it. And yet it's still a mystery."

"Is it real?" I asked foolishly. "You speak of what I saw as if it's something real and solid . . ."

"*Not* just a dream?" I could hear the smile in her tone. "And *you*?" Grinning more broadly now. "Are *you* real and solid? Am I? Is anything?

Can you be sure you're now awake? Are you certain you're not still dreaming?"

"I know all that," I thought impatiently, "but it doesn't answer my question. Is it real? I mean is it really happening? If it is, how could this be? Last I recall, the visitors' garden and dwellings were being overrun by the Nodite tribes—isn't that what really happened? Don't we both know what really occurred?"

"Do we?" she whispered. I could hear that smile again.

She was starting to become enigmatic, and I realized that there was nothing more to be learned from her at this point. I could feel that this wasn't a matter she particularly wanted to dwell upon, and after a pause she returned to the original matter at hand.

"As I told you," Astar settled into her teaching mode, "the female visitor finally consented to Serapatatia's plan. She must have been aware she was directly breaking MA's rules, but Serap assured her that the coupling would only occur with one very special male of the finest Nodite blood and that it could never create the cultural anomaly they'd been warned about so severely. In this way they were able to justify their transgression to themselves."

"Still, she didn't tell her mate? That's a sign she knew it probably wasn't right."

"It wasn't as simple as that," the Watcher snapped back. "She knew perfectly well she was taking a big risk. But it's hard for us Watchers to identify with how really badly she thought their mission was progressing. After all those years of effort, I'm sure she felt the whole affair was just about to collapse. Serap's cooperation and friendship was the only bright light in the entire mess. No. Oddly, I think she sincerely felt it was worth the risk. She was using her initiative and doing her best."

"She thought MA would understand? Really?"

"I guess. But we're getting ahead of ourselves . . . that is if you still want to hear what I saw happening?"

"How do I know that what you observed was any more real or unreal than the dream vision about the . . . what did you call it? . . . the Helianx?" I asked, forming the question that had bothered me since I'd awakened from the dream.

"Perhaps you won't," she said. "Perhaps all our stories are real and unreal. But if by 'unreal' you mean 'it didn't actually happen,' perhaps you should ask yourself whether you can be quite sure that *your dream* actually happened."

This was hard to grasp. Within the dream everything I had experienced seemed so real and solid that had I stayed there any longer, I might well have become convinced it was the dominant reality. Yet, while I'm "awake," what I observe seems just as real and solid to me.

I felt caught, oscillating between these two different realities, and it was starting to get painful. You might think that because I'm a Watcher who appears to move fluidly between third, fourth, and fifth dimensions that I might have had a better understanding of Dreamtime and the part it plays in our lives. I have a better grasp on it now, but sitting there in the cool of the night listening to Astar, Dreamtime—let alone this Helianx creature—was still a mystery to me. I really wasn't expecting an explanation, but she was on a roll, and she might know something about Dreamtime that I didn't. Astar was one of the more knowledgeable of the few Watchers permitted to remain on the planet after the uprising.

The Watcher was continuing to talk in my mind, her tone more patient than I'd have expected given my ignorance of what we were discussing. I was still deeply puzzled. Here was I, dreaming of an ecstatic union of both visitors and the Helianx, while at the same time Astar was relating what was happening to the visitors.

"History, as you likely think of it, isn't really that straightforward. Many versions of the same event occur simultaneously, each one producing a different resolution. Then, whichever resolution serves the greater purpose, and it can be positive or negative, will become the primary time line, if I can call it that."

She must have felt my confusion, because she let her surprising statement sink in before continuing. "Imagine a theater with the same actors on many different stages, all saying their lines slightly differently and each group resolving similar situations in their own way. Usually the differences are so small mortals don't notice the subtle transitions when they wake up from sleeping . . ."

I interrupted, "But this Helianx creature . . . how does that fit with what you're saying?"

"Slow down, sister. I know you're curious about your dream. But first, do you understand what I'm saying about these time lines?"

I wanted her to know I'd been listening. "These different lines of probability resolve into one primary time line, that's what you mean? But, how? Why?"

"How? I can only guess—I've heard better minds than mine say the multiple time lines are simply artifacts of the multidimensionality of the Multiverse. Why? Perhaps it's to do with choices or, let's say, with freedom of choice, allowing the consequences to play out. Something like that, perhaps. So every one has a chance to learn from the results of their actions even if the actions and their consequences aren't included in the primary time line."

"Freedom of choice?" I was confused again. Where did choices come into it?

"Each of those time lines allows a different degree of freedom for the beings involved. The reason this is difficult to grasp, for us anyway, is because mortals have the experience of being entirely free to choose their thoughts and actions in a manner almost impossible for us to identify with. We're not really built that way. We function as we've been created to function; mortals, and let's assume the Helianx, for example, *is* some sort of mortal being, well, you might say they too are on a learning curve. They're the upwardly mobile ones. And to learn and grow they need the freedom to succeed or fail on their own terms. It's the results of their choices that build the time lines, and it's the Supreme Being's momentum, you might say, that collapses all those time lines into the primary one."

"Okay, now I'm starting to see what you're saying. And it's we from the inner realms who nurture and administer this primary time line. Is that what you're saying?" With this I thought of the Melchizedek Brothers—who run the great Multiverse universities—and how they're devoted to teaching ascending souls. I also pondered the fact that the Prince's mission—before the revolution anyway—was so completely devoted to caring for, and uplifting, human beings. That was why we were there. And what about the System Sovereigns and the

Constellation Fathers, do they too exist primarily for the advancement of mortal souls?

The more I thought about this, I felt I was starting to understand what Astar meant when she'd once told me that she considered the Multiverse as a vast teaching machine.

I knew she heard my thoughts, so I turned back to the vision I'd seen in my dream . . . the creature she'd called the Helianx.

"Ah yes," she sighed, "it's your dream that concerns you."

She was right. Caligastia's machinations could wait. I was aware I was still avoiding knowing the details of what had happened to the visitors. However, that dream of mine was suddenly far more interesting.

"Any of these time lines," she was saying, "can be subject to the insertion of novelty. It's relatively rare, but it happens. Didn't I hear, for example, that a Pleiadean ship recently inserted itself into Vanu's primary Lemurian time line?"

I thought I was starting to understand. "So what you're saying is there will be a time line in which the Pleiadeans *did not* come with their warning . . ."

"Yes. And one in which they came but didn't believe the Lemurians worth telling about the oncoming disaster, and another in which they only picked up Vanu and Amadon and left everyone else to their fate . . ."

"And one in which the comet didn't approach Earth so closely and didn't cause disaster?" I asked.

"Yes," she said, "that too."

"And the Helianx is like this? An insertion of novelty in the time line I was dreaming?" I could feel her smiling. She was enjoying being the knowledgeable one.

"If you understand that, you'll find the next step more illuminating. From a mortal's point of view, for example, each individual will perceive and experience what appears to them to be the same solid 'reality' you spoke of before. Yet, each mortal will experience it slightly differently. This may be quite evident to us, but it's rarely appreciated by humans unless the novelty inserted is sufficiently out of the ordinary. In that case, what do you think happens?"

I was startled at the unexpected question. "Well, it would depend on the impact the novelty adds, I suppose. If its effects were strong enough, then wouldn't its effects become the primary time line? There. Did I get it right?"

"Well, let me ask you another question." She paused, and both of us turned to watch the sun seeming to rise behind the eastern mountains, etching the shaded folds of dark against the rose-pink light. In the face of such beauty we moved to the other side of our dolmen to bathe in the first rays of the sun as it peeked over the mountains bowing before it.

"How do, let's say, a woman and her two children . . ." she asked thoughtfully "step completely unharmed from a physical catastrophe, a wildfire perhaps, when everyone around them died? Or a tornado that seems so oddly selected in what it destroys or how it kills?"

"Humans would think it's their gods at work, wouldn't they? Or fate, or destiny." I trailed off, groping for a deeper insight, which seemed to elude me.

"Luck, indeed! You've been observing humans too long! Why do some people attract trouble, and others don't? It's hard to put that down to luck. Perhaps destiny is getting closer to the truth. If you think it's luck or blind chance, answer me this . . . and I'm sure you'll have seen this either here or on Zandana. If a group of mortals perceives a rare event, such as the appearance of an extraterrestrial craft in their skies, you may have noticed that some people in the group will see it while others will see nothing. Does that make my point clearer?"

"Obviously that's not luck . . . but those are fairly extreme examples."

"That makes my point," she said firmly. "These sorts of discontinuities become more obvious the greater the novelty, but they're really happening all the time. Every moment. Same for the person who attracts trouble."

There was another long pause. Three fandors circled high overhead, and I watched as the sun caught the underside of their transparent wings and ignited momentary flashes of color. I was surprised; I'd not seen fandors penetrating this dimension before.

"So, certainly mortals," she stressed the word mortals, "can think of it as personal destiny—it's their learning path. That's why I suggested you best consider the Multiverse as a vast teaching mechanism. It's almost infinitely malleable. It serves everything and everybody. Every part of the whole is responsive, both to every other part, but also its responsive to the living Multiverse, in the form of the Supreme."

This was starting to get a little too complicated for me, but although Astar had paused I didn't want to stop her. Besides, I was happy she'd spend time with me. I confess I must have drifted off because I only heard a few words here and there, something about the heart of matter . . . about the interaction between Creator and Creation.

I pulled myself together before she'd noticed I was starting to over-load. Besides, I couldn't resist a little dig; she'd been enjoying showing off her knowledge of the Mutliverse long enough, I wanted to get back to my original question. "And history?" I asked her. "You were saying I didn't understand it . . . that it wasn't as . . . what? . . . as 'straightforward' as I thought."

But, of course, I couldn't deceive her.

"I haven't been able to be with other Watchers very much recently," her tone softer now with a hint of self-deprecation. "I'm sorry if you've found me tedious. These are not simple matters. And it helps me to sort out my thoughts if I extend them to another Watcher."

It was at this point that I realized she was just as off-balance as I was about what she was doing as a Watcher following the revolution. Her lofty attitude was merely her way of covering up her lack of certainty. I should have seen that before. Yet I had grasped the basics of her explana-tion of the time lines and how they were resolved into one primary line, and I felt grateful for that insight.

"Which brings us back to history," she said, reading me again. "If I'd told you at the start that history weaves its way like a serpent through a field of probabilities, you would never have known what I was talk-ing about, would you? Or, if I'd said that history is no more than the resolved primary time line embodied in the Supreme Being, you would have needed a context within which to understand me."

Fair enough, I thought. She had given me some helpful insights, although I had not received a complete answer on what the Helianx really was, nor what the creature was doing with the two beautiful visitors.

As I was thinking these thoughts, Astar disappeared.

13

An Arranged Marriage

Spontaneous Telepathy, Angelic Cosmology, and Getting to Know Cano

I could appreciate the difficult situation Mein Host had found himself in when Catherine had arrived announcing she was pregnant. He had no obvious reason to disbelieve her when she claimed the child was his, and yet his intuition, which was getting progressively sharper, told him otherwise. He clearly didn't believe Catherine wanted to marry him any more than he wanted her for a wife. She was also one of the first of the women to have conceived a child while living within the Process community, and that had posed an entirely new problem for the Omega.

Yes, he'd had orders to marry the girl, but was marriage really the answer? The Process was already known in England for its eccentricity, and the times were becoming far more lax in their formalities. Then again, Mary Ann was the only one of them who knew anything about American values regarding children born out of wedlock. So perhaps she had a point.

Mein Host had made it obvious over the course of his life that he hadn't considered himself the marrying type. In fact, he'd discussed marriage only once, and then it had been in general terms. He'd broached the subject once with Jean some four years earlier, before he had joined the community. I could see his relief when she'd showed no interest. He'd loved Jean as deeply as he was capable of loving anyone at that age, but he was still so cut off from his feelings that his emotional body showed little sign of being wounded by her lack of interest.

Now, four years after that, my ward was being presented with this fait accompli. He was ignorant of the true story of Catherine's impregnation—and would remain so for twenty-five years—and appeared to feel no choice but to accept her word that he'd fathered the child.

In his talks with Catherine after she arrived I could see his dilemma being played out. He could scarcely claim not to be the father, because, as far as he was aware, he was the only man who had had a sexual relationship with Catherine. To insist otherwise clearly would be a cowardly evasion of his responsibilities—and he was gentleman enough to know that. And because he remained devoted to Mary Ann, I could see that he'd decided to view the situation simply as an arranged marriage—a challenge his Goddess had set him for his own good.

And so it was that the couple married in Chicago's Cook County Courthouse on a rainy spring day, witnessed by two other Processeans who'd taken valuable time off from selling magazines on the street to attend the ten-minute formality.

It was not a joyous occasion; it would not be a joyous marriage. In reality, it was no kind of marriage at all. It appeared to exist solely to add a veneer of respectability. In retrospect, these attempts at respectability are somewhat ironic for a group that in a few short years would be blamed—completely falsely, I should add—for provoking Charles Manson, in some mysterious way, to commit his crimes. Even though there was never any connection to Manson, the accusations themselves were enough to end any remaining pretense of respectability.

In the months prior to the child's birth the couple lived uneasily together in the same room at the Chicago Chapter house beside the lake. Both of them were evidently trying to make the best of the situation, but it was such an inherently fractious relationship that it was an unavoidably unhappy time. Trying to stay calm for the baby's sake resulted in a general atmosphere between them of barely repressed resentment, which appeared to explode every few weeks in Catherine's unpredictable rages. They barely knew one another and had spent only that one erotic week together in London for their Absorption—and that hadn't gone spectacularly well!

Evidently one week of wild sex hadn't necessarily equated with any level of genuine appreciation for one another.

As the time of the birth approached, both were continuing to work to get the Wells Street Chapter and coffeehouse up and running, while also spending hours out on the streets selling magazines. When they retired for the night, exhausted, the couple seldom spoke and made sure to avoid touching each other in bed.

Mein Host, I've now had the chance to observe over time, has something of a visceral distaste for the sight of the female body distended by pregnancy. Whatever the reason that lay behind this aversion—which he wouldn't know for many years—it was merely one more factor that contributed to the atmosphere of low-level hostility hanging between them. His emotional body was in a constant state of turmoil throughout this time—he clearly hated being in this situation. He must have felt trapped by his obligations; guilty about his antipathy to his new wife's dysmorphic body; angry at Catherine for putting him in this situation; ashamed of his lack of empathy for her; and torn apart by the conflict within his intuition as to the wrongness of the paternity on the one hand and on the other, his desire to do the right thing. To be a good father.

The only way my ward appeared to be able to handle this inner tumult was to cut himself off from his feelings and assume a cold, unemotional affect. Unfortunately, there seems to be no more infuriating a pose, when confronting someone who is emotionally disturbed, than extreme emotional detachment. This led to further rows, and worse, to the grimly suppressed hostility of an old married couple who'd long disliked each other and knew the pain of inflicted silence.

Given all these emotional stresses it wasn't surprising that the issues surrounding the child's birth became yet another source of Catherine's long-simmering resentment directed toward her putative husband.

On top of this, they were under a lot of pressure to keep the chapter going. They now had two rents to pay and were also routinely forwarding a healthy percentage up to the Omega. Additionally, they were responsible for keeping the Cavern buzzing with activity and the organization's assemblies and meditations well attended. Much of this fell on Mein Host's shoulders. These preoccupations, and a general indifference to his wife's condition, resulted in his being on the street magazine selling and out of contact when Catherine was taken off to the hospital. Thus he was not present for the birth. Evidently he was in no hurry to get there and arrived late the following day to drive her and the baby back to the chapter house.

Now if you recall, Catherine was the daughter of an immensely wealthy and corrupt Anglo/American family, and although her childhood had been extremely difficult, she had experienced it in the most elegant and opulent of surroundings. Being rudely carted off to a maternity ward in a broken-down general hospital on Chicago's South Side, and then finding herself in the agonies of childbirth—being the only white face among a sea of black women—might likely have been a disconcerting scenario for any young woman from a wealthy background.

Catherine, I hasten to say, was no racist. That was evidenced a few years later when she traveled on her own into the depths of Haiti to interview Voodoo priests about their ceremonies and practices for PROCESS magazine. In fact, it was her experience in the maternity ward with those kind and openhearted black women that allowed her the courage and confidence to move around the deeply occulted Voodoo circles with such complete impunity.

However, the depth of her resentment made it impossible for her to do anything but blame my ward for the terrible conditions and the personal shame she felt at giving birth "in the poorhouse," as she termed it. There was no talk of her closeness to the black culture and the warmth with which she was received by the other mothers. Admitting to all that might have mitigated her anger at being, in her terms, "so poorly treated." No doubt she was also resentful that Mein Host hadn't been present for the birth. He hadn't been chain-smoking and pacing nervously back and forth outside either, as she'd imagined he might be, in a scene she must have lifted from the movies. Nor had he bothered to call. Instead, he had left her at the hospital for two days, after she had undergone an extremely painful delivery with the minimum of analgesics. She felt entirely justified in holding my ward responsible for all of these lapses.

You will have noticed, I'm sure, that neither of them saw Mary Ann as culpable in any way. Catherine, because she was holding back a crucial secret; my ward, because he was ignorant of the truth.

Prior to the birth, both of them had tried to stay calm "for the sake of the baby," and had ended up with a repressed silence between them. Now, with a vigorously noisy baby boy back with them in their shared little room, the situation went from bad to worse. Catherine's explosions of fury became more uncontrollable and were now invariably amplified by the cries of the child. The screams of the baby pierced the walls as if they were made of paper, and this, in turn, infuriated the other three exhausted Processeans who were living with them in the small, poorly built house.

Mein Host seemed to be completely lost. He'd never been anywhere near a tiny baby and had none of the genetic or sentimental attachment he might have had if he'd been certain the child was his own son. He also clearly made the point of trying not to bond with a child with whom he felt no sense of kinship. He must have known it was an ungenerous attitude to take toward the boy, yet he simply could not bring himself to be more generous-hearted under these circumstances. I've heard him since trying to justify his actions by saying he'd never wanted to usurp the true father's role in the boy's life, but I know he regretted how he behaved at this time. It was one of the lowest times in his life.

I believe he is now honest enough with himself to accept that it was primarily his self-concern and his sense of personal powerlessness, more than his irritation with Catherine and the boy, which caused him to act in a way that he now understands as cruel and self-indulgent.

Over the following few months, seeking to build revenues from sales of the magazine, new members were transferred from the London Chapter to Chicago, and the house was filling up. This led to further disruptions and sleepless nights for more people, more general irritation, and more stress on all of them. The pressure to make money was constant, and what they made was never enough. The more money they made, the more they were expected to make in an endless round of increasing effort, and an increasing annoyance with the little family who seemed to be at the center of their troubles.

Something had to break, and although Mein Host would never have thought of himself as a Jonah, his transfer to the recently formed New Orleans Chapter instantly changed the dynamic in Chicago in a positive way. For Mein Host, the relief of leaving the contentious hothouse atmosphere was clear for everyone to see. He was palpably delighted to move to New Orleans. He would, at a later point in his life, live in Chicago again, but not under such trying conditions as those he had experienced with Catherine and the baby.

New Orleans made a curious impression on him, a young Englishman who'd only known the furious pace of Chicago. There was a looseness and ease, almost European in tone, to the city's atmosphere that evidently felt familiar and comfortable to him.

A small chapter had been set up on Royal Street in the French Quarter, and its coffeehouse was already overflowing with interested young people. The Vietnam War was reaching its peak, with the draft becoming the major preoccupation of young Americans. The recent Tet Offensive had exposed the truth of American vulnerability and the absurdity of fighting for a corrupt South Vietnamese administration. Young people were in turmoil. Their friends, their brothers, and their cousins were dying in the thousands, or returning maimed and forever changed. New Orleans seemed to be one of the cities that attracted those who were the most rebellious opponents of the war and the administration that so cynically promoted it.

It was in the New Orleans Process Cavern that Mein Host had another spiritual experience, which—although he was becoming well practiced in empathy—clearly astonished him. To this day he is unable to fully comprehend precisely what occurred.

He was sitting at a low table talking to a young man while both sipped their coffees when, for no reason that I could ascertain, they suddenly fell silent. The noise in the coffeehouse, the buzz of conversation, the Beatles' "Sgt. Pepper's Lonely Hearts Club Band" playing loudly, along with the chink and tinkle of cups and glasses, all this continued unabated around them.

It seemed to me they remained silent for over half an hour before the man got up and wordlessly left. He appeared to be quite ordinary. Mein Host didn't know his name and never saw him again. It was such an internal mental experience for him that I wasn't privy to what happened during that time; however, I did observe that his emotional body was far more settled after the experience.

Mein Host has no memory of what happened during the silent interchange except to say it was the first time he'd ever had an extended telepathic encounter, and it was with someone he didn't even know. I believe that's what surprised him, although he took the encounter in his stride and didn't make very much of it at the time. I suspect he thought it might be a more common event than, in fact, it is. If he had known that such an experience would only be repeated twice more over the following thirty-five years, he might have made better note of it.

Yet, of course, there was a very good reason he wasn't any the wiser at the time—such an insight would have been premature. My ward needed to keep his feet as firmly on the ground as possible as he had a lot of purely practical issues that would consume his life for the foreseeable future. The young telepath he'd met was, in fact, a relatively highly developed incarnate rebel angel who'd recognized my ward and swept him into a telepathic intimacy. That much I know. What they conversed about remains a mystery, both to my ward and to me.

So why would this have occurred if Mein Host has no memory of the content of the interchange? What would have been the purpose?

As I write these words, I feel more confident in asserting what I only had glimpses of forty years ago when the incident happened. There have been a rapidly growing number of rebel angels entering human incarnation over the previous half-century. I now understand this is a truly massive plan, and it concerns every level of the Local Universe. It is also extremely challenging for the incarnated rebel angel.

As must be evident so far from the narrative of Mein Host's gradual spiritual awakening, with all its struggles and sacrifices, it has taken me every bit of thirty years to build up our collaborative relationship to reassure him that I mean him no harm. That I wasn't going to take him over or possess him and use him for my own nefarious purposes. I also needed to be secure that my ward could handle my energy under a variety of different circumstances—which is why it took as long as it did. Of course, for much of that time, Mein Host had no idea my intention was to develop a working relationship whereby ultimately we could collaborate together on these volumes.

It was only in the first decade of the twenty-first century that we were both ready to work together. He'd tested me, as I'd tested him, and he'd come to peace with my presence in his life. His study of *The Urantia Book* had given him a context within which to understand that my claim of being a discarnate rebel angel might be authentic.

We chose to trust one another and see where the collaboration took us. My ward knew I wanted to explore the impact and the consequences of the angelic revolution on life on Earth, while I was aware of his intense desire, almost a need by this point, to know himself and to understand how he'd come to be the way he was. It promised to be a collaboration that would be deeply satisfying for us both. At that early stage, and until we'd completed the first volume, my ward had no thoughts of bringing the work to the public. He believed it too personal for general interest. It was when I confirmed for him that there were more than 90 million rebel angels currently living out their lives as human beings and that the information in the books would be of great benefit to them as they became aware of their own angelic heritage that he saw the value of sharing our collaboration.

As I have previously related, my ward has encountered incarnate rebel angels on a handful of occasions prior to his telepathic meeting but had no conscious awareness of who they actually were. Before he joined the community, two of his girlfriends were incarnate rebel angels, but neither he nor they had the conceptual framework to be able to understand this. The only thing they did know was that they felt an unaccountable closeness, which they didn't feel with other people.

However, if I place this telepathic incident in the larger context of Mein Host's seventy-four years, it becomes meaningful when viewed as part of a highly considered and incremental program of gradual spiritual awakening. In spite of having no conscious memory of what was communicated, the fact of the incident and the clarity of the telepathic contact when it was occurring had a profound effect on my ward's subconscious mind and was a further preparation for what lay ahead. This is so much the case that I can say with certainty that I would not be able to be here writing these words were it not for a whole series of progressively mind-expanding incidents as the one I've just described.

And Mein Host is no exception. There are many who have been

going through a lifetime of spiritual preparation for the upcoming global transformation without being consciously aware of what was happening.

* * *

I really did want to hear what the Watcher Astar had observed while I'd been away on Zandana and thought by now I had a better grasp of what she was telling me about multiple time lines. I suspect she felt the need to go into that digressive exposition as a way of warning me of the inherent unreliability of any historical account, including, to her credit, her own.

When we met again at the next full of the moon to continue our discussion of what had happened to the off-world visitors and their plans for the planet, I began our conversation by expressing my gratitude for her insights into an area I knew little about.

"It's my area of specialization," she replied modestly, "but there's so much more to know."

She was answering my thought: "Before the revolution I studied cosmological physics with the Melchizedek Brothers. In the middle of the course, however, I had to leave, so I still have much to learn."

I formed the thought, "So what you're telling me is your narrative of the visitors' troubles and their ultimate departure is not only one of many versions but the one that is being impressed into the historical narrative . . ."

"Yes, the primary historical *time line,*" she corrected me. "The event or the version that carries its consequences forward on the primary time line."

"Because this particular narrative is the one from which the most can be learned?" I asked.

"From which the most can be learned by *all participants,*" she corrected me again, "as well as everyone who is involved in such planetary affairs in the future."

She paused while we both made ourselves comfortable against our favorite dolmen, the moonlight flooding the stone circle with its whispery light. I was wondering whether all this implied there was some sort of meta-plan driving the choices as to which version of an event becomes included in the primary time line. But I didn't want her to launch in to another digression drawn from her "area of specialization," so I quickly tried to mask off the thought from her.

She laughed in a friendly way, and I knew she'd read me again. She said, "Let's leave that one alone for the moment, but I think you're catching on."

I liked that she'd studied an area I knew so little about. I was learning from her, and, knowing her better by now, I was content to overlook her slight condescension. And I was still cautious about revealing too much of my growing ambivalence at how Prince Caligastia, who technically was our superior, was carrying out Lucifer's revolutionary plans.

Of course I wasn't consciously aware at the time of the conversation in which Lucifer had told me about his alchemical experiment, since he'd closed my memory down. But a hint of it must have leaked out, because the Watcher suddenly became more alert. No doubt she had caught the tail end of my thought. I realized that for all of her knowledge of time lines that she hadn't had the advantage of hearing Lucifer expound on his plans. She hadn't even been to Zandana, as it turned out, or even left this planet. I reckoned she must be one of those stationary Watchers assigned to a particular world and not given permission to leave. I, on the other hand, have been able to come and go much as I pleased.

"I too can leave . . ." she said, slightly offended by my assumption, "if I so wish. But have you not yet understood that this is becoming the most interesting of the revolutionary worlds? So I ask myself, Why go anywhere else? Everything's happening here."

I wasn't going to argue the point. To each her own, I say. And then, before I could stop the thought, I wondered whether it was really me who was instigating her digressions. I knew I wasn't in the best of states—I must have seemed most confused to her.

However, my thought faded into irrelevance when she continued. She had returned to the fate of the visitors. "Serapatatia and the female visitor finally fixed on a plan, which they both were convinced would be for the best, given the trying circumstances they were all in."

Remembering her admonition about the inherent unreliability of multiple time lines I settled back against the still-warm stone to hear the Watcher's story.

She smiled at my mock caution and continued: "As with any of Prince Caligastia's projects," she began again with some noticeable pride, "this one was exquisite in its subtlety and in the patience that had gone in to its planning. As I mentioned last time, it took five years of gentle persua-sion for the female visitor to come around to Serapatatia's obsession to get some of that violet blood into Nodites veins. . . . No, not more than one; they finally settled on a single mating. She felt sure she could justify just that one coupling, given the drastic need and the increasingly disappoint-ing state of the visitors' mission."

Recalling my tutorials back on Jerusem, I said, "But surely that was one of the major stumbling points. Absolutely no interbreeding before there was enough violet blood to go around . . . what was the number needed? One million pureblood offspring . . ."

She interrupted me: "That's just what took the five years . . . if you've been listening. Of course it wasn't easy to persuade her to break her oath. Yes, it was a challenge, you know how those Material Daughters are stick-lers for the law. They *have* to be tough."

"So what happened to change her mind?"

"Perhaps she fell a little bit in love with Serapatatia, to tell you the truth. I don't think she wanted to disappoint him. He is a beautiful man, and one who is completely sincere. And she'd met with the Council of Grandmothers who were pushing Serap for a happy conclusion. She liked them, yes. And they made a convincing case for it, pointing out that the two projects weren't incompatible; that the introduction of violet blood into a single Nodite bloodline would allow the visitors to turn their dete-riorating situation around far more rapidly than waiting for all those million offspring. There was no reason they couldn't both happen simul-taneously. They even recommended a young Nodite aristocrat of the pur-est possible bloodline to do the deed. But I think it was Serap's sincerity and his decency that finally convinced her."

"They're descended from Nodu, right? One of the rebel staff. Wouldn't that be falling straight into Caligastia's clutches?"

She smiled encouragingly, and I took that as a hint to show off some-thing of what I've observed in my time. "Nodu of the Prince's staff— the leader of the sixty staff who'd followed the Prince? How could she ever have thought Nodites could be trusted? Did she really believe the Grandmothers would be satisfied with just one bloodline?" I hadn't really taken in the full absurdity of their justification.

"Well," she said, patient again. "It's not hard to understand when you've watched human behavior enough. Stealing something or murdering someone, for most humans, that first time they do something wicked, they'll likely feel guilty. Their conscience will prick them. The second and third times appear to be easier, because they've deafened themselves to their conscience. Going ahead with Serap's plan would almost certainly lead to more and more couplings, because the rules have already been broken."

The shiver that ran down her body told me everything I needed to know. Her pain was so evident that my mind went back to the time the rebel staff, deprived of immortality and slowly dying appalling deaths, had been instructed by their Prince to mate and procreate with as many highborn mortals as possible. It was from this that the Nodite tribe originated and emerged.

It had been a terrible time for all of us Watchers, given that we had been unable to do anything but observe those fine beings dying horrible deaths after their thousands upon thousands of years of continuous life. These were the true Nephilim, not the "fallen angels" of popular Judeo-Christian belief, but the revolutionary supporters of Caligastia and Lucifer's plan. However, while they were not angels by any means, they certainly were almost superhuman in their attributes. And, I might add, Nodu and the other rebel staff were all the more influential for their very human capacity to interbreed with mortals.

Watchers such as myself and my sister here obviously cannot have sexual intercourse with mortals. Even if we possessed the appropriate genitalia, we don't have access to shared dimensions or the material frequency domains to make such a mating possible. Nodu and the other staff had their material bodies grown for them by the Avalon surgeons and prepared especially for third-density frequency domains. All one hundred of the staff were grown or gene-spliced from purely human stock—their one hundred clone-donors (of which Amadon was a stirring example)—and they evidently shared a remarkable reproductive compatibility.

Although members of the staff were much superior to humans and were magnificent in appearance, they also needed to look and be human enough so as not to unnecessarily frighten the locals. They were on this world to help humans along, after all—at least they were until the rebellion struck . . .

"And now . . ." she finished the thought for me ". . . it feels like everything is up for grabs."

I immediately felt a new caution. Was she leading me on? "Up for grabs?" That wasn't exactly what I'd been thinking. Was she trying to trap me? Lure me out? I really didn't want her to know how mixed up my feelings had become.

Then I felt her smiling again in my mind, and I softened somewhat. I knew I was being silly—paranoid even—which was one of the risks of focusing too closely on third-density emotional turmoil.

I took a few moments to relax and gather my wits. Then I went back to those moments when Caligastia had instructed Nodu and the others to make as many hybrid children as possible. It was the Prince's way of maintaining his influence—as much as he could, anyway—over what remained after his staff's demise. And that's very much what happened. Caligastia, through his priests and now the Nodite grandmothers, controlled the destiny of the Nodite tribes every bit as effectively as he once controlled his staff. So while both Serap and the female visitor genuinely believed it was for the best—if I'm to accept my sister Astar's account—I had a growing sense that Caligastia's plan was simply so corrupting that it would be the final ruination of the visitors' whole mission.

"When the female visitor finally met with the chosen one, Cano," Astar picked up her account again, "she'd already agreed in principle to the transgression. And Cano turned out to be an even more exceptional specimen than Serapatatia—and a lot younger! It seems she'd already spotted him working alongside those Nodites who'd been friendly to the visitors . . . no, it was before their meeting. I heard she'd already been admiring him from afar . . ."

The Watcher paused while we both wondered what that must have been like for her. Not being sexually reproductive beings, we Watchers tend to puzzle over this entire business. Naturally we are drawn to some beings and not so much to others, but these are matters of function and timing. We experience nothing of the tumultuous emotions we observe in human sexual relationships.

"Not only was he physically magnificent," Astar continued, "he was

also extremely bright and gently persuasive in his own way. He understood immediately what was required of him, and besides, because the
female visitor was eternally youthful, she was the most beautiful creature
he'd ever seen. He couldn't stop telling her how beautiful she was, how
much he worshipped her."

"Dangerous territory!" I thought.

"Oh! She loved it! Couldn't get enough. I heard her tell him, as they
got to know each other better, how she felt her mate had been taking her
for granted . . . how he was so depressed she was afraid he was becoming
impotent. It seems there hadn't been a pregnancy in a couple of years."

Now, *that* I hadn't heard. A couple of years! For what was primarily a
reproductive mission, that couldn't have been encouraging.

"It just added to the pressure she felt. Not that the visitor needed too
much pressure to push her over the edge after getting to know him. Odd,
but she really convinced herself she loved him."

"Didn't last long, I guess," I said, thinking of the devastated condition of the garden as well as the apparent absence of the visitors and their
retinues and followers.

"It was a terrible situation. You were *most* fortunate not to have been
around for it," she replied, the emphasis in her tone letting me know she
found my absence somewhat suspicious.

"I could see from the troubled state of her emotional body," she swept
on smoothly, "that almost immediately after they'd consummated their
reproductive act, she knew she'd done something utterly awful, although
I don't think she was fully accepting of it until she had to tell her mate
about it the next day. He was appalled, of course; and utterly bewildered.
He couldn't believe she'd betrayed her most solemn oath."

"Really!" I found that hard to believe. "You're telling me he hadn't
picked up on something going on that was being hidden from him?
Really?" That baffled me. Aren't Material Sons meant to be bright? "You
mean in all those five years of plotting and planning behind his back he
never had a clue?" It was really hard to believe, considering how closely
bonded the pair must surely have been.

Astar's tone was smiling again. "Kind of makes more sense of her
complaints about her mate's indifference, doesn't it?!"

"He must have immediately known they'd blown the mission," I said, appreciating how important following instructions from MA had always been, especially for the male visitor.

"He was thrown into a complete turmoil." Astar agreed with a sigh. "He deeply loved his mate and obviously must have realized, when he heard what had happened and how long they'd been scheming, just how out of touch he'd become. Frankly, I don't know what horrified him most: her act of betraying MA's injunction, or his own blind ignorance that this horrifying plot was being hatched in his own household.

"They'd been arguing about it all day, and by evening she was still trying to protest that it would be forgiven. 'MA will know I meant well!' I heard her muttering repeatedly between the wails. Then, they'd start arguing again. It was pathetic. He couldn't bring himself to stay angry with her. He obviously hated seeing his mate in that distraught state and loved her far too much to continue berating her . . ."

"Besides," I thought out loud, "he would have known they were in this mess together—even if *she* believed she'd acted independently."

"It was only later," Astar told me, "around midnight, that our sister Solonia lay down the law for them . . . she really ripped in to the pair, in the most courteous of ways, of course . . ."

I recalled encountering the seraphim Solonia a couple of times prior to the revolution, and I didn't think we'd ever become close. She'd always been a straight arrow and was proud not to have fallen for Lucifer's revolutionary rhetoric. As the revolution broke over us, forcing us to choose to either stay loyal to Multiverse Authorities and everything that MA represented or to align ourselves with Lucifer and the glorious freedoms he was promising, I never thought she was the type to take the risk.

Astar broke in to my thoughts again. "Solonia scorned me too, although I knew her quite well before the troubles. Better than you, it sounds like."

This was true. When we all made our decisions, and Solonia had remained loyal to MA, I no longer was good enough for her and she would have nothing to do with me. Solonia was one of the seraphim appointed specifically to guard over the visitors' garden, so I had seen something of her. But she'd always turned away.

"They all do that!" Astar said, with more resentment in her tone than I'd have expected. "It's like we're criminals. They despise us."

"What did the good sister Solonia tell the visitors?" I had a rather nasty feeling that I was going to enjoy at least this part of Astar's story.

She paused again, this time to arrange her thoughts. Had she revealed too much of herself with those critical comments? I hoped she'd sense I was being kind and reaching out to her by asking her about Solonia's statements. I appreciated her long and thoughtful pause before she formed her reply. I knew I must have raised a personally painful issue. Was I perhaps pressing her to reveal too much of herself? Was her talk of feeling like a criminal a bit too compromising for her own comfort? I realized I needed to be more guarded with this Watcher. Emotional oversensitivity is one of the dangers for any Watcher who identifies too closely with what she observes of mortal life. Without noticing it, we can get sucked into an emotional vortex that we're hopelessly ill-equipped to handle. It's all par for the course in the larger context of our eventual mortal incarnation, if that is to be . . . Oooops! . . . I hadn't meant to let that consideration leak out. But it was too late.

Astar broke in with a battery of questions. "A future incarnation? As a mortal? Watchers? As mortals? Are you losing your mind?!" There was part astonishment and part horror in her tone as she picked up on my thoughts. She evidently hadn't yet pieced together this particular part of the ongoing drama.

"No, no, it's just my theory," I tried to reassure her. "It's just what I think *might* be happening. Don't take it too seriously. Of course, if it feels right, if it makes sense of all this we go through, then give it some more thought and let's meet once more at the next full moon. I have yet to hear your conclusion to what sounds like a tragic tale."

"Tragic indeed, for MA's plans," she reminded me with a sharp look.

Had I given away my sympathies with that thoughtless slip?

"Yes, but not without a certain, very human, poignancy," she said softly. Although whether Astar was genuinely touched by this so-called poignancy or simply playing with me I wouldn't know until we next met, when we'd sit once more, our backs against this friendly dolmen and basking in the light of a full moon flooding the sacred circle.

* * *

Sadly, the city of New Orleans is currently known worldwide for the tragedy wrought by Hurricane Katrina in 2005.

In 1968 the city was just as vulnerable to wind and tide as it had been when Katrina savaged it thirty-seven years later. It was just as susceptible to flooding from the Mississippi and the canals and, considering that much of the town continues to slowly sink into the soft sand and marshy soil, it was, due to recent climatic changes, only marginally less likely to be overrun by a storm surge.

Yet none of these concerns rose to the degree of agitation and uncertainty that were aroused by the Vietnam War. For many young people coming of age in the 1960s the war was becoming the fulcrum of their discontent with the entire repressive culture of their parents. This resulted in the widest and most vociferously fought intergenerational rift in countries—primarily in the West—that the modern world has yet seen.

It was the revolutionary sixties and the time of the youth rebellion.

And there was much to rebel against.

The history and details of this rebellious era are well known, and I've no need to reiterate them here. Of more interest to me are a couple of less evident observations.

When understood in the broader context of the massive social transformations occurring across the globe over the subsequent half-century, the 1960s were far more widely influential in breaking old and atrophied social patterns than has been generally accepted. Many of these effects have been subtle; they manifested in the emotional and spiritual realms by touching hearts and minds of the following generations. The consequences of these subtle impulses can be appreciated as much in the recent impulse for social justice and the right to individual freedoms among the young of the world as in the unlikely reconciliations that have occurred in national and political spheres.

I don't want to overstate the positive outcomes here, which, like the collapse of Soviet communism or the end of South African apartheid, had a wide variety of causes. The period from 1987 to 2012 was primarily a time in which the corruption and inequality baked into the world's social and political systems, after 203,000 years of Prince Caligastia's behind-the-scenes machinations, were being exposed. Thus, this twenty-five-year period has felt particularly harsh and difficult for many people.

However, that's by way of a digression. More significant to the theme of my narrative is the increasing appearance of righteous revolutionary zeal in so many young people. This is what first showed itself en masse in the 1960s and was one of the consequences of the first large wave of incarnate rebel angels born after the Second World War and growing into their maturity in the '60s and '70s. Since then, and as mentioned earlier in this narrative, other more recent waves of incarnate angels have been able to build on the emotional security and spiritual insights of those who preceeded them.

As I'm fairly sure that anyone who has taken the care to read this far is likely to be a reincarnate (if you are not then you may not have made much sense of my words), I feel I can speak more freely. If you haven't already discerned your spiritual heritage by this point in your life and are pondering this possibility—because it just might explain why you have always felt so different from most people—I can only urge you to explore this matter more deeply for yourself.

Being discarnate myself and hoping to enter into mortal incarnation allows me to speak with more authority on these delicate matters than can Mein Host, for whom such claims could be all too easily dismissed as delusions of self-importance. And I say these are "delicate matters" because many of your predecessors have met with particularly unpleasant ends, as you may well have experienced yourself in a previous lifetime.

Even today there are many places in the world where "normal people" would happily kill you in the name of their religion if they discovered who you really are. Even in the more developed cultures of today, academia will likely scorn you; your neighbors would avoid you; lovers and spouses won't understand you; and shrinks will make far too much money trying to rid you of your "delusions" and will enrich Big Pharma still further. And the priests of at least three major religions will deride you (and some would even condemn you to death).

It's perfectly natural for reincarnates to have kept knowledge of their angelic or extraterrestrial heritage to themselves. It is dangerous knowledge. But, equally, if it feels true and helps you understand yourself and your behavior more fully, then hold the knowledge in your heart and nurture it and observe the way in which it will enrich your life. You will possibly have had flashes and insights as a child of previous lifetimes that were discounted by adults or explained away; I suggest you revisit them in your meditations. If images or visions come to you then assume they'll have something of value to pass along. If you have had previous lifetimes (which are not required of "normal" human beings) you will likely find most value in examining the manner of their deaths to understand how the unresolved issues, or the suffering, have been passed down and touch you in this life. If you are following Mein Host's chain of experiences you'll be having an opportunity to observe this in action.

I know I've said this more than once, but it's of paramount importance. Incarnate rebel angels are frequently unaware of who they are and where they come from, because you are here to live and experience a mortal life under the conditions that ultimately resulted from the choice we all made to follow Lucifer's revolution. The mortal life you are leading today is an extremely challenging experience for a reincarnated rebel angel, given the unfortunate state of the world. Your life here can be understood as a righteous blowback for having followed Lucifer into rebellion, every bit as much as it's an opportunity to experience what was sewn as a result of past choices.

In a sense, it is a path of personal redemption—and a very rich one too.

It has truly been said that "Man is the highest God"—a phrase that has been much misunderstood by humans but not by angels! As I've mentioned before, angels are not indwelt by the Creator God. The Atman, as we know, appears to be the sole privilege of all mortals of sound mind. And it's the mortal soul that ascends.

We angels do not ascend from our posts in the manner of mortals. In fact, as some of your more astute theologians have correctly surmised, it is precisely the gift of this Indwelling Spirit that was the cause of much of Lucifer's complaints. He would never have admitted it—although I can't be expected to know the mind of a System Sovereign—but some commentators have claimed that Lucifer was deeply envious of human sovereignty at the time of the revolution. Thus it was not only the freedom of choice naturally accorded to all mortal beings that Lucifer so coveted, and most likely unacknowledged by him, but an ambition to be indwelt by this Creator God he was said to have rejected. Does this mean that Lucifer too is awaiting mortal incarnation? Or, is he perhaps already in human form? Or, coming soon to a planet near you? Or, in some future time . . . no, no, I must stop this right now. Such speculations are unfair to Lucifer, and it's quite beyond my present pay grade to know or reveal such things. But I observe that this is the first time I've allowed in the thoughtform that Lucifer himself might also incarnate as a mortal.

I've been coming to understand over the course of these volumes that an opportunity to experience these human freedoms is precisely what the rebel angels are getting. Yet there is also a profound mystery unfolding here that I've no doubt will become clearer to me as my narrative continues.

* * *

It was in New Orleans that Mein Host was starting to become more aware that there was something rather different about him (as well as some of the others in the community) from almost everyone he'd met or come to know. It wasn't a new thought—I'd heard him express the sentiment a number of times before. But it was said unknowingly and from frustration. Nor did it appear to be an expression of superiority—rather the opposite. From what I observed he seemed more inclined to believe he was somehow being singled out for special punishment.

"Why would I have chosen to be born prematurely, into a war that would ensure I'd be traumatized as a child?" I'd seen him write in his journal. "What impelled me to defy authority at school so as to be constantly caught and beaten? Or to explode against Mary Ann and walk out like I did?"

With the rare exception of some, like his ex-girlfriends Jennifer and Jean, and the few people in the community he felt close to—all of whom were reincarnates without being aware of it—he was suddenly encountering more people on the streets of New Orleans with whom he was experiencing this strange and unaccountable resonance. As with the nameless young man who had engaged my ward in telepathic dialogue in the coffeehouse and then melted away, others seemed to recognize something of themselves in my ward and thought of it, perhaps, as mere charisma.

It was this factor, this charisma, that led to my ward's being appointed the one to conduct the First Progress. This was a weekly gathering held at the chapter—an evening introducing all that the Process had to offer to potential members. Whether from meeting a Processean on the streets and buying a magazine from them, or from sitting with a delicious Ogmar (precursor to the Smoothy) in the coffeehouse and being "chatted up" (their words) by a remarkably attractive young woman in a striking uniform, with sparkling eyes (and remarkably dilated pupils) and a charming manner, everyone with the least bit of interest or curiosity in the Process started off by attending the First Progress. This was the gateway to their Mystery School.

Mary Ann and Robert had just arrived in the States from Europe with all their dogs. They'd taken up residence in a fine house on the other side of Lake Pontchartrain and were just starting to play their part behind the scenes in the New Orleans Chapter. Thus I'm inclined to think it was Mary Ann's clever use of her people that resulted in my ward giving this key weekly introductory event.

It was in giving the First Progress week after week that I observed another of his subpersonalities, his alters, starting to make himself felt. This wasn't the sacrificial Gabriel Stern I'd come to readily recognize. He now only made rare appearances when Mein Host was in extremis. This personality didn't display any of my ward's natural emotional reticence or his desire to keep out of the limelight. This one was quite different.

As I observed the skill with which my ward (for whomever he is manifesting he remains my ward) managed the frequently bumptious groups attending the First Progress, I realized I'd seen this subpersonality once before. It was when my ward was fourteen years old and Diana, his mother, had arranged for him to spend a couple of weeks living with a group of about forty teenagers, all boys from all over the country, on an eighteenth-century British warship.

The magnificent old ship was safely berthed in harbor and used now, somewhat ironically, for introducing young nautical enthusiasts to a life on the ocean waves. It was clear that my ward was no particular nautical enthusiast, and he'd been surprised at his mother's choice to send him there. He'd shown no great affection for the sea and never had any interest or the opportunity to learn to sail, yet from the first day on the craft he clearly enjoyed the rough-and-ready life. He threw himself into all that was to be learned of an era in which such vessels indeed ruled the waves, winning their battles, and then serving to police the ever expanding British Empire.

Mein Host was by no means the oldest of the boys, and he certainly didn't appear the most self-confident, or the most sturdily built, so he was taken aback when, on the second day, the naval staff appointed him in overall charge of all the boys. He was to be their captain!

This was the first time my ward ever had the experience of being a leader, and I knew that leadership was not something he'd ever coveted. He'd always preferred to keep his head down. To remain unnoticed.

And yet he played the part remarkably well.

He seemed to be a natural leader.

I was astonished and a little afraid for him.

Yet he easily handled his often unruly crew by setting a rigorous example and doing this with humor and charm and, when required, with an authority that must have surprised him. However, he took it in his stride, and I don't believe he gave it much thought at the time. It would be many years before he recognized this as the doing of one of his subpersonalities.

When Mary Ann chose my ward to be in charge of the First Progress she was tapping in to the same hidden leadership potential as those who'd selected him to captain the crew. Might it be these demands from authority figures he could respect, ones urging him to step up to the plate, that created the space for this particular subpersonality to emerge? Or might it have been the subpersonality's desire for expression that was noticed and exploited by those in authority?

At around this point in time, when the Omega still knew all the members personally, instructions came down that everyone's name was to be change. Presented as a cutting off from the past identity and claiming the new, each was given two new names by Mary Ann.

So it was that my ward would now be named as Micah Ludovic. I don't think he knew what the names meant, or what Mary Ann had intended, but I heard him tell Juliette that he liked the sound of them. "They're both hard and slick names. They sound like they mean business. Nice three-syllable bounce in Lu-do-vic . . . cool, huh?"

"And Micah's pretty snappy too," agreed Juliette.

But that was only how the names sounded. There'd be another side to this Micah Ludovic identity that could never be described as pleasant. And yet it was a tribute to Mary Ann's intuitive intelligence that she knew my ward well enough to use him for her own purposes. For, yes, Micah Ludovic was smart and charming, and yes, charismatic in his way. But he was also intensely self-contained and emotionally unreachable, and he was becoming increasingly cynical and manipulative. He seemed to care little for people outside the group, and his success with the First Progress—drawing him once again back into Mary Ann's inner circle— was not endearing him to the others less favored in the Oracle's constant shuffle of affection and intimacy.

Micah Ludovic, in short, was a real piece of work.

* * *

I took some time over the following month—before I met with Astar again—to try to make more sense of what she had told me about multiple realities. Even though I was familiar with the multilayered nature of the Multiverse, the concept of different events occurring in . . . what? In parallel realities? I found that a lot harder to grasp. I kept wanting to know which of these realities was actually real.

It was frustrating, and I couldn't stop trying to puzzle it out. I constantly felt on the edge of understanding how they might function. Yet, even as I struggled with this problem, I had another of those insights that were happening with increasing regularity. So this is what it's like, I thought, to be an embodied mortal! To want to know the truth . . . to be curious! This was what it was like to feel the drive to get to the bottom of an elusive problem. It was the intensity of my curiosity that changed.

Looking back I can now see that I simply didn't have the vocabulary to describe what I was trying to understand. Had I been able to think in terms of quantum physics and the so-called many-worlds interpretation, I might at least have had the words necessary to throw some light on the mystery. I say the "words" of quantum mechanics, because for all the theory's inclusion of the observer into the equation, scarce emphasis is ever placed on the state of consciousness of the observer. After all, it's always the observer who either simply observes, or who "makes the measurement," or the one who "collapses the wave function." It will always end up with the observer.

While this isn't the place to tackle quantum mechanics and the theory's possible implications, it is helpful for me to use some of that theory's insights as I retrospectively review my thoughts during that tense month I spent roving the desolated peninsula. With this in mind, I can condense my conclusions down to a single factor.

If I give due credit to the quality of the consciousness of the observer, and when the single hypothetical observer is expanded to include a nested hierarchy of observers—each collapsing their wave functions appropriate to their responsibilities, their experience, and the quality of their consciousness—then the pieces of the puzzle have a chance to start falling into place.

As a Watcher, this seemed a reasonable assumption. I know there is a hierarchy of celestials of which I am but a lowly member. Although I was created as seraphim, when I chose to follow Lucifer and the Local System was isolated, my status changed. Prior to that I'd been trained in the arts of "mind stimulation," as well as how to promote equable social relationships by subtly supporting the moral and spiritual decisions of mortals. Like others of my kind, we thought of ourselves as extensions of the Seraphic Over-government, although in my case I was posted specifically to the Prince's staff.

That was before the troubles, of course. Now everything has changed. I could accept I was thought of as lowly by MS's agents who were making my life increasingly difficult. No, it was this new curiosity that was almost overwhelming me.

I just had to understand how it all fit together.

And it frightened me, as my ward might say, half to death.

14

Nested Hierarchies

The Watcher's Tale Continues,
Tragic Deceptions, Creation Myths,
and a Voodoo Ceremony

I wrote previously of these nested hierarchies from a celestial viewpoint as a way of trying to put words to the observer's dilemma. As I now understand it, the primary historical time line—to use the Watcher's phrase—of a planet such as Earth is driven by the choices and decisions that mortals make. On a mundane level, it's the emotional intensity of your interests and the focused value of your choices that go to shaping the reality you experience. Clearly, these decisions depend on the state of consciousness of the mortals making them.

This much should be self-evident by now.

Less obvious is how that reality is then modulated by the choices and decisions of those celestials whose function it is to further refine the primary time line to satisfy the requirements of their superiors in the Local Universe and the continuing needs of the mortals.

I can clarify this with my twist on the classic philosophical question: If a tree falls in the proverbial forest and there is no mortal present to observe it, does it mean its falling has gone unobserved by the nature spirits whose function it is to oversee the forest? Just so, when you are alone in a crowd or a desert, you are observed, and being observed you are unknowingly influenced by the observer.

In this way I was able to understand how those celestials modulating the primary time line could have chosen for their own purposes to lay greater emphasis on the story the Watcher was telling me than was placed on the reality I watched simultaneously unfolding in Dreamtime. Both realities, both stories, were equally real—yet only one of them was incorporated into the primary time line. This must have been the narrative deemed to carry the most spiritual value for the maximum number of entities, both human and celestial, and stretching into the future.

A revolution among the angels is a rare enough event. As I've already stated, the Melchizedek teach there have only been three previous rebellions in this Local Universe in all its long history. As you'll know from my narrative so far, I've been pondering whether the Lucifer Rebellion could have been covertly sanctioned from above, or if there was any degree of intentionality to what appears to be a continuing pattern of failure of MA's missions and agents. From what I was learning about the recent debacle with the off-world visitors being imprinted on the primary time line, I realized that a planet such as Earth appears to become a "teaching machine," from which other planetary civilizations can learn.

I found my musings, however, were rendered somewhat irrelevant as I surveyed the hard reality of the devastation the Nodite tribes had made of the visitors' beautiful garden. When I inquired as to the direct cause of this I was surprised to hear it had been started by the actions of some of the followers of the visitors. Apparently, after these followers had seen the deplorable state of their once-magnificent leaders and learned of the betrayal, they had run amok. They were so infuriated by what they saw as a Nodite conspiracy to subvert the visitors' mission that they had swept out over the broken and battered wall like a swarm of vigilantes. In a mad bloodlust, they completely obliterated the nearby Nodite settlements, murdering every man, woman, and child they could find.

The victims were not only innocent of any conspiracy against the visitors' mission, but the nearby Nodite villages had largely overcome their tribal loyalties and were enjoying bonds of affection with the visitors' followers as well as building trusted trading alliances. They knew nothing of Serapatatia. As far as they were aware, they were on the warmest of terms with the visitors—so much so that there was a constant trickle of their young people "crossing the wall," as they called it, to join the visitors' training programs.

When the maddened hordes poured into their villages, the attacks caught the villagers entirely by surprise. Many families were burned alive in their tents and reed-roofed huts. Those lucky enough to escape immolation staggered about in the smoke, bewildered by fear and horror, until they were cut down and killed without mercy.

I managed to thread together the facts of these atrocities from the little I was able to overhear as I moved around the peninsula. I gathered it was only when the rampaging horde had returned from the slaughter that the full impact of what they'd done came home to them. They felt so deeply ashamed of themselves for betraying the visitors' nonviolent principles that they were trying to banish any mention of the bloodbath.

The visitors, of course, were utterly horrified by the atrocities. That they believed themselves to be the cause of the mindless violence, coupled with their inability to do anything to stop it, must have compounded dreadfully on the misery they were already feeling.

Yet there was clearly no time for self-pity.

Everything the pair had labored to build over this past century was falling apart all around them—and now they had to deal with their followers' orgy of indiscriminate killing. Both of them had been appalled at the massacres and were harshly blaming themselves for losing control of their faithful followers. They'd been preaching peace, mutual respect, and cooperation for the past hundred years—and here were their followers running amok, slaughtering entire families.

The visitors felt that their sacred principles had been betrayed by their followers as much as they themselves had betrayed MA's sacred trust. Then, on top of that shock, the visitors would have to have known there would be terrible repercussions when the main Nodite tribes learned of the massacres of their brothers. I believe it was this threat that the visitors took as a sign to leave the peninsula and their beautiful garden behind without putting up a fight.

The gossip I overheard between two of the highborn faithful confirmed this. They'd both been in the inner circle of the visitors and had attended them throughout the recent troubles. When I came across them, they were languishing in prison, having been injured during the fighting when the Nodites counterattacked. Of course, they didn't know I was listening to their conversation.

The visitors were painfully aware that the carnage would just be the start of a pattern of violent retribution, of revenge killing, of eyes for eyes and teeth for teeth, a pattern they knew would repeat itself down through history in an endless succession of ethnic cleansings, pogroms, and genocides.

As if to add to the female visitor's woes, I heard that the lover she'd been persuaded to take by Serapatatia had been among those killed by the mob when they swarmed the nearby settlements. This appeared to be sheer coincidence, because it was the first time he had gone to that particular settlement to visit a distant relative, a cousin he'd never met, who'd been living and building a trading network there. They'd both been hacked to death and their bodies burned along with those of most of the traders' wives and children.

The visitors' decision to leave the peninsula had, by all accounts, created even further division among their followers. Some had angrily rejected the visitors' nonviolent retreat as cowardice and vowed to stay to try to repulse the inevitable Nodite invasion. A smaller group remained loyal to the visitors and were said to have left in the same caravan on their long journey eastward to find a new home.

I saw devastation and destruction all around me: the beautiful buildings were rubble, the visitors' ambitious horticultural projects were returning to the wild, and, most surprisingly, every tree in and surrounding what was left of their compound had been completely stripped of its leaves and fruit. These were all sights that unexpectedly ripped at my heart. I found it particularly painful to observe this desecration of nature in midsummer, when the trees should have been strong and healthy and covered with leaves and berries.

That was as much as I discovered before I met up once again with my sister Watcher at the full of the moon. I knew I could rely on her for more personal details if I could learn to be patient with her condescension.

"The fools!" the Watcher interrupted, scorn dripping from her words. I hadn't sensed her presence. My thoughts about her must have drawn her in.

"Of course the Nodite aristocracy knew about the tree! Everyone did! But they didn't know which one it was!" she ended with a snort.

It was when I was thinking about those stripped and dying trees that she must have picked up my concerns again.

So that's what the Nodites must have been after! The "Tree of Life," the visitors called it. They were always protective of it. The visitors were the only ones ever permitted to eat its fruit. Of course that very prohibition was temptation enough for the word to get around about this "immortality tree." They all wanted a taste of *that*!

"Those foolish people!" the Watcher sneered again. "They thought they'd be immortal too if they ate the fruit of that tree. Thought they'd live forever, like the visitors. Except they didn't know which tree it was!" There was more caustic laughter from the Watcher.

"But even if they did," I replied, "the fruit wouldn't have any effect on them, right?"

"They didn't have the visitors' biology," she agreed. "The fruit would never work with normal mortals. Also some of the fools fell sick and died eating poisonous leaves of the other trees . . . that put off a lot of them."

As the Nodite bloodline was descended directly from Nodu, one of the leaders of the rebel Nephilim had made sure the history of the original Tree of Life had been kept alive by the Nodite priests. When the Nodite aristocracy discovered there was another of these legendary immortality trees in the visitors' garden, not a tree there would be safe.

We laughed together at their muddled thinking. We both knew that a specific chemical in this Tree of Life was the causative agent that allowed for immortality. As was true with the Prince's staff before the revolution, when the visitors with their especially prepared bodies ate its fruit, its chemistry interlocked with specific cosmic frequencies in their bodies, thus ensuring their continued longevity.

In the staff's case, it was MA's decision to cut off those specific frequencies after the rebellion that led to the deaths of the erstwhile immortal rebel staff. It was their immensely long lifetimes, more than their superhuman attributes, which led them to be remembered as the Nephilim.

It is in the Book of Enoch that the Nephilim have been inaccurately called "Watchers" and identified, again inaccurately, as fallen angels. Not true. Fallen they may have been, but the Nephilim were no angels. Enoch then further muddies the waters by claiming it was these "fallen angels" who mated with the "daughters of men."

All quite impossible had they been angels.

The Nephilim were MA's agents, granted, but they were most definitely not of angelic heritage. They may well have been given superhuman vehicles of extraordinary longevity, but the rebel Nephilim proved to be all too human.

Watchers—fallen rebel angels such as myself, as I've said before—are incapable of mating with mortals, even if we so desired, until, of course, we are incarnated as mortals. But I wondered what it would be like and pondered how the female visitor must have felt having Cano for a sexual partner, if only for that one night's coupling. My thoughts next turned to the ramifications of her actions, and with this I heard the Watcher's voice once more.

"It astonished all of us who were observing it," Astar began. "When the male visitor grasped what his mate did, that she'd doomed the whole mission, he still could have walked away. He'd known nothing of what she and the Nodites were cooking up behind his back. Serapatatia hadn't told him about the scheme. He was completely innocent in the eyes of MA's courts. He could have taken the first transport back to Jerusem and washed his hands of the whole affair. That's what *I'd* have done!"

She paused to let me take that in.

"Do you know what he did?" She still couldn't quite believe it herself. "Can you imagine? He went right out and screwed a young native girl for himself . . ."

"In revenge? To get back at his wife?" I was just as surprised. He must have known that meant certain death.

Astar laughed, a dry scratching in my mind. "I thought that to start with. But, no! He did it for love! For love! Can you imagine?!"

"He loved the girl?" I queried. This was getting hard to believe.

"No, no, not the girl. His mate!" Astar said, mildly irritated. Then her tone turned wistful. "He must've really, really, loved her. He said he couldn't imagine wanting to go on living without her. Of course he *didn't* love the *girl*. It wasn't vengeance; that wasn't it."

It seemed Astar couldn't help making me feel like a simpleton. Was *that* how I made others feel? I hoped not. I would have stopped her if I hadn't been so interested in what I was hearing.

"I heard him claim that if his mate was going to die . . ." she paused, and I heard the crinkle of disbelief in her tone when she continued. "He said then he was going to die right alongside her. So that's what he did. He went out and deliberately had intercourse with the girl . . . all for the love of his mate. So that they'd face mortal death together. Can you believe it?"

I was curious. "Was this after Solonia had spoken the law to them back in the garden?"

Astar inclined her head.

I took that as encouragement. "So, he knew the consequences of following his mate's lead?"

"Of course he knew!" she said. "That's why he did it!"

I felt that cutting scorn again. I'm sure she was as flabbergasted when she first saw this happening as I was at hearing it. You must understand, the visitor's action really was hard for us to believe. I'd certainly never observed such a profound act of love and compassion among individuals of the mortal races in all my time on the planet. And, now that I think about it, I'd never seen anything like this from among the populace of Zandana. I suspect they might consider such altruism absurdly sentimental.

Yet given the unfortunate state of Caligastia's world, such an act of selfless love would have shone like a single rose in a burned and blackened landscape. So yes, my sister was right. There really was a delicate poignancy here that I might well have missed in surveying the catastrophe.

"And then he disappeared!" she said triumphantly. "He went on a walkabout. From new moon to new moon. No one knew where he'd gone. She almost went mad with worry and guilt. It wasn't pretty."

It must have been a terrible time for his mate. She'd dragged the whole mission down on both of their heads. And they were unlikely to have another opportunity.

"Serapatatia's drowning himself didn't help."

This bit hit home. I hadn't heard what happened.

"The very next day," she said proudly. "When he heard what had happened in the garden. What Solonia had told the visitors got around like wildfire."

"But didn't you say Serapatatia was innocent?"

"Innocent, no," she said firmly. "All I said was that he truly believed his plan was noble and good. He was in complete support."

This time it was my turn to pause.

I had to admire the Prince's cunning. He must have been setting up the deception ever since those first visits he'd made to the visitors' compound. He'd have been probing the pair for any weakness he could exploit. He would easily have read the female's impatience and ambition and must have started to concoct his plan as early as that. And Serap? When did he come into play?

"They'd no idea!" Astar answered my thought. "Neither of them. And Serap, even when he killed himself, still didn't know Caligastia had been using him."

"Did the visitors know they'd been duped by the Prince?"

"Oh yes!" she said with a cackle that made no pretense where her sympathies lay. "Oh dear me, yes! Solonia made it very clear. Up until then I think they were both in denial . . . she was, anyway. Until Solonia, it felt to me like she was still hoping MA would see the good sense of what she'd done. Or at least that Solonia would dismiss the whole affair when she heard it was really Serap's idea."

"Some chance!" I said, trying to match her cackle.

But even though I was laughing, I wasn't happy.

Perhaps I should have been reveling in another of Caligastia's strategic triumphs—he was my titular superior, after all. Oh yes! And the God of this World!

I just couldn't do it. I couldn't control the sense of sadness that seemed to come out of nowhere and almost overwhelm me. I tried to mask the emotion before the Watcher picked up on it, but when I turned back to her she'd slipped away as silently as she'd arrived.

The moon stood high overhead as I sat on, pondering what I'd just learned. I hoped she hadn't made too much of my uncertainty and, if she had, that she wouldn't report it back to Caligastia. I had to remind myself that I had spoken highly of the Prince's patience and cunning.

It was an unspoken rule among us Watchers that we didn't inform our superiors about one another, but I could never be quite sure who abided by this and who didn't. Caligastia had his special agents everywhere. He maintained the psychic ability that all Planetary Princes possess and was able to activate any one of his Watchers at any time. We follow his instructions implicitly—because it's our function to do so. We have little choice in such matters.

For reasons I'd been unable to understand at the time, I hadn't yet been drawn that closely into the Prince's web. I had never yet been activated, for example, despite hearing something of this activation from other Watchers who'd spoken of being temporarily possessed by the Prince. They told me they never knew when it was going to befall them. And sometimes the possession was so subtle, so aligned with their own intentions, that they were unaware it was occurring until after the Prince had withdrawn his presence.

One of them told me she never felt as though Caligastia was forcing her to any action on his behalf. No indeed, nothing so obvious. "He plays on our angelic natures," she continued with a slight simper, "on our joy to be of service and our desire for order. However distasteful the tasks he might set us, when he activates us we feel this pleasant sense of satisfaction and find ourselves devoted to accomplishing the objectives."

I knew that for all of Caligastia's power over us, he could only activate and work through one of us at a time. The instruction I received from him some time ago to track down the location of the recently arrived offworld visitors could barely be called an activation. I had taken my time to fulfill the mission, and I certainly wasn't touched by any mysterious sense of satisfaction on accomplishing it.

I recall fervently hoping the Prince wasn't holding back my activation for some particularly heinous activity of his in the future.

I have to admit the idea terrified me.

* * *

It was clear to me that Mein Host was happy and relieved to be free of Catherine and her son. The last few months in Chicago before being transferred to New Orleans had been among the most trying of his young life.

Catherine held him responsible for having her "dumped in a public hospital" for the birth of the child. This wasn't true. The decision had nothing to do with him, but, nevertheless, her blame would rise to the surface in rows and constant quibbling. I've no need to record the substance of their rows or the suppressed silence of their truces; they are not hard to imagine. Nor did he and Catherine have the solace of sexual intimacy on which to fall back, as would most loving parents, because by this time both had their reasons for heartily disliking the other. They'd had little choice but to share a bed, with the baby in his crib at its foot, but neither of them had shown any interest in renewing their sexual relationship. It was never to be one of those situations in which the birth of a child was destined to draw its parents closer together.

While I'm sure this period was as trying for Catherine as it was for my ward, his intuitive sense that the child was not his and that he was not being told the whole truth clearly persisted in troubling him. While I am proud he never used this against his wife in their rows—it would have been far too hurtful for Catherine—I could see from the state of his emotional body that it never stopped worrying him. He tells me he now feels it was his emotional immaturity that had prevented him from overcoming his self-concern and restrained him from expressing more love for the child.

However, I should also mention what he has sensed intuitively since becoming an adult: that he was never intended to have children. He wasn't to know this consciously, but this had been agreed upon in his pre-incarnational life-planning discussion. It has held true to this day, despite an active and generally unprotected sex life. There have been no unwanted pregnancies and no children.

Although my ward had no conscious memory of the pre-incarnational discussion—and wouldn't have for many years—he would have been subconsciously aware of this decision. While this doesn't justify Mein Host's indifference toward the baby, it does help explain his reluctance to ever fully own the child as his son. I've heard him since claim that he simply couldn't force himself to do it—that he'd be living a lie and, as mentioned previously, usurping the role of the true father.

Naturally, Catherine interpreted this disinclination as a personal insult, both as a vulnerable woman who'd just given birth and as someone who had knowingly lied about her child's conception. She was a proud, highborn young woman who had been indulged over the course of her life by those with no investment in exposing her deceptions, and as a consequence she'd become a consummate liar. She'd grown up with no sense of moral direction from her con man father and even less loving attention from her alcoholic mother, so it's scarce wonder by this time that Catherine believed her own lies.

However, the predicament in which she now found herself was sorely testing her already unbalanced state of mind. She'd been instructed by Mary Ann to tell my ward that he was the father of the child while concealing what would turn out to be the source of the child's true paternity. To give the young woman dubious credit, I've no doubt that the Oracle's instruction encouraged her to believe her lies were for the best of all, which for liars is not so different from believing they are telling the truth.

Yet despite her efforts to convince him the child was his, Mein Host's quite evident lack of fatherly spirit became, for Catherine, a constant reminder of her duplicity—which then in turn further infuriated her. (There seems to be nothing that enrages liars more than being disbelieved when they think they're telling the truth!)

You can, I trust, appreciate the delicacy of this matter for a young woman who already possessed a somewhat tenuous grip on the truth before joining the community. For example, had she *really* killed her mother? And if she hadn't, why would she want to make such a callous claim? And, to Mein Host's knowledge, she never denied it.

If it appears I've dwelled too long on the confusion engendered by Mary Ann's deceptive manipulation as well as Catherine's willingness to play along with the Oracle's lie, it has been to sketch out just one of a number of equally confused situations. These will arise with increasing frequency as more children will be born to members of the Process community, some under just as uncertain circumstances.

And these uncertain circumstances?

I hope you, patient reader, won't feel unfairly treated if I hold back that information for now. I'm not trying to create a mystery so much as doing my best to avoid getting ahead of myself—a constant temptation, as I'm sure you'll have noticed. Although mine is a narrative approach, I have already transgressed with regards to what my ward knew of Mary Ann's past. In the case of Catherine's claim of her child's paternity, the truth took so long to emerge that to reveal it now would throw little light on the couple's subsequent behavior.

So it was that when Mein Host was transferred to New Orleans he knew nothing of how he'd been deceived and had only his intuition to whisper that something very wrong was going on behind his back. It would take him many years, long after he'd left the community, to disentangle all the lies and finally learn who the child's true father really is.

New Orleans kept my ward sufficiently busy that his distressing marital situation was the last thing appearing to trouble his mind. If he thought about it at all it was only with the pleasure of being out of it.

The Royal Street Process coffeehouse was becoming known as a haven for young people of a more serious bent. Many of the men were facing the draft and were trying to come to terms with a decision that, whatever they chose—the military or an uncertain future in Canada or Sweden— would forever change the trajectory of their lives, if it didn't kill them.

The intensity of the era added a life-or-death quality to the animated discussions taking place in the Cavern. It forced young Americans to confront for the first time the hypocrisy of the power elite and the corruption at the heart of American politics. The assassination of President Kennedy four years earlier had briefly threatened to expose the malevolent currents running beneath the surface of political life, only to be prevented by a brutal cleanup of the loose ends. The Warren Commission's findings may have reassured the older generation, but, for the more attentive and intelligent among the young, the killing of the president under such transparently suspicious circumstances opened their eyes to the reality of criminal misconduct at the highest levels. The murders of Martin Luther King and Robert Kennedy in the spring and summer of 1968, both sadly the result of high-level conspiracies, merely reinforced their mistrust of authority. The justifications the government was making for the war were becoming increasingly tenuous and unrealistic, as the body count was rising day by day. It was the first war to be widely televised and, with a TV in almost every home, no future soldiers had any doubt as to what awaited them when they were called up for service.

As can frequently happen when humans first realize how deeply corrupt the state of their leadership actually is, the future can appear so bleak that any demand to contribute to its continuance can feel like a betrayal of conscience. I know it's a deeply unsettling revelation to know so many of your political leaders have only their self-interest at heart. It was the inverse of such a dilemma that we who followed Lucifer into revolution had to wrestle with when MA's agents sought to persuade us of Lucifer's madness.

It is such a harsh and unpalatable vision for a species whose animal nature is to instinctively trust strong leadership that few people will have the stomach to dig much deeper. Thus it is perhaps fortunate that they are unlikely to discover that the power elites of the contemporary world have been in thrall, mostly unknowingly, of Prince Caligastia, self-proclaimed God of this World, for more than 200,000 years.

The level of the corruption seems to be so unsettling that a glimpse is sufficient for most people to close down to the awful possibility that they are being duped and therefore choose to maintain a state of denial. Some are so horrified by what they find out that they believe the only solution is violently opposing the powers that be. These were the people who joined militant groups like the Weathermen and the Black Panthers.

For other young people in the 1960s that brief and ugly glimpse beneath the surface of life was enough for them to reevaluate their allegiances and turn their backs on their families and social obligations. These were the beatniks and hippies of the late sixties, the ones who dropped out of straight society. They tended to be sexually liberated, resolutely individualistic, suspicious of authority, and frequently too distracted by utopian delusions to summon the enthusiasm and self-discipline necessary to become a member of a Mystery School. But they were all too happy to find refuge in the Process coffeehouse, to sip their herbal teas, smoke their incessant cigarettes, and endlessly discuss the inequities of a society they'd both rejected and yet on which they still depended.

Finally, there were those who were perceptive enough of the world to understand the scope of the tragedy and had no illusions about the depth of the corruption and greed that permeated the political classes in the Western cultures. It was largely from among these few who could see the world clearly and were starting to become overwhelmed by what seemed to be a future without hope that the Process was collecting its American followers.

* * *

If there are those who are curious as to why I would choose to concentrate on the sad story of the visitors and the apparent failure of their mission, the reason is that I have the benefit of some retrospective understanding.

Surveying the primary historical time line of the planet as it extends back 500,000 years, as I'm attempting to do here, I find there are a number of fundamentally key circumstances that have further tilted the deck in Prince Caligastia's favor. These are the events to which I have needed to pay most attention if I wish to clarify for myself the various events that have led so irrevocably to the present times.

I have also learned enough by this time to know that my interpretation of these incidents, or indeed the very choice of one incident rather than another, is personal. Therefore, this review should be taken simply as my interpretation. Of course there have been other key events that have occurred, which I have not described in this narrative, because either I wasn't present for them or because the impact of the events themselves haven't risen to a sufficient level of global significance. Naturally such events as these will have been observed and recorded by other agents with their own priorities.

You will have to decide for yourself which resonates most strongly with your own Spirit of Truth.

Here I can only confirm what must have been obvious: the narrative I've been relating has descended into the modern era as the biblical story of Adam and Eve—and has become something of profound consequence in the mythic history of your species.

Creation myths are curious affairs. They both shape the cultures that create them, and at the same time they also reflect some of the deepest fears and prejudices of those cultures. The traditional Adam and Eve story lays the blame for the Fall on Eve's behavior, thus giving formal religious authority to the subsequent second-class status of women. And then, by casting Adam and Eve as the first humans, the myth as interpreted by Christian dogma portrays every subsequent human being as inherently sinful. And in what now would be thought of as a blatant act of gender discrimination Eve, and therefore all women, become the source of this sinfulness.

Not only is the very idea absurd and an obvious piece of priestcraft, but it also seeks to legitimize the inferior role of women by giving it the divine stamp of approval. Yet it is an unfortunate truth that women have been subjugated by men in almost all cultures throughout the world—and have always been—long before the Genesis account became the West's sanctified justification for degrading women. Contemporary feminists may be disappointed to hear that it was simply men's relatively larger size and greater strength, coupled with their independence from child-bearing that, with very few exceptions, has invariably permitted men to dominate women. It is only when a culture achieves a certain degree of maturity that the issue of gender disparity even comes up for discussion—and there have been few enough of those cultures over the history of the planet.

Within the larger context of my examination, the Adam and Eve of whom I speak were most definitely not the original humans of biblical repute. If that was so it would imply the human race was a mere 38,000 years old—which is at least a small improvement over the 6,000 years that some biblical fundamentalists believe to be the age of the planet.

However limited their understanding may be, such fundamentalists are correct to believe that the traditional story of Adam and Eve was an extremely significant event in human history. They are correct too in their belief that choices were made that turned out to have a profoundly disturbing impact on the course of human development. While these two factors are perfectly true, the arrival and the very existence of Adam and Eve was a far stranger and more complex affair than the children's story sketched out in the Bible. Their failure, if that is what is was, lay not so much in some sexual indiscretion or betrayal of trust, although that too occurred, but in the minimal amount of violet blood that had entered the human genome and the consequent imbalance this has produced in the evolving human races.

When the visitors left the peninsula there were only four genera-tions of pureblood offspring, comprised of some sixteen hundred indi-viduals. Two-thirds of these chose to take up the Melchizedek's offer to be returned to Jerusem rather than remain on the planet with their disgraced forebears. Thus, rather than the hundreds of thousands of pure violet-blood offspring spread all over the world interbreeding with the different human races, there were less than six hundred direct descendants of the visitors left to fulfill their genetic mission.

Yet it is also true that with even the extremely limited amount of violet blood that was ultimately to enter the veins of the local Nodite tribes, the impact the visitors and their progeny have made on human development has far outweighed their limited numbers.

Although I included something of my Watcher friend Astar's admiration for the cunning efficiency with which Caligastia had subverted the visitors' mission, I didn't share it. The truth was that the whole situation was a miserable failure, with continuously regrettable consequences. Even that tiny amount of violet blood worked its way into the bloodlines of primarily the Nodite aristocracy. Astar had been correct when she told me the Nodites couldn't be trusted to keep it to one bloodline. Yet it was still a rare gift that brought with it a significant boost to both intelligence and their immune systems.

The preservation of these limited genetic bloodlines became of almost pathological concern to the various highborn clans who spread throughout the Middle East, into the Indian subcontinent, and up into southern Europe. They intermarried; they formed truces and alliances; they raised armies and fought each other; and they pushed farther and farther into territories previously held by the far less aggressive Neanderthal tribes. Within 15,000 years almost all of the Neanderthals had been wiped out. With the exception of small clans of Neanderthals who'd lived on, escaping detection by living in inaccessible caves, these new men and women, with the gift of a splash of violet blood, came to dominate life throughout much of the European Continent, and stretched through to the Near and Middle East.

Adam and Eve, our two once-illustrious, off-world visitors, now also deprived of their immortality, and along with some of their younger offspring and their followers, trekked east from the Mediterranean across the desert. A year of hard traveling later, they arrived and set up their new encampment in a fertile area between the Tigris and Euphrates Rivers.

The local nomadic tribes, on learning of the influx of this clan of godlike, blond-haired, "blue-eyed demons," fled from the area and continued to avoid it until they were finally befriended by descendants of the visitors.

The pair lived remarkably long lives and had another crop of more than sixty children, who themselves had children and grandchildren. The two original visitors tried their best to make their amends and redeem themselves before both died thoroughly mortal deaths. Their descendants lived out their long lives, interbreeding with the indigenous tribes and, in contrast with the earlier Nodite disaster, seeking to spread the genetic gift as widely as possible.

If I've compressed the last stages of this unfortunate affair into a few paragraphs it has to be because at that time I became terribly confused. I'm afraid I lost my composure. I didn't have the heart to follow the caravan to the Euphrates, or take the time to observe the visitors settling into their new place. I felt the last fragment of joy slipping away—a joy that's the natural spiritual heritage of all angels. Even those of us who are said to have defaulted on our responsibilities are able to retain some semblance of that original joy. But when I observed the terrible dejection that followed the collapse of the visitors' mission, I felt myself drawn down into an unfamiliar and terrifyingly dark place.

I think it was then that I slid into what I've since learned was a state of mental depression that, if painful for a human, was pure torture for a Watcher. I had no doubt it was precipitated by the mix of unaccustomed emotional reactions I was having on hearing about the collapse of the visitor's mission and then observing for myself the distressing consequences. I felt trapped in this overwhelming pit of utter hopelessness—when I should have been exulting at Caligastia's successful sabotage. Yet I simply couldn't take any pleasure in it. I felt there was something happening that was desperately out of balance, something terribly wrong.

Besides, this wasn't the reason I'd aligned myself with Lucifer's cause! This wasn't why I'd signed up! This wasn't the greater freedom promised for all beings! This was the greater freedom being used for malice and trickery and for personal ends of those in power.

This was a world that was rapidly becoming the sole province of Prince Caligastia and the rebel midwayers. With the potential genetic impact of the violet blood so radically minimized, Caligastia had little difficulty in coopting and corrupting almost all of the primary bloodlines in what I had to admit was an increasingly naked lust for total power.

Prince Caligastia had long proclaimed himself God of this World, and now it seemed to me he was intent on making absolutely sure that human beings knew it. The Prince's previous attempt to unify humans under his direct "divine authority" had resulted in the terrible war that had devastated much of North Africa and the Middle East some forty-five thousand years earlier. I had a sense the Prince wasn't going to make the same mistake twice.

I'm embarrassed now to admit how filled with self-pity I was, but I really didn't know which way to turn, or quite how I'd got myself into this wretched mess. Whether it was my desire to avoid the emotional agony I was experiencing or the accompanying obsessive thought that I may have condemned myself to an eternity of uncertainty and despair through my affiliation with the Prince, I could take the stress and strain no more.

The last thing I recall was a feeling I'd never experienced before. It was as though I was fading out—as if I were becoming invisible to myself. It was not an altogether disagreeable feeling, if only because it relieved me of the horrible, out-of-control, spiritual pain I had been experiencing.

When I found myself restored to full consciousness I discovered I'd been transported back to the Islands of Mu through no volition of my own.

I certainly felt clearer of mind and was momentarily grateful for that. Yet when I recalled the predicament in which I'd previously left Vanu and Amadon and the people of Lemuria, I almost fell back into the black depression.

I'm happy to say I was in for an unexpected surprise.

* * *

Mein Host hadn't been in New Orleans more than three weeks when the strangest story filtered down to him from the Chicago Chapter, one that cast yet further light on Catherine's unusually disturbed state of mind.

Those first few weeks had been a happy time for my ward. He was clearly popular with the others, and his moneymaking abilities always made him an asset to any chapter. I believe his relief at being away from Catherine and the baby was soon eclipsed by the more genuine pleasure of being in a city in which he clearly felt increasingly at home and at ease.

I'd have thought, therefore, that it would have been all the more shocking for him when he was shown a letter written by his friend Chris, the head of the Chicago Chapter. Yet he seemed wholly unfazed, even amused, by the curious story. The letter hadn't been sent to my ward but to Wendy, the young matriarch we've met before when she dispatched Mein Host and her protégé Nick off to Sicily, and who'd been appointed the head of the New Orleans Chapter.

The note was short and to the point.

Catherine had been discovered a few days prior at around two o'clock in the morning, long after everyone had gone to bed, in the basement of the Chicago Chapter house. Apparently she'd been found in the dark, lit only by the flickering flames of the white candles surrounding her.

Then there was a joke in the letter about the clouds of incense being so thick (it had been the smell drifting up to the bedrooms that had alerted them) that it was next to impossible for Chris to make out what was happening. He wrote that he'd tiptoed down the stairs and made his way gingerly through the smoke without Catherine hearing him, and having no idea what he was going to find.

When he'd got closer, and the billowing smoke had cleared enough so he was able to see, he found Catherine in a long white nightdress, in what might have been a light trance. She was muttering incantations and was sticking needles into a small wax figurine, which she admitted later she'd molded in the likeness of her husband, my ward. She was practicing Voodoo magic on him! If she wasn't attempting to kill him, she was certainly trying everything she could to make his life as painful as possible.

When Wendy had finished reading the letter she looked over at Mein Host with a leer in her smile. I knew the woman enjoyed a good gossip, and this was obviously a rare and juicy piece of scuttlebutt—too good not to relish. Even I, who've witnessed some bizarre behavior in my time by mortals on all of two worlds . . . even I found myself taken aback by the strangeness of it. He was aware he hadn't treated Catherine particularly well, but he clearly had no idea it had become this bad for her.

"Well, I knew she didn't like me . . ." my ward said with a bemused look at Wendy. "I didn't much like her myself! But this? No, I never imagined she'd do something like this . . . it's weird!"

"Has she ever talked about doing something like this before?"

"Never. This is something out of the blue." My ward was shaking his head while replying, and I could feel his genuine bewilderment. "It was a difficult situation, you knew that, right?"

Wendy lit a cigarette and smiled with encouragement.

On hearing that I thought of course she would have known about the state of their relationship. She probably knew more about it than Mein Host, who seemed to have put any painful thoughts of Catherine aside soon after arriving in New Orleans.

In close communities, word of troubled relationships travels fast. Any such news tends to feed the ever present impulse to analyze and endlessly discuss the psychic, psychological, and spiritual implications of every word and action in question. As communities in general are, at their very essence, about relationship, about human interactions under a wide variety of challenging circumstances, there should be nothing unusual in this. However, gossiping was generally not encouraged among well-mannered young English girls and boys from good middle-class homes and university educations. Thus, framing gossip within a psychotherapeutic context had become an acceptable way of indulging in it. In fact, many of the discussions I've overheard under these conditions were so overloaded with Process terms that they were all but unintelligible to the uninitiated.

In my opinion this was an unnecessary pretension, and they all knew it. Such heady talk was really only the emotional need to gossip dressed up in whatever fancy jargon currently in vogue with the community. There need be no shame in this, as gossip has always been an integral part of communal life. But early habits are evidently hard to break. The shame associated with "talking behind someone's back," drilled into well-bred young English schoolchildren at their boarding schools, would never entirely disappear, however artfully camouflaged it might be by clever rhetoric and perceptive observations.

Mary Ann, in turn, was never burdened with such tepid middle-class reticence. By this time she was entirely dependent on the gossip relayed to her by her inner circle—although they'd have thought of it as verbal reports—about what was going on with various individuals in the Process chapters. In fact, it was largely through the Oracle's example that the urge to gossip (yet always remembering to frame it in arcane Process precepts) would come to be a continuing pattern, which only became more abstruse with the development of the group's increasingly complex religious terminology.

Yet it did create a secret language of sorts, a way of viewing and interpreting the world, which distinguished the Elect from the uninitiated herd. It also served to bond them into an illusory sense of shared identity and a common cause.

"After I wasn't there for Catherine at the hospital . . ." Mein Host was telling Wendy ". . . at least that's what she accused me of . . . it just got worse and worse. Then, after being stuck in that little room together with the kid shrieking and everyone blaming us for keeping them awake . . ."

"But needles? Sticking needles into a doll of you?" Wendy wasn't going to let it go. "That's pretty extreme! You must have done something to deserve that!"

"I've no idea." My ward was shaking his head, bemused again. "It could have been anything. I'm sure I didn't treat her well. I know that. Probably wasn't just one thing, just a whole pileup of stuff. I'm more sorry for her than anything."

"Didn't you love the baby?" Wendy was pressing deeper. "Couldn't you at least have kept the peace for his sake?"

"It was nothing to do with him, poor little creature," he admitted. "It was all between Catherine and me. Of course we tried to keep the noise down. It was just an impossible situation. You know what a hot-tempered girl she is . . . it was a lot harder for her than me . . ."

"Well trained in the arts of suppression, as you are," Wendy replied with a smirk; she knew her Englishmen.

"Seriously, I'd no idea it was that bad for her. But needles in the basement?! Really?!" They were both laughing by this time. It was just *too* absurd.

"And you know what? I never felt a thing!" More laughter. "Nothing! Not a pinprick. I haven't even thought much about the girl since I've been here."

"Perhaps she was just practicing!" Wendy couldn't help blurting out between giggles. "Perhaps she hadn't got to the good part yet!"

In spite of the weirdness of Catherine's position—after all, what do you do with someone caught in the act of voodoo witchery?—I'd noticed before this tendency of the matriarchs to stick together, however outlandish the reasons. I assumed it was a sisterhood sympathy.

But apart from that there was something else rather more dishonest happening on Wendy's part. What Mein Host wasn't to know throughout this exchange was that Wendy had been part of the discussion back in London about what to do with the pregnant Catherine. So Wendy would have known about the unusual circumstances of the child's conception, as much as she was aware of the fact that the child was unlikely to be my ward's son.

In addition to Wendy, there was of course Diana, my ward's stalwart mother, to be taken into account. Like all mothers, Diana was thrilled to learn of her first (and only) grandson. She'd been as surprised to hear the news of the baby as she had been to learn about her son's marriage but was predictably delighted at the prospect of a grandchild.

When the child was born Diana must have been overjoyed. As the oldest of three sisters herself, with the younger two sisters already blessed with grandchildren, Diana was bound to have felt an extra touch of satisfaction. Although very different, the three sisters loved one another but with that slight competitive edge found in some families.

As Mein Host settled into a busy life in the New Orleans Chapter of the Process, this business of Diana and her grandson would become just one of the challenges facing him as the community grew rapidly in size and influence.

In my ward's opinion the community was once a Mystery School; soon it would become a religion. A religion, no less! All official and now called The Process Church of the Final Judgment.

"A church! For heaven's sake!" My ward couldn't help a wry snort at the irony of it.

The community's new name and official position sounded like just the sort of organized religious institution that had turned my ward in to an atheist in the first place.

I could only wonder at what was going to happen next.

Unknown Territory

Catching Alight and
the Emergent Wisdom of the Watchers

When I started working with Georgia on her *Confessions of a Rebel Angel* I had no idea it would turn out to be a multi-volume labor of love; and I certainly didn't anticipate that she would be exploring the past history of the planet in such detail or with quite the passion she brings with her evident need to unravel the many competing threads that weave through Earth's prehistory. And I say she has a "need" rather than merely a passing interest in unraveling those pesky threads, because that's how it feels to me. She really *needs* to do this. And this is why the impulse to carry this project through to wherever it leads us feels so much in Georgia's hands. Perhaps I should have known better!

When Georgia and I began the first volume together the process of writing was itself so fascinating and I was learning so much that I paid scant attention to where our collaboration might be leading us. I'd already had some inkling of the immense time spans involved from my reading of *The Urantia Book*. That I came to intuitively find the book authentic had allowed me a broad appreciation of those thousands of millennia prior to recorded history, when human beings not so very unlike us were living out their lives as best they could under the most difficult of circumstances.

The Urantia Book, and what it revealed, was something of a personal revelation to me. I'd always had, as long as I recall, the uneasy feeling that something had gone desperately awry at some point in Earth's history. Possibly being born in a war may have initially prejudiced me, but as I grew up and came to know better the ways of the world I found no reason to change my opinion. Something must have gone horribly wrong; I had nothing on which to base this uncomfortable feeling, but the recurrence of the thought that this just cannot be the best way for a planet to be organized and managed has never left me.

An amorphous and admittedly naive thought perhaps, yet any reasonable assessment of just the past four or five thousand years of which we have some historical knowledge points to something being already deeply amiss and throwing its shadow over all human activities.

I began to realize this uneasy feeling might have its roots in an actual event when I started coming across references in so many different ancient cultures of what can be characterized as the "War in Heaven." I remember thinking that if Heaven itself is at war then what kind of chance did we have? It was a horrible reality, made worse by an equally persistent and disturbing feeling that I may have had some hand in it. I'm aware that this must sound pretentious and a bit silly, yet although the feeling persisted, it never rose to delusions of persecution or self-importance but simply remained in the back of my mind.

I've since learned that a number of people who've used entheogens as tools for self-knowledge have also encountered somewhat the same sense of errors made in some distant past for which we now have a chance to redeem ourselves. Where this insight sprung from, and what the idea of redemption might entail, are just two of the developing themes in these books.

It was when I came across *The Urantia Book* in my earlier forties that I found this so-called War in Heaven far more clearly delineated and referred to there as the "Lucifer Rebellion," the results of which have indeed rippled down through history to affect us all today. There was something unsettlingly familiar about this rebellion among the angels. I seemed to feel more emotionally invested in this drama than I could ignore and thus began the trail of investigation that ultimately led to working with Georgia on these volumes.

It took about fifteen years of what I later realized was an intense training period in which we both learned to trust one another. It was some years before Georgia revealed herself as a "rebel angel" or, as she prefers, an angel who aligned herself with Lucifer at the time of the rebellion. I'm not particularly superstitious by nature, nor am I easily spooked, but I was clearly getting myself into unknown territory. I am only thankful to the Urantia papers for at least giving me a context within which to have some limited understanding of who Georgia might be and what she was doing in my life.

During the years we were getting to know each other I was writing my three books exploring the behind-the-scenes impact that nonhuman intelligences were having on the world, and yet I was constantly being drawn back to focusing on this angelic revolution that seemed to have had such a powerful influence on shaping life on Earth. I knew I had to try to write about it. By my early sixties I'd made three failed attempts to find the right voice to approach and tell the story I felt brewing inside me. It was only when Georgia made it clear she wanted to explore much of the same area for her own purposes that I knew I'd found the voice I was looking for; and perhaps more importantly, I felt sure Georgia's observations and the depth of her knowledge would be far beyond anything I could bring to the table.

My familiarity with the unusual words, terms, and concepts in the Urantia papers allowed us a shared vocabulary, and because my mind had already been expanded by the material in the book, I wasn't freaking out at every turn of Georgia's narrative. Rather the opposite. I found myself utterly fascinated. It wasn't like channeling, or taking dictation. I didn't want to do that anyway. While I could hear Georgia clearly in my mind, the actual composing and writing is a thoroughly collaborative effort in which we discuss the best way of expressing this or that, or what metaphor is most appropriate, or she might ask me to do a little research to fill out or substantiate one of her observations. She's invariably courteous and tolerant of my frailties, and I continue to be surprised and fascinated as her narrative rolls on revealing events, personalities, and insights of which I have no conscious awareness.

It was with this, the third volume of Georgia's *Confessions,* that I felt we really caught alight. We were picking up a small but devoted readership from the first two volumes, and I know Georgia was encouraged by the response. It hadn't been my original intention to publish this work as I thought it too personal and idiosyncratic to be of interest to other people. However, it appears that Georgia's words are striking a familiar chord in others, which I take as a validation of the narrative as it continues in the next volume, published by Inner Traditions • Bear & Company, titled *Wisdom of the Watchers.*

Although we try to make these volumes as stand-alone as possible, the story Georgia is unfolding of her half-million-year posting on Earth is turning out to be a lengthy process, and many of the key nonhuman personalities continue to appear in Georgia's narrative down through time. Here in the third volume, for example, we find the Lemurian people being warned of the approaching disasters and yet the catastrophe itself, as well as the Pleiadean evacuation operation, will have to wait for the *Wisdom of the Watchers.*

In this third volume Georgia reports on Prince Caligastia's undermining of the visitors' mission, while in the next volume, she writes of how the consequences of the visitors' failure continue to wreak havoc as the indigenous people fall further under Caligastia's control.

In this volume she describes an important interchange with one of the Planetary Princes of Zandana, a neighboring planet that Georgia likes to visit when matters get too hot for her on Earth, and yet how this relationship will play out, and the unfortunate effect it will have on Prince Caligastia, appears in later volumes.

In volume 4, Georgia is given the opportunity to expand her interplanetary travels, visiting and exploring a handful of other worlds that have aligned with Lucifer's revolution, and starts to realize that Earth seems to have been selected for some special destiny.

As for my life as surveyed and analyzed by Georgia, it's proving nothing short of a revelation. I'm able to get glimpses of what was going on behind the scenes, of what I never understood or even noticed at the time. Here, as in the next volume, I remain very much in thrall to Mary Ann, my putative incarnate Goddess, yet these are early days and the Process will continue to grow in numbers and influence throughout the late 1960s and the early '70s as the community expands into America.

Here, in this volume, I've been finding my way—I'm still in my late twenties—while in the next volume I have the chance to travel widely in the States and get to know a number of well-known but unconventional public figures, including a long and memorable three days spent in a tepee with Dr. Timothy Leary on the Millbrook estate.

Yet throughout these early volumes there seems to be a number of developing themes, some evident, like Prince Caligastia's thirst for power and his claims of divinity; other themes are less apparent, though pregnant with future significance, as in various clues that the angels who followed Lucifer have been, and are being, permitted to incarnate as mortal beings. Unaware consciously of their angelic heritages, there are signs of such human beings just starting to appear in Georgia's narrative of prehistory, as they will be found in greater numbers as we approach the Atlantean era in the next volume.

Georgia seems to have been extremely cautious in giving credence to what was happening to the rebel angels. Such a fusion of angel and mortal was apparently considered unheard of as the implications of such an angel/human hybrid would be far-reaching and unpredictable. She slowly becomes less reluctant to hope for a mortal incarnation for herself over the course of these books. Her wariness will gradually change as Georgia grows more familiar with observing this unlikely phenomenon and how it will manifest in Atlantean times.

It is in her telling of my life that Georgia becomes less guarded in making this claim and relates incidents, like my telepathic encounter with the man in the New Orleans Chapter coffeehouse, in which she makes no bones about stating that the young man is an advanced incarnate rebel angel. Astonishing as this might seem, Georgia continues to identify incarnate rebel angels and, in some cases, the part such individuals have played in the historical narrative. She makes plain that this opportunity to incarnate as a mortal is no picnic for a rebel angel.

As she relates in her brief analysis of Aleister Crowley in this volume, his real impact, as with a small number of other contemporaneous incarnate rebel angels, was to help pull down and expose the smug pretensions and delusions rooted in the false certainties of the previous age. Thus it is not for his magical workings, nor for his arcane theories, and not for his poetry, nor for his recondite philosophizing, as Crowley well might have hoped to be remembered, but, as Georgia points out, it will be for his true influence as a courageous and determined rebel who faced off against the stultifying social and religious order of the time.

In the *Wisdom of the Watchers,* the next volume, she will continue with her narrative of Earth's ancient history as it evolved between 39,000 BCE and 16,500 BCE, as well as her ongoing examination of my own life as viewed through her unique perspective. Throughout that critical period of the planet's development, and in her observations of my own life, Georgia describes how the influx of rebel angel incarnates, always relatively small in numbers, has been increasing over time, becoming more numerous and in some cases even influential in their cultures as they leave their marks on the social and cultural developments of the nineteenth and twentieth centuries.

What I've come to understand with Georgia's guidance over the course of this study is that the rebel angels who incarnate as human beings, while almost always unaware of their previous existence as angels who once aligned themselves with Lucifer, invariably feel unaccountably different from their parents, their siblings, and most of the people they encounter in life. They seldom have easy lives, and even if they are sometimes successful in worldly terms, their lives are often overshadowed by disappointment.

A rebel angel will need to undertake many lifetimes to become fully accepted into the mortal ascension program. Georgia has confirmed that there are now well over a hundred million such beings on Earth at the present time, and from the letters I've been receiving it's clear that her words are proving valuable to those readers drawn to these books. And I can reassure them from personal experience that if they are recognizing themselves as incarnated rebel angels they are more than likely to have concluded their long cycle of mortal lifetimes and will ascend as mortals when they've completed the tasks taken on in this lifetime.

I have received such personal support and encouragement from writing these books with Georgia, and it's my hope that you, now reading these words, will find the same value in following Georgia's narrative into the next volume and will be as enriched by her insights and revelations in *Wisdom of the Watchers* as I've been in recording her words.

The Angelic Cosmology

I, Timothy, have now read so many versions of this so-called War in Heaven appearing in different myths and legends from all over the world, as well as in the sacred books and traditions of major religions, that the war is more than likely based on a real event. I believe the most authoritative account can be found in *The Urantia Book,* where it is referred to as the Lucifer Rebellion.

Thirty years after first reading *The Urantia Book,* I still regard it as the most reliable source of information about both extraterrestrial and celestial activities. It is broken down into four parts devoted to the following subjects: the Nature of God, the Central and Superuniverses; the Local Universe; the History of Urantia (their name for this planet); and the Life and Teachings of Jesus Christ. (For a definition of terms common to both *The Urantia Book* and this book, please refer to the glossary.)

According to the Urantia model, there are seven Superuniverses, which together compose the material Multiverse. These seven Superuniverses form the substance of the finite Multiverse and circle the Central Universe, which can be visualized as the hole in the center of the toroidal form of the Multiverse.

Each Superuniverse contains one hundred thousand Local Universes, each of which has its own Creator Son (ours is Christ Michael or Jesus Christ) and its own Divine Mother—these are the Creator Beings of their domain. This pair of high beings modulate the energy downstepped from the Central Universe to create and form the beings and the planetary biospheres within their Local Universe.

Each Local Universe sustains ten million inhabited planets broken out into ten thousand Local Systems. Each Local System, in turn, contains one thousand inhabited, or to be inhabited, planets, and each has its pair of System Sovereigns (ours were Lucifer and Satan) appointed to govern the System. Each planet has two Planetary Princes (ours were Caligastia and Daligastia) who oversee their particular worlds.

According to *The Urantia Book,* Lucifer and Satan came to believe that an elaborate conspiracy had been concocted by the Creator Sons of the Local Universes to promote the existence of a fictitious Unseen Divinity, which the Creator Sons then used as a control device to manipulate the orders of celestials and angels within their creations. Having announced the existence of this conspiracy, Lucifer demanded more autonomy for all beings and for System Sovereigns and Planetary Princes to follow their own approaches for accelerating the spiritual development of their mortal charges.

The revolutionaries quickly gained followers, and the rebellion spread rapidly to affect thirty-seven planets in our System, with Urantia, our planet Earth, being one of them. Choice was given to the many angels involved with supervising System activities as to whether to join the rebel faction.

Lucifer's charge—that too much attention was being given to ascending mortals—appeared to ring true to a large number of angels as well as the thirty-seven pairs of administrative angels: the Planetary Princes and their assistants, who were responsible for the orderly progression of mortal (human) beings on their worlds. The revolution was effectively suppressed by the administration authorities who recast it as a heinous rebellion, two immediate consequences were the replacement of Lucifer and Satan and the isolation of the System and a quarantined Earth.

At the time of the Lucifer Rebellion, the vast majority of the 50,000 midway angels on Earth—40,119—aligned themselves with Lucifer and Satan. They were destined to remain on our planet until the time of Christ, when, according to *The Urantia Book,* it was one of Christ's occulted functions to remove them. It is a brief reference and no further details are given in the book as to where the rebel midwayers were taken. However, with the removal of these rebel midwayers, a mere 9,981 loyalist midwayers remained here to fulfill the tasks of five times their number.

As a result of all of this, in contrast to a normal planet (one not quarantined) on which angelic companions and the presence of helpful midwayers and extraterrestrials must be a commonplace experience, we Earthlings have slumbered in our corner of a populated Multiverse, unaware of who we are and how we got this way. Having been quarantined and isolated from normal extraterrestrial activity for the long 203,000 years since the rebellion, we first lost touch with, and then forgot entirely, our rightful place in the populated Multiverse. Given this, we were bound to evolve as a troubled species. Our planet is one of the few worlds that, due to the Lucifer Rebellion, was thrown off course from its normal pattern of development.

This disquieting situation, this planetary quarantine, has persisted for more than two hundred thousand years, only to have finally been adjudicated, or so I understand, in the early 1980s.

Given that the planetary quarantine has finally been lifted, the rest of the Multiverse is now able to make legitimate contact with us. More recently, what we are witnessing is the return of the rebel midwayers (the Beings of the Violet Flame), who are now coming back to assist us in the coming transformation of our world. While perhaps of more personal interest to my readers, the many angels who aligned with Lucifer at the time of the rebellion incarnating as mortals. It appears these rebel angels and Watchers are being offered human incarnation as a path to personal redemption as the world is emerging from an interminably long Dark Ages to shake off the shadows and fulfill its remarkable destiny.

Glossary

Many valuable insights from many different sources have contributed to the themes and fundamental questions that this series of books seeks to explore, but the most reliable and comprehensive exposition of God, the Universe, and Everything that I have come across remains, after thirty years, *The Urantia Book*. A number of the concepts and words below are drawn from it and marked (UB), but the definitions are mine.

Albedo: the second stage of the alchemical process resulting from the slow burning out of the impurities present in the first stage.

Angel: a general term for any order of being who administers within a Local Universe.

Atman, Indwelling Spirit, Thought Adjuster (UB): an essence of the Creator that indwells all mortal beings, human and extraterrestrial.

Bioplasm (UB): a constituent of an individual's genome required to reconstitute a biological duplicate of the bioplasm's donor, or for calibrating a cloned physical vehicle to its intended environment.

Caligastia (UB): a Secondary Lanonandek Son who served as Planetary Prince of this world and who aligned himself with Lucifer.

Cano (UB): Young Nodite aristocrat who mated with Eve, the female visitor.

Central Universe (UB): the abode of the original Creator God/s—the Father, the Mother/Son, and the Holy Spirit (UB). If the Multiverse is a torus, then the Central Universe is the hole in the middle existing on a far finer frequency and from which energy is downstepped to form the building blocks of the material Multiverse.

Citrinitas: advanced state of spiritual enlightenment whereby the alchemist can make an ultimate unification with the Supreme.

Creator Sons (UB): co-creators—each having a female complement, the Mother Spirit (UB)—of each of the 700,000 Local Universes (UB). The co-creators of the Local Universes modulate the downstepped energies from the Central Universe to design the life-forms for those beings existing within all the frequency domains of their Local Universes.

Daligastia (UB): a Secondary Lanonandek Son who served as Caligastia's right-hand aide.

Demons: negative thoughtforms.

Devas: the coordinating spirits of the natural world. All living organisms are cared for by devas (or Nature Spirits). In the human being the deva is that which coordinates and synchronizes the immense amount of physical and biochemical information that keeps the body alive.

Extraterrestrial: mortal beings such as ourselves, some of whom hail from more developed worlds with access to our frequency domain.

Fandor (UB): a large, semitelepathic, passenger bird said to have become extinct about 38,000 years ago.

Frequency domain: the spectrum of frequencies that support the life-forms whose senses are tuned to that specific spectrum.

God: in *my* personal experience, God is both the Creator and the totality of Creation, manifest and unmanifest, immanent and transcendent.

Guardian (Companion) Angels (UB): function in pairs to ensure their mortal wards grow in spirit over the course of their lifetimes.

Indwelling Spirit, Atman, Thought Adjuster (UB): an essence of the Creator that indwells all mortal beings, human and extraterrestrial.

Janda-chi: the second of the two Planetary Princes on the planet Zandana.

Jesus Christ: the Michaelson (UB) of our Local Universe (UB) who incarnated as Jesus Christ in the physical body of Joshua ben Joseph; he is also known as Michael of Nebadon (UB).

Lanaforge (UB): a primary Lanonandek Son who succeeded Lucifer as System Sovereign.

Lanonandek Order of Sonship (UB): The third order of Local Universe Descending Sons of God who serve as System Sovereigns (Primary Lanonandeks) and Planetary Princes (Secondary Lanonandeks).

Local System (UB): our Local System, named Satania (UB), is believed to currently possess between 600 and 650 inhabited planets. Earth is numbered 606 in this sequence (UB).

Local System HQ Planet, Jerusem (UB): the political and social center of the Satania System.

Local Universe (UB): a grouping of planets that comprises ten million inhabited worlds.

Lucifer (UB): deposed System Sovereign and primary protagonist in the rebellion among the angels.

Lucifer Rebellion (UB): A System-wide rebellion among the angels occurring 203,000 years ago on Jerusem that affected thirty-seven inhabited worlds, of which Earth was one.

Master Universe (UB): the Multiverse that contains the seven Superuniverses (UB).

Melchizedek Sons/Brothers (UB): a high order of Local Universe Sons devoted primarily to education and who function as planetary administrators in emergencies.

Midwayers or Midway Creatures (UB): intelligent beings, imperceptible to humans, who exist in a contiguous frequency domain and serve as the permanent planetary citizens.

Mortals (UB): intelligent beings who emerge as a result of biological evolutionary processes on a planet. Souls are born to their immortal lives as mortals, whose physical bodies live and die before they are given the choice to continue their Multiverse career.

Mortal Ascension Scheme (UB): the process by which all mortal beings who live and die on the material worlds of the Local Systems pass up through the seven subsequent levels to Jerusem, where they embark on their Universe career.

Mother Spirit (UB): with the Michaelson, the female co-creator of a Local Universe.

Multiverse: the entire range of frequency domains, on every level of the Master Universe (UB).

Multiverse Administration (MA) (UB): a general term for the celestial administration, with special reference to Local Universe bureaucracy.

Nebadon (UB): the name of this Local Universe of ten million inhabited planets.

Nodites (UB): descendants of the illicit interbreeding between selected mortals and, on realizing they were doomed to physical death, those of the Prince's staff who followed Caligastia's uprising.

Nodu, Nod (UB): Nodu is Georgia's informal, but respectful, name for the member of the Prince's staff who opposed Caligastia and who, in time, led his people to the Islands of Mu.

Satan (UB): Lucifer's right-hand aide who co-instigated the angelic rebellion 203,000 years ago.

Serapatatia (UB): Nodite prince who persuaded Eve to accelerate the visitors' mission by mating with Cano and creating a singular Nodite bloodline with a healthy dash of violet blood.

Seraph(im) (UB): a high order of angels whose functions include that of companion (guardian) angels, or, like Georgia, observing angels.

Seraphic Transport System (UB): Transport Seraphs, living beings who carry non-material beings, Watchers as well as Ascending Mortals, to the other worlds on a variety of frequency domains within the Multiverse.

Solonia (UB): the Seraphic "voice in the garden" (UB) who admonished the visitors and had them leave their garden home and start their long journey to settle in the Land of the Two Rivers.

Superuniverse (UB): a Universe that contains 100,000 Local Universes (UB).

System of Planets (UB): a grouping of planets consisting of a thousand inhabited, or to be inhabited worlds.

System of Satania: The System of planets within which Earth is but one of the more than 650 inhabited worlds of the 1,000 planets within its administrative domain and the locale of the Lucifer revolution.

System Sovereign (UB): the administrative angel, together with an assistant of the same rank, who is in overall authority of a Local System. Lucifer and Satan were the pair in charge of this System of planets.

Thoughtforms: quasi-life-forms existing in the astral regions, drawing their limited power from strong emotional thoughts projected out from human mentation, both conscious and unconscious. Thoughtforms can be negative or positive. Localized negative ones are referred to as fear-impacted thoughtforms.

Transport Seraphim: order of Seraphim specifically created as sentient vehicles to make interplanetary transit available in the fourth and fifth dimensions.

Ultraterrestrial or Intraterrestrial Beings: the beings who inhabit our neighboring frequency domain and who *The Urantia Book* calls the midwayers or midway creatures.

Unava: chief of staff to Prince Zanda, the senior of the two Planetary Princes of the neighboring planet Zandana.

Universe Career (UB): a mortal's destiny, unless chosen otherwise, to rise through the many hundreds of levels of the Multiverse to finally encounter the Creator.

Violet Blood (UB): the potential of an infusion of a slightly higher frequency genetic endowment, which results in more acute senses and a deeper spiritual awareness and responsiveness.

Zanda: senior Planetary Prince of Zandana, a planet named in his honor and to which Georgia has made frequent visits.

Zandana: a neighboring planet developing within approximately the same time frame as Earth and whose Planetary Princes also followed Lucifer into revolution.

Index

About the Author

Timothy Wyllie chose to be born in London in 1940 at the height of the Battle of Britain. Surviving an English Public School education unbroken, he studied architecture, qualifying in 1964 and practicing in London and the Bahamas. During this time he also worked with two others to create a Mystery School, which came to be known as the Process Church, and subsequently traveled with the community throughout Europe and America. He became art director of PROCESS magazine, designing a series of magazines in the 1960s and '70s that have recently become recognized as among the prime progenitors of psychedelic magazine design. In 1975 he became the director of the New York headquarters, organized a series of conferences and seminars on such unorthodox issues as out-of-body travel, extraterrestrial encounters, alternative cancer therapies, and Tibetan Buddhism. After some fractious and fundamental disagreements with his colleagues in the community, he left to start a new life in 1977. The record of Wyllie's fifteen years in the Mystery School of the Process Church and the true account of this eccentric spiritual community appears in his book *Love, Sex, Fear, Death: The Inside Story of The Process Church of the Final Judgment,* which was published by Feral House in 2009. It is slowly becoming a cult classic.

301

A profound near-death experience in 1973 confirmed for Wyllie the reality of other levels of existence and instigated what has become a lifetime exploration of nonhuman intelligences. Having created his intention, the Multiverse opened in a trail of synchronicities that led to his swimming with a coastal pod of wild dolphins, two extraterrestrial encounters—during one of which he was able to question the ET mouthpiece as to some of the ways of the inhabited Multiverse—and finally to an extended dialogue with a group of angels speaking through a light-trance medium in Toronto, Canada.

Wyllie's first phase of spiritual exploration was published as *The DETA Factor: Dolphins, Extraterrestrials & Angels* by Coleman Press in 1984 and republished by Bear & Company as *Dolphins, ETs & Angels* in 1993.

His second book, *Dolphins, Telepathy & Underwater Birthing,* published by Bear & Company in 1993, was republished by Wisdom Editions in 2001 under the title *Adventures Among Spiritual Intelligences: Angels, Aliens, Dolphins & Shamans.* In this book Wyllie continues his travels, exploring Balinese shamanic healing, Australian Aboriginal cosmology, human underwater birthing, dolphin death and sexuality, entheogenic spirituality, the gathering alien presence on the planet, and his travels with a Walk-In, along with much else.

Wyllie's work with the angels through the 1980s resulted in the book *Ask Your Angels: A Practical Guide to Working with Your Messengers of Heaven to Empower and Enrich Your Life,* written with Alma Daniel and Andrew Ramer and published by Ballantine Books in 1992. After spending time at the top of the New York Times religious bestsellers, *Ask Your Angels* went on to become an international success in eleven translations.

The Return of the Rebel Angels continues the series he began with *Dolphins, ETs & Angels* and *Adventures Among Spiritual Intelligences,* presenting further in-depth intuitive explorations of nonhuman intelligences. It draws together the many meaningful strands of Wyllie's thirty-year voyage of discovery into unknown and long-taboo territories into a coherent and remarkably optimistic picture for the immediate future of the human species, with the inconspicuous help of a benign and richly inhabited living Multiverse.

The Helianx Proposition or The Return of the Rainbow Serpent, also thirty years in the making, is Wyllie's illustrated mythic exploration of an ancient extraterrestrial personality and Hir occult influence on life in this world. Published by Daynal Institute Press in 2010, it includes two DVDs and two CDs of associated material. The CDs contain 19 tracks of the author's visionary observations augmented by Emmy-winning musician the late Jim Wilson, master of digital sonic manipulation.

Confessions of a Rebel Angel, Wyllie's first collaboration with Georgia, emerged in 2012, published by Inner Traditions • Bear & Company, who followed up with *Revolt of the Rebel Angels* in 2013, *Rebel Angels in Exile* in 2014, and *Wisdom of the Watchers* in 2015. Wyllie carries on working in collaboration with Georgia on her *Confessions* series and can only hope that his stalwart publisher and his small but growing readership will continue to be as fascinated and educated by this multidimensional, multiplanetary, multivolume overview of the past half-million years of global activity.

Wyllie lives in a house of his own design at the foot of a mesa somewhere in the wilds of the New Mexico high desert.

BOOKS BY TIMOTHY WYLLIE

The DETA Factor: Dolphins, Extraterrestrials & Angels, 1984 (currently in print as *Dolphins, ETs & Angels,* 1993).

Ask Your Angels: A Practical Guide to Working with the Messengers of Heaven to Empower and Enrich Your Life, 1992 (cowritten with Alma Daniel and Andrew Ramer).

Dolphins, Telepathy, & Underwater Birthing, 1993 (currently in print as *Adventures Among Spiritual Intelligences: Angels, Aliens, Dolphins & Shamans,* 2001).

Contacting Your Angels Through Movement, Meditation & Music, 1995 (with Elli Bambridge).

Love, Sex, Fear, Death: The Inside Story of the Process Church of the Final Judgment, 2009 (editor, with Adam Parfrey).

The Helianx Proposition or the Return of the Rainbow Serpent, 2010 and 2014.

The Return of the Rebel Angels, 2011.

Confessions of a Rebel Angel, 2012.

Revolt of the Rebel Angels, 2013.

BOOKS OF RELATED INTEREST

The Return of the Rebel Angels
The Urantia Mysteries and the Coming of the Light
by Timothy Wyllie

Confessions of a Rebel Angel
The Wisdom of the Watchers and the Destiny of Planet Earth
by Timothy Wyllie

Revolt of the Rebel Angels
The Future of the Multiverse
by Timothy Wyllie

Wisdom of the Watchers
Teachings of the Rebel Angels on Earth's Forgotten Past
by Timothy Wyllie

Dolphins, ETs & Angels
Adventures Among Spiritual Intelligences
by Timothy Wyllie

Bringers of the Dawn
Teachings from the Pleiadians
by Barbara Marciniak

The Pleiadian Agenda
A New Cosmology for the Age of Light
by Barbara Hand Clow

The Pleiadian House of Initiation
A Journey through the Rooms of the Wisdomkeepers
by Mary T. Beben
Foreword by Barbara Hand Clow

INNER TRADITIONS • BEAR & COMPANY
P.O. Box 388 • Rochester, VT 05767
1-800-246-8648
www.InnerTraditions.com

Or contact your local bookseller